Imperi

G000229701

EDUCATIONAL
SERVICES

DEATH BY DESIGN

THE FATE OF BRITISH TANK CREWS
IN THE SECOND WORLD WAR

PETER BEALE

SUTTON PUBLISHING

First published in the United Kingdom in 1998 by
Sutton Publishing Limited · Phoenix Mill
Thrupp · Stroud · Gloucestershire · GL5 2BU

British Library Cataloguing in Publication Data
A catalogue record for this book is available from the British Library.

ISBN 0-7509-0802-5

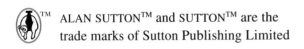
Typeset in 10.5/13.5 pt Times.
Typesetting and origination by
Sutton Publishing Limited.
Printed in Great Britain by
WBC Ltd, Bridgend.

Contents

Acknowledgements

The main sources used in writing this book were those of the Tank Museum Library at Bovington and the Public Record Office (PRO) at Kew. The help and courtesy of the staff of both organizations is most gratefully acknowledged, particularly that of the Tank Museum Librarian, David Fletcher. His knowledge and experience have been of immense value, and the prompt and willing attention given by all Tank Museum Library staff is much appreciated.

Discussions with Paul Harris of the Department of Military Studies, Royal Military Academy (RMA) Sandhurst, provided valuable direction and orientation, as did many discussions with former tank soldiers, in particular Lt Col P.N. (Berry) Veale, DSO, MC. Jonathan Falconer of Sutton Publishing was, as always, encouraging, helpful and prompt. My secretaries, Colleen Jones and Kristie Franks, converted manuscript into typescript with clear mind and nimble fingers, and then did the whole thing over again at least three times. And my most grateful thanks to my wife, Shirley, for all her help, encouragement and patience, and for taking such a vital part in researching the original documents at the Tank Museum and the PRO.

Abbreviations

A/A	Anti-Aircraft
ACIGS	Assistant Chief of the Imperial General Staff
ACE	Associated Equipment Company (makers of heavy engineering equipment)
AFV	Armoured Fighting Vehicle
AG	Adjutant General
AP	Armour Piercing shot
APC	Armour Piercing Capped
APCBC	Armour Piercing Capped Ballistic Capped
APDS	Armour Piercing Discarding sabot (generally abbreviated to 'sabot')
A/T	Anti-Tank
BEF	British Expeditionary Force (elements of the British Army sent to France in 1939 and 1940)
CAFV	Chairman, Armoured Fighting Vehicle Division of the Ministry of Supply
CCRA	Commander Corps Royal Artillery (senior artilleryman in an Army corps, accountable to corps commander for effective use of all corps artillery)
CETD	Chief Engineer Tank Development
CGME	Controller-General of Mechanical Engineering
CGRD	Controller-General Research & Development
CID	Committee for Imperial Defence
CIGS	Chief of the Imperial General Staff (the senior soldier in the British Army)
CIM	Chief Inspector of Mechanization
CRA	Commander Royal Artillery (senior artillery man in a division, accountable to the divisional commander for effective use of all divisional artillery)
DA	Director of Artillery
DAFV	Director, Armoured Fighting Vehicles
DDGFVP	Deputy Director General Fighting Vehicle Production
DESE	Director, Engineer & Signals Equipment
DFVI	Director, Fighting Vehicle Inspection
DFVP	Director, Fighting Vehicle Production
DGA	Director General of Artillery
DGES	Director General of Equipment and Stores
DGFVP	Director General, Fighting Vehicle Production
DGM	Director General of Munitions
DGME	Director General of Mechanical Engineering
DGMP	Director General of Munitions Production
DGTS	Director General of Tank Supply
DGTT	Director General of Tanks and Transport
DM	Director of Mechanization
DMGO	Deputy Master General of Ordnance
DMI	Director of Military Intelligence
DMO	Director of Military Operations

DMT	Director of Military Training
DNLE	Directorate of Naval Land Equipment
DOF	Director of Ordnance Factories
DOI	Director of Operations and Intelligence (later split into DMO and DMI)
DOS	Director of Ordnance Services
DRAC	Director, Royal Armoured Corps
DSD	Director of Staff Duties
DTD	Director of Tank Design
DTE	Director of Transportation Equipment
DTP	Director of Tank Production
DTS	Director of Tank Supply
EMF	Experimental Mechanical Force
FGS	Fancy Goods Store (the canteen at the Royal Military Academy, Sandhurst)
Flak	*Flieger Abwehr Kanone* (anti-aircraft gun)
FVPE	Fighting Vehicles Proving Establishment
GMC	General Motors Corporation
GSO	General Staff Officer
HE	High Explosive
HQ	Headquarters
HV	High Velocity (relating to a tank or anti-tank gun)
KwK	*Kampfwagen Kanone* (tank gun)
LMSR	London, Midland & Scottish Railway Company
MGO	Master General of Ordnance
MV	Medium Velocity (relating to tank or anti-tank guns)
NCO	Non-Commissioned Officer
OCTU	Officer Cadet Training Unit
OP	Observation post
PAK	*Panzer Abwehr Kanone* (anti-tank gun)
PRO	Public Record Office
QMG	Quarter Master General
RA	Royal Artillery
RAC	Royal Armoured Corps
RAOC	Royal Army Ordnance Corps
RE	Royal Engineers
REME	Royal Electrical and Mechanical Engineers
RHA	Royal Horse Artillery
RMC	Royal Military College
RTC	Royal Tank Corps
RTR	Royal Tank Regiment
RUSI	Royal United Services Institute
RYPA	Roll, yaw and pitch apparatus
SCNE	Select Committee on National Expenditure
SP	Self-Propelled (often refers to artillery on a tracked chassis)
TOG	The Old Gang
TR	Training Regiment
VCIGS	Vice Chief of the Imperial General Staff
WOSB	War Office Selection Board

Prologue

Vigilance Sleeps

Owing to the large number of casualties the full story of the Royal Wiltshire Yeomanry action will never be known. It is known that the leading Crusader squadron met six 88mm anti-tank guns and unhesitatingly charged on to them, destroying four out of the six at the cost of the whole squadron. Their Grant and Sherman tanks were also in action, but again owing to casualties their deeds are not known. The commanding officer and the squadron leaders were all casualties at an early stage, and the rear link tank lost touch in the smoke and dust. By 0900 hrs there were only five tanks of the Royal Wiltshire Yeomanry left.

FROM AN ACCOUNT OF THE ACTION OF 9TH ARMOURED BRIGADE, EL ALAMEIN,
2 NOVEMBER 1942

Actions such as this took place throughout the Second World War. Tank crews were ill equipped, undertrained, badly led, uncertain what they should be doing, but generally courageous. The genesis of this book was the observation from reading many accounts, and the direct experience of tank battles, that the development of British tanks before and during the Second World War was a disgrace. Further investigation and discussion led to the view that the ineffective performance of British tank units – particularly when compared with that of German and Russian tank forces – was not due only to the poor design and construction of the British tanks they used.

The original thesis suggested the title *Death by Design*. The title has been retained, even though the causes of unnecessary wastage of the lives of tank crews can be attributed to incomplete training, uncertainty of doctrine and poor leadership, as well as sub-standard design. These four causes were the main contributors to the ill-pre-preparedness of British armoured forces not only at the beginning of the war in 1939, but also before the war and during the whole of its course until early 1945.

Tank crews were murdered because they were sent into battle so ill prepared. The thing that should make us angry and indignant is that with a little thought and planning these murders could have been avoided. In November 1918 Britain's tank forces were more advanced than any others in the world, and ideas were being developed for the provision and use of progressively more effective tank forces. Had progress been maintained, even on a modest scale, it would have been possible for Britain to have tank forces comparable with those of Germany in 1936. This was the year when Hitler reoccupied the Rhineland, the first manifestation of his aggressive intentions. A determined and well-equipped British Army, including appropriate armoured formations, might well have acted as a deterrent.

A Crusader knocked out in the Western Desert, 1942. It probably did not belong to the Royal Wiltshire Yeomanry, because an encounter with a German 88mm would have left it far more battered. (Tank Museum)

This was not to be, and at no time until 1945 did Britain's armoured capability meet that of the Germans. There were fleeting moments of equipment parity, provided in particular by the Matilda Tank in 1940 and early 1941. But Matildas were available only in small quantities in the places where they were needed, and their design did not lend itself to further upgrading.

The purpose of this book is to review the significant history relating to the development of British tank forces up to 1945, and to identify as far as possible the causes that led to those forces being so ill prepared to fight. The principal sections of the book cover the main international events of the period from 1919 to 1939, and the response of the British government to those events, particularly relating to the provision of the armed forces; the development of tank doctrine, tanks and tank guns; and the training provided at all levels of the tank forces.

The review of what happened allows us to see some of the reasons why Alistair Horne could make the statement: 'The story of Britain's tank inferiority all through World War II is one the great disgraces of her military history.' Evaluation of the reasons suggests

A Matilda – 'The Queen of the Desert' – which was equal to the best the Germans could produce, but the period of parity was only from 1940 to mid-1941.

many ways in which things could have been done better. It is all too late for those tank soldiers who lie buried in a foreign field, and it is a long time ago anyway; but a nation must always be prepared to defend itself, and it should take all reasonable steps to ensure that those entrusted with its defence are properly prepared to do so.

Si vis pacem, para bellum
(If you want peace, prepare for war)
Vegetius (AD fourth century)

CHAPTER I

Atrophy of an Army

INTERWAR HISTORY
1918–39

At the beginning of 1919 the forces of Germany lay defeated, and those of Britain and her allies were strong and all-conquering. But by 1939 Britain's army was small, ill equipped and ill trained, while Germany's army was vigorous, well equipped and about to be triumphant. Why such a reversal? The answers lie largely in the terms imposed on Germany in 1919, and the national attitudes and reactions of Britain and Germany in response to international events as they unfolded.

This chapter reviews briefly the main historical events from 1919 to 1939, beginning with the features of the Treaty of Versailles that set those events in train. The reactions of progressive British governments are then considered, leading on to the effect those reactions were to have on the state of the British Army in 1939.

The Treaty of Versailles was the formal instrument for ending the hostilities of the First World War. Most countries who fought against Germany were invited; the significant countries not invited were Germany and Russia. There were three people of outstanding importance at the conference to determine the terms of the treaty: France's Georges Clemenceau, known as Le Tigre (the tiger), who stood for an earnest desire to fetter and cripple Germany forever; America's Woodrow Wilson who was full of ideas (his Fourteen Points) but no plan; and Britain's Lloyd-George who felt initially that Germany should be treated with justice and compassion, but his self-serving political instincts, and an imminent election, made him change his view and promise that he would ask for the trial of Kaiser Wilhelm II, punishment of those responsible for atrocities, and the fullest indemnities for Germany.

With one main leader withdrawn into the clouds and the other two bent on hammering Germany it is hardly surprising that the terms of the treaty (see Appendix I) were considered by Germans at the time, and by historians subsequently, to have been unreasonably harsh. Like any other proud nation Germany was not going to take these perceived injustices lying down. There was a mood which would compel them, under a suitable leader, to right these wrongs.

In contrast to this determined attitude the British wanted only to sit back peacefully and not have to be involved in a similar conflict ever again. They would look after the empire, of course, but the League of Nations would look after any international unpleasantness.

SIGNIFICANT HISTORICAL EVENTS LEADING TO THE OUTBREAK OF THE SECOND
WORLD WAR:

3 January 1925:	Mussolini becomes dictator of Italy
October 1929:	Wall Street Crash
18 September 1931:	Japan invades Manchuria; League of Nations does nothing
2 August 1934:	Hitler becomes dictator of Germany
3 October 1935:	Mussolini invades Abyssinia
7 March 1936:	Hilter reoccupies Rhineland
12 March 1938:	Hitler invades Austria
August/September 1938:	Czechoslovakia under pressure of invasion; war seems inevitable
September 1938:	Chamberlain meets Hitler and finally gets his 'letter of intent' (so-called 'peace in our time')
15 March 1939:	Hitler invades Czechoslovakia and occupies Prague
31 March 1939:	Chamberlain promises aid to Poland in the event of aggression
23 August 1939:	Germany and Russia sign a non-aggression pact
1 September 1939:	Germany invades Poland
3 September 1939:	Britain and France declare war on Germany

BRITAIN'S DEFENCE NEEDS

A nation's survival can be defended and upheld by three main means: diplomacy, economic strength and armed strength. During the period 1919–39 these methods were used to achieve the objective of Britain's national survival, and in the early part the main thrust was by diplomatic and political means. Britain, along with many other countries, considered that the League of Nations would provide collective security for all member nations – and, indeed, all the world. It was therefore considered that the need for armed strength as a complement to diplomacy was of secondary importance. Indeed, soon after the end of the First World War the government promulgated the policy called the Ten Year Rule. This stated that in the government's view there was no likelihood of a war for ten years, which clearly meant that there was no need to keep substantial armed forces in being during those ten years. In 1920 it was assumed that there would be no war until 1930; in 1921 no war until 1931; and so on. Thus the provision of armed forces was allowed to slip back by a process of progressive procrastination.

Britain's defence requirements were more complicated than those of many other countries because she had to consider not only the defence of the home islands, but also that of her imperial possessions. This defence was required not only for those possessions themselves but also because they provided much of the raw material and food that Britain required. It was necessary not only to protect those countries themselves from external or internal threats but also to protect the sea lanes between those countries and Britain. A particularly important locality that required protection was the Suez Canal, forming as it did a vital link between Britain and India and other British possessions beyond Suez. So to the first requirement for the employment of armed strength, home defence, was added the second, maintaining imperial holdings and communications.

The third area where armed forces might have to be employed was what was called the Continental Force. This requirement was for an armed force which could go to the aid of Britain's allies, specifically those on the European continent. This had been done in 1914 when Britain sent the expeditionary force to help the French and Belgians, which over a four-year period became a very substantial army. There was much debate as to whether Britain still required to maintain the capability of sending such a force. This debate was renewed from time to time during the course of the 1920s and the 1930s.

METHODS FOR ACHIEVING DEFENCE OBJECTIVES

Assuming that the three main defence objectives are home defence, protection of imperial holdings and the communications with them, and the provision of a continental force, what are the ways in which those objectives can be achieved, and what are the requirements for the Army, Royal Navy and Royal Air Force (RAF) respectively?

A Light Tank Mk VI B (Indian pattern) leaves a fort at some point in the mid-1930s. (Tank Museum 1623/B6)

A Light Tank Mk VI B (Indian pattern) ascends – with difficulty – the Nahakki Pass; the light tanks could at least move in such country, and there was therefore a significant demand for this type of tank. (Tank Museum 268/A4)

Home defence depends on all three services, in particular the Royal Navy, to prevent any forces landing on Britain's shores. That task can also be undertaken by the RAF who can intercept aircraft supporting invasion forces; the RAF can also repel those invasion forces themselves. The British Army assists in preventing hostile forces from landing, and then has the major role in combating those forces once they have landed; another role is the provision of anti-aircraft defence.

Imperial holdings and communications needed to be protected particularly by the Royal Navy because of the Navy's great mobility and ability to move quickly from one trouble-spot to another with substantial firepower. The role of the RAF in defending imperial holdings and communications was to assist the Navy and to carry out bombing and other attacks on insurrections within the countries which form part of the empire. The role of the Army was to provide a force which could defend the countries of the empire against invasion and against internal insurrection or other troubles. In some countries, particularly India, the troops from Britain were very substantially supported by troops of the country itself, but there was still a need for British forces in various roles in all of those imperial possessions.

The Continental Force was a much more contentious item. Basically the requirement was to provide support to Britain's European allies. Britain provided substantial forces in the First World War and gave great support to the French. If Britain were allied to France at any future time would France expect a contribution from Britain in her defence? The answer was obviously yes. But what form could that support take? One view put forward very strongly was that the most effective form of support would be by an air force, and a land force would not be necessary.

The role of air forces was a subject for intense debate after 1918. Their expansion during the First World War had been very substantial considering that, in effect, there were no air forces at the beginning of that war. By the end Germany had 200 squadrons of aircraft, France 260 and Britain 100. These forces were mainly used as fighter squadrons or for reconnaissance. There was certainly some bombing, and the bombing which took place over England created a very strong impact on both the people who were bombed and the British government. It was felt that bombing alone could destroy both the will and the capability of a country to defend itself. This was put forward in particular by an Italian, Giulio Douhet, in his book *The Command of the Air* (1921). His thesis was that there was no effective defence against the bomber and that both civilian morale and industrial and defence installations would be destroyed very quickly after the employment of substantial air power.

This then presented the government with two major choices for providing support to a continental ally. The first was by building up a substantial bomber fleet, the second by providing a substantial armed force on the ground. In both cases the Royal Navy would provide support, particularly to the armed force on the ground. There was at that time a reluctance on the part of the RAF to provide air support, both in protection of supply routes to the Army and in a direct tactical fashion.

BRITISH GOVERNMENT REACTIONS TO THE EVENTS, 1918–39

In this section we consider the reactions of the British government to the historical events which occurred between 1920 and 1939, and consider in particular the actions that were taken to maintain the defence objectives mentioned in the previous section.

The first significant action to be taken was obviously to demobilize all the enormous forces that Britain had raised during the First World War. Because it seemed clear that this had been 'a war to end wars' it was not necessary to consider the need to fight another war for a long time. Some people thought that there would be no more wars. The decision regarding no more wars resulted in the Ten Year Rule mentioned in the previous section. Ministers could assume that there would be no serious assault on Britain itself, nor would there be any need for the Continental Force. The only requirement that had to be met was that to defend the imperial possessions and the lanes of communications with those possessions. This requirement involved mainly the Royal Navy, which would make sure that the sea lanes were not threatened by any hostile powers and would protect any troops being sent to any area where hostilities had broken out on land.

On the land itself there was a need to provide British troops to deal with local insurgents either from within or outside the particular British territory. The British would be supported generally by troops belonging to the imperial possession itself. The

A Light Tank Mk III in Palestine, 1936; it belonged to the 6th Battalion, Royal Tank Corps.
(Tank Museum 367/E6)

particular areas of initial concern were Palestine and the north-west frontier of India. Other trouble spots arose during the years from 1920 to 1930, but generally the number of troops required was small. The British Army did have a commitment in the Rhineland, where, with the French, they formed the force occupying the demilitarized zone. This was to be occupied for a total period of fifteen years but troops were to be withdrawn progressively, first after five years and then after ten years. In fact they were all withdrawn after ten years and the last allied occupation troops left the Rhineland in 1930.

It was not until the 1930s that significant international trouble began. Italy had a dictator in the person of Mussolini, but his intentions were not taken to be aggressive up to that time. In Germany Hitler had not yet come to power, although his Nazi Party was becoming more powerful. Up to 1930, however, Germany was not seen as an aggressor nation partly because she had no significant forces with which to be aggressive. The other possible country that could disturb the peace of the world to any large degree was Japan, and again up to 1930 there was no significant indication that Japan had any aggressive intentions.

The first overt action to create a disturbance in international affairs was the Japanese invasion of Manchuria. On the night of 18 September 1931 a small charge of dynamite exploded in the marshalling yards just outside of Mukden, Manchuria's capital. The bomb did little harm but was used immediately by the Japanese as an excuse to protect imperial interests in Manchuria. They promptly invaded, seizing towns and communication centres throughout the southern part of that land. Immediately after the Mukden incident, Chiang Kai-shek, representing China, counselled a policy of no resistance and announced that China would take its case to the League of Nations. This might have restrained the Japanese if any of the major powers had been prepared to espouse China's rights; unfortunately no one was. The Japanese representatives at Geneva insisted that they had acted only to restore order, that they had no territorial ambitions and that they would certainly withdraw once safety of life and property had been assured.

In the end the league appointed a commission to investigate the affair. In February 1932 Manchuria was proclaimed by the Japanese as a separate nation and given the new name of Manchukuo.

The Japanese installed Henry P'u Yi, the last of the Manchu dynasty, as head of the government of the new country. He was, of course, entirely dependent upon Japan. The league's investigative committee, under Lord Lytton, finally reported in 1932. It flatly condemned Japanese aggression. Japan, however, had no intention of apologizing or surrendering what it had gained. When the other nations at Geneva accepted the report the Japanese walked out and left the league. They then began pushing their Manchurian invasion further inland in China.

This created concern in the British cabinet and they decided on 23 March 1932 to revoke the Ten Year Rule in response to the increasing threat posed by Japan. The whole cabinet accepted the cancellation of the Ten Year Rule without dissent; however, it went on to state that this did not justify immediate increases in defence spending, and that in view of the disarmament conference the whole spending question should be studied further. The armed services had won the right to plan but not to spend.

The dominant department in the cabinet was HM Treasury. Through its control of finance it became the central body for the development and coordination of policies on most matters, but particularly those where significant sums had to be spent. (This of course applied to all the three service departments.) But HM Treasury had also to consider Britain's economic condition. Because of the Wall Street Crash in 1929 and the spread of economic depression throughout the world during 1930–1 the Treasury had to pay very close attention to Britain's ability to spend money on defence without suppressing economic recovery. The balance between the economy and defence was one which was to occupy the Treasury and the War Office from 1932 until 1939.

On 30 January 1933 Hitler became the Chancellor of Germany. That appointment and the Nazi Party's subsequent consolidation of power was a source of great concern to the British Foreign Office and government generally. There were fears about Germany's rearmament which led the government to view with dismay the possibility of aggression in Europe as well as in the Far East.

In the light of this change in Europe the British Chiefs of Staff drew up a new assessment of the imperial defence situation. They considered that Germany would be a profound threat to British security within 3 to 5 years and emphasized how unprepared the Army was for any type of continental role. This unpreparedness would take years to remedy because Britain was lacking not only the weapons of war and the service people, but also the plant to produce those weapons. The delay between nominating the requirement for a weapon and the production of that weapon in battleworthy form with people trained to use it can be as long as 3 or 4 years. The Chiefs of Staff recommended that the deficiency in the defence forces should be dealt with immediately.

The paper in which this was proposed was presented to the Committee for Imperial Defence (CID). The CID decided that a group called the Defence Requirements Committee (DRC) should be instituted to formulate plans for Britain's rearmament.

The Defence Requirements Committee was set up in November 1933 and had on it the most powerful and influential civil servants in British government at the time. The chairman was Maurice Hankey, the Secretary to the Cabinet and the Committee for Imperial Defence. Other members were Warren Fisher, the Permanent Secretary to the Treasurer; Robert Vansittart, the Permanent Under-Secretary of State; and the three heads of the services: Adm Chatfield, Sir Edward Ellington and FM Montgomery Massingberd. The first meeting of the Defence Requirements Committee took place on 14 November 1933 and agreed in principle to concern itself primarily with the nation's military needs. They considered the threats to Britain as they were at that moment. Vansittart expressed the belief that Germany was the primary threat in the long term. The committee agreed and then came to grips with the question of how Japan should be dealt with in view of the position of Germany. Fisher of the Treasury argued that because the nation lacked the resources to engage two first-class powers at the same time it had to decide which was the more serious threat and concentrate on that. Fisher suggested that it would be as well to gain Japan's respect by a show of resolve in the Far East. He therefore recommended the rapid completion of the base in Singapore and the modernization of part of the fleet for operations there.

To deal with the German threat the committee proposed a five-year programme to remedy the deficiencies of the armed forces. Under this programme the Royal Air Force would be brought up to fifty-two squadrons, a strength recommended and approved in 1923 but never achieved owing to subsequent economies. The Army was to be able to put 4 infantry divisions, 1 tank brigade and 1 cavalry division on the continent within five years. For the Royal Navy the committee recommended that the existing fleet should be modernized, new bases built and the air arm increased. This report resulted from the DRC's first meeting and was discussed by the cabinet on 14 March 1934. Their initial discussion reached no decisions and they had a second meeting on the matter five days later.

Nothing was settled at this meeting and it was decided that an outside committee should make a decision on the terms of reference. In effect the report was shelved as the cabinet was unwilling to come to grips with the unpleasant and expensive realities it set forth. Pressure from the Chiefs of Staff on 20 April forced the cabinet to make a decision. Their decision was that those questions should be turned over to the Ministerial Committee on the Disarmament Conference.

Thus the matter of rearmament was discussed by a disarmament committee. The membership of this committee consisted entirely of politicians, and it was therefore going to consider the political and economic implications of any proposed course of action. In the political climate of the time, with pacifism still a dominant force and an election a little more than a year away, the committee was not going to go out of its way to adopt programmes that would upset large segments of the electorate.

The first meeting of the Ministerial Committee on the Disarmament Conference discussed the DRC report. Having decided that it was better to improve relations with Japan rather than spend money on Singapore and the modernization of the Royal Navy in the Far East, the committee then considered the German threat. Chamberlain questioned the need for the Continental Force. It was pointed out that if Germany was going to control Belgium and Holland she would have an ideal area from which to bomb England. Chamberlain replied that if the RAF were built up it could provide a deterrent to Germany's even thinking of such a move. This in part stemmed from a statement made by Baldwin in November 1932 in a speech to the House of Commons when he spoke about air attacks by hostile bombers and said: 'In the next war you will find that any town which is within reach of an aerodrome can be bombed within the first five minutes of war from the air. It is well for the man in the street to realize that there is no power on earth that can protect him from being bombed. Whatever people may tell him the bomber will always get through.' Chamberlain's counter to this threat by German bombers was to suggest the building up of a strong bomber force for the RAF. The report from the Defence Requirements Committee was also sent to the Treasury. As a result of the Treasury report and further discussions by the disarmament committee it was resolved on 12 July 1934 that the Army should receive a budget of £20 million to be spent over five years, while the RAF should receive a further forty new squadrons to act as a deterrent to Germany and inspire confidence at home.

The actions over this period of time illustrate the way in which requirements were formulated by professional defence people for the defence of all of Britain's interests and were dealt with by politicians in a way that can only be described as vacillating. This approach, coupled with the Treasury's reluctance to spend money on defence, resulted in a very slow improvement in the quality and size of Britain's forces. However, there were two sides to this question.

On 4 March 1935 a White Paper on Defence stated that the government had to increase defence expenditure because of the deterioration of the international situation and the failure of the Disarmament Conference. On 9 March Hitler used the White Paper, which he claimed was directed against Germany, as a pretext to announce the existence of the German Air Force to the world. This made the government sit up and ask the Air Ministry for an assessment of the relative strengths of the two air forces.

The cabinet appointed a sub-committee of the Disarmament Committee on Air Parity to look into the situation. The committee recommended that to obtain parity it would be necessary to spend almost £10 million more than the current air estimate. On 21 May 1935 the cabinet authorized that the numbers and types of planes suggested be ordered immediately, subject to Treasury review.

This was called Scheme C, and required the purchase of 3,800 planes between then and April 1937. This would not only enable Britain to maintain parity with Germany, but would encourage the expansion of the aircraft industry.

While Scheme C was being debated in parliament, the Defence Requirements Committee was assessing what was needed for all three services to provide adequate defence of the country. The resultant plan was called the Ideal Scheme and was presented on 11 November 1935; each of the services was considered.

The RAF reserves were to be expanded (in addition to the already authorized Scheme C); the Royal Navy would have a fleet sufficient to meet Japan in the Far East, while still being able to deal with a simultaneous threat in home waters; and the Army was to be able to put a Field Force of 4 infantry divisions, 1 tank brigade and 1 cavalry division on the continent within a time-frame to be determined.

The main problem with the Ideal Scheme was its cost, which was more than £400 million above and beyond expenditure planned for the next four years. The Treasury position on the Ideal Scheme was put forward by Neville Chamberlain, then Chancellor of the Exchequer. He considered that it would exceed Britain's capacity to pay, and would thus dislocate the national economy. Therefore it would have to be scaled down to the point where it would be in line with the nation's resources. Scaling down demanded allocation of priorities, and Chamberlain argued that an RAF with a powerful strike capability was the best investment. The Royal Navy would receive second priority, and the Army a distant third.

Neville Chamberlain was Chancellor of the Exchequer 1931–7, and Prime Minister 1937–40. More than any other single person he was responsible for the ill-preparedness of Britain's armed forces at the outbreak of the Second World War.

These views were reinforced in respect of the Army by the industrialist Lord Weir, who considered that the logistics of equipping a Field Force made such a force unrealizable for several years. For the Army the decision was taken in February 1936 that plans be prepared for a Field Force to be ready in five years, and that all plans to expand the Territorial Army be cancelled.

The rearmament expenditure agreed in the 1936 budget continued to make the Treasury very uncomfortable. This discomfort was greatly reinforced when the defence services' estimates for the 1937 budget were received. The Treasury became determined that defence spending, and the borrowing required for it, could not be allowed to exceed certain prescribed limits. A memorandum was prepared by Richard Hopkins of the Treasury on the future of defence finance and was ready for Chamberlain when he became Prime Minister on 28 May 1937. Chamberlain then authorized the Treasury to draw up a plan for the complete re-evaluation of the rearmament programme based on the Hopkins paper. This plan, drawn up in a few weeks, recommended a detailed review by the services of their current and anticipated expenditures. The Treasury also recommended that until the review was completed, decisions on new defence programmes should be postponed.

During the summer of 1937, while this review was being carried out, the cabinet assigned to the Minister for the Co-ordination of Defence, Sir Thomas Inskip, the task of preparing a report recommending the direction and shape that rearmament should assume.

Inskip issued an interim report in December 1937, and the final report in February 1938. The basic strategy advocated was to limit Britain's military preparations to those sufficient to protect the country from a 'sudden knock-out blow'. This strategy meant that the order of priority for defence resources was: security of the United Kingdom; keeping the sea lanes open; defence of British territories; the fourth priority, and a bad last only to be undertaken after the other priorities had been met, was the Continental Force.

The Army felt, with good reason, that it had become the 'Cinderella' of the services. The Continental Force would have been made up of operational field units and would have been able to move quickly to combat aggression against continental allies. The table (Figure 1.1) shows that in the three really significant years for preparing an Army for 1939 (1936, 1937 and 1938) expenditure on the Army was lowest or equal lowest for the three services. Although the increases in expenditure were substantial in 1938 and especially 1939, by then it had become far too late to provide a well-trained and well-equipped Army for the Second World War when it broke out. The lead times for the design and manufacture of equipment, for the training of soldiers to man the equipment and for the development of leaders to command those soldiers, are measured in years. Months were all that were allowed by the blinkered, cowardly, appeasing politicians of pre-1939 Britain.

FIGURE 1.1: DEFENCE EXPENDITURE BY THE BRITISH GOVERNMENT 1930–9 (£ MILLION)					
Year	Navy	Army	Air Force	Total Defence	Total Government	Defence as % of Government
1930	52	40	18	110	881	13
1931	51	39	18	108	851	13
1932	50	36	17	103	859	12
1933	53	38	17	108	778	14
1934	57	40	17	114	797	14
1935	65	45	27	137	842	15
1936	81	55	50	186	902	21
1937	102	73	82	257	979	25
1938	132	122	143	397	1033	38
1939	182	242	295	719	1490	48

The various delays imposed by the government on the development of even the most modest Army impacted on all its branches; infantry, tanks, artillery, engineers and signals. The greatest impact was felt by those branches of the Army where lead times for the design and manufacture of equipment was the largest. The lead time for a new tank – from the initial specification to receipt of operational tanks by field units – cannot be fewer than three years and may be as many as six. This assumes that there is a reasonably firm specification at the outset, i.e., the users of tanks or their superiors can state clearly what the tank is required to do. The broad requirements are translated into specifics, such as: what main gun or guns are needed, and what ancillary armament; how fast the tank must move, and over what sort of country; what range of operation is needed, and thus how much fuel; what opposition is to be expected, and what protection or thickness of armour is appropriate.

A major problem for British tank designers and manufacturers in the interwar years was the lack of a detailed specification. This stemmed in turn from uncertainty as to how tanks should be used. The first matter to consider is therefore the function of an armoured force. What are the useful contributions that tanks can make as part of an Army? This forms the subject of the next chapter.

APPENDIX 1.1   THE TREATY OF VERSAILLES

1. Chronology
President Woodrow Wilson developed a statement of fourteen points to serve as a basis for the cessation of hostilities between Germany and the Allied Powers. He presented this statement to the US Congress on 8 January 1918. He amplified the points in various speeches during 1918. (A summary of the fourteen points and the chronology for 1918 are given in Section 2.)

The terms of the armistice had to be formalized into a treaty. The Paris Peace Conference debated this treaty, starting on 18 January 1919. On 7 May 1919 the terms of the treaty were presented to a German delegation summoned to hear them; Germany had not been represented at the Peace Conference.

The Germans were outraged by many of the terms and the differences between them and the Fourteen Points. But they were in no position to take any action by force, and signed the treaty on 28 June 1919. The main heads of the treaty are described in Section 3. Finally, treaties were signed with Germany's supporters; those treaties are listed in Section 4.

2. President Woodrow Wilson's Fourteen Points, presented to the US Congress on 8 January 1918.
1. Open covenants of peace openly arrived at, with no subsequent private understandings.
2. Absolute freedom of navigation on the seas.

3. Removal of all economic barriers between all nations consenting to peace.
4. National armaments to be reduced to minimum consistent with domestic safety.
5. Impartial adjustment of colonial claims.
6. Evacuation of Russian territory.
7. Evacuation and restoration of Belgium.
8. All French territory to be freed, invaded portions restored, including Alsace Lorraine.
9. Italian frontiers to be readjusted.
10. Peoples of Austria–Hungary to have freest opportunity of autonomous development.
11. Romania, Serbia and Montenegro evacuated; territorial integrity of Balkan states to be guaranteed.
12. Turkey be to assured secure sovereignty; Turkish-occupied territories to be given opportunity for autonomous development.
13. Independent Polish state to be set up and guaranteed: Poland should have free and secure access to the sea.
14. A general association of nations to be formed to afford political independence and territorial integrity to all nations great and small.

President Wilson developed his theories during 1918 with the following statements:

11 February 1918, to US Congress: The Four Principles.
4 July 1918: The Four Ends: these can be summarized into one sentence: 'We seek the reign of law, based on the consent of the governed and sustained by the organized opinion of mankind.'
27 September 1918: The Five Particulars: these stress the need for impartial justice and the avoidance of any covert groupings of league members for any purpose whatsoever.

On 4 October 1918 the German government requested President Wilson to bring about an armistice on the basis of the Fourteen Points. After discussions with Germany President Wilson asked the Allied governments if they would grant an armistice on the basis of the Fourteen Points. They agreed, but with two modifications:

• Exclusion of Point 2, freedom of navigation on the seas
• Inclusion of a reparations clause: 'Compensation will be made by Germany for all damage done to the civilian population of the Allies and their property by the aggression of Germany by land, by sea, and from the air.'

These conditions were presented to the German government by President Wilson on 5 November 1918. The German government gave no written reply to these terms, but accepted them by asking FM Foch, Generalissimo of Allied Forces, for an armistice. This was granted on 11 November 1918.

3. Analysis of the Treaty of Versailles, 1919

Signed on 28 June 1919 and brought into force by exchange of notifications on 10 January 1920. Note that this treaty was only between the Allied Powers and Germany. The treaty had fifteen parts; there was no direct relationship between the parts and the Fourteen Points, although some of the points found expression in the treaty.

Part I: The establishment of the League of Nations, intended to unite all its signatories in a league guaranteeing their territorial independence and integrity.

Parts II & III: Territorial dispositions: Germany lost territory in the west, north and east.

West: Belgium acquired from Germany the frontier districts of Moresnel, Eupen and Malmedy; Luxembourg ceased to be associated with Germany in a customs union and later entered into an economic union with Belgium; the Saar basin was placed under the control of the League of Nations, with a plebiscite to take place in 1935 (it was, and the Saar voted to return to Germany); Alsace and Lorraine were ceded to France by Germany; the left (west) bank of the Rhine and the right bank to a line drawn 50 km to the east were demilitarized.

North: Germany lost northern Schleswig to Denmark in a plebiscite; the Flensburg zone elected for Germany.

East: Germany ceded West Prussia and most of the province of Poznan to Poland. This created a corridor separating East Prussia from the rest of Germany. Danzig was created a free city under the league.

Part IV German rights and interests outside Germany: Germany ceded all its overseas colonies to the Allied powers, who distributed them to various mandatories.

Part V Military, naval and air clauses: Germany agreed to reduce its Army to 100,000; the size of the Navy was restricted, and no replacement ship was to exceed 10,000 tons; all naval and military air forces were prohibited, and all aircraft and other equipment were to be destroyed.

Part VI Prisoners of war were to be returned, and graves were to be maintained.

Part VII Kaiser Wilhelm II was to be tried as a war criminal; however, the Dutch government refused to release him and the matter lapsed.

Part VIII Germany was to accept responsibility for losses and damage caused by Germany and her allies, and to pay reparation for it.

Part IX Financial clauses: these relate to the technicalities of German reparation payments and other financial matters.

Part X Economic clauses: these clauses dealt with the restoration of commercial relations; the most important provision was that securing 'most favoured nation' treatment from Germany for five years without reciprocity.

Part XI Aerial navigation: Allied aircraft had full liberty of passage over Germany until 1 January 1923.

Part XII Ports, waterways and railways: the main aim of this section was to secure international control over rivers which flow through more than one country. International commissions were set up to control the Rhine, Elbe, Oder and Danube rivers.

Part XIII Labour. This section created the International Labour Organization through which the league members would endeavour to secure and maintain fair and humane conditions of labour for all workers.

Part XIV Guarantees: the Rhineland, and bridgeheads across the Rhine at Cologne, Coblenz and Mainz, were to be occupied for varying periods up to fifteen years.

Part XV Miscellaneous provisions, none of great significance for subsequent history.

4. Other Treaties Determining the Outcome of the First World War

The Treaty of Versailles was between the Allied Powers and Germany; it did not include those countries that at one time or another during the conflict had supported Germany. Treaties with those other countries were signed at different places and at different times as follows:

10 September 1919:	Austria signed the Treaty of St Germain.
27 November 1919:	Bulgaria signed the Treaty of Neuilly.
4 June 1920:	Hungary signed the Treaty of the Trianon.
10 August 1920:	Turkey signed the Treaty of Sèvres.

CHAPTER 2

How are Tanks Used?

Scene: Salisbury Plain, 3 March 1932

The three young officers all wore the cap badge of the Royal Tank Corps (RTC). They shivered as they stood on the ridge and looked over the farmlands and woods towards the river. It was 7 a.m.

'Hell of a time to meet.'

'CO always likes an early start, but he could have chosen a warmer day.'

'Do we know it's going to be him that's coming?'

'That's my bet. Look, isn't that a scout car coming up the hill there?'

They watched as the scout car came to a halt. A tall figure dismounted, leaned in to say something to his driver, and walked across to the three officers. As he approached they came to attention and saluted.

'Good morning, gentlemen. Right time, right place; good. At ease, and I'll tell you what this is about. But first, you've all prepared your thoughts on the paper I sent you?'

'Yes, Colonel.'

'Well then. This is part of a programme to get ideas from throughout the Tank Corps as to how tanks can be used. It started at the top, and the General reckoned that it would be useful to get the thoughts of forward-thinking officers in an informal way. He asked me to select one subaltern from each squadron, give them a major tactical problem, and get their thoughts on what forces they would need and how they would use them. You've all had the same problem outlined to you in my confidential memo, and now I want your ideas. As I said in the memo, don't be restricted in your thinking.

'One final point before we start. Don't get too carried away with being selected for this. Your squadron commanders have given good reports on all of you, but there are plenty of others not far behind.

'Right, let's start with you, Pat. That village over there, Parbury, is held by what appears to be an enemy division. We can assume they have artillery, but haven't identified any other supporting forces. As you've been told, you are in command of a mobile force of about divisional strength, but you've been given a choice of what's in the force. Tell me how your force is organized, and what you're going to do with it.'

'Yes, Sir. First, my force would be based round the tank brigade with mediums. I'd have a brigade of light tanks, a regiment of artillery, and a battalion of infantry. We would advance to the line of that road there' – Pat pointed to a road about a mile short of the river and parallel to it, indicated by a line of trees – 'with the tank brigade. The light brigade and the artillery would advance to the same place. As soon as the artillery were ready to fire we would start to shell Parbury, and advance with the light brigade to assault the bridge. From there we'd be guided by enemy reaction.'

'Fine, Pat, I'll ask you some questions and raise a few points when we've heard the others. You next, Bob.'

'Sir. Like Pat's, the central part of my force would be the tank brigade. I'd reverse the size of the infantry and the light tanks by having a brigade of infantry and a single regiment of light tanks. The light tanks would be used for reconnaissance, and the infantry would have lorries to move them forward quickly. I'd have three regiments of artillery, and a bridging company of engineers. The general plan would be to make a diversionary attack on Parbury, but with the main attack slightly later on the bridge about three miles downstream.' He pointed. 'I'd bring the artillery up to a position where it could support either attack, a mile back from the river and half-way between the bridges. The main attack would be an infantry assault, with the intention of seizing the downstream bridge and putting the tank brigade across. The infantry would hold the bridgehead, and the tank brigade would start to roll the enemy position up from the downstream bridge to Parbury. That's it broadly, Sir.'

'Thanks, Bob. My comments later, as for Pat. Now you, Charles.'

'My force would be almost the same as Bob's, Sir, and you know that none of us knew who else was going to be here. The only addition to my force is a squadron of RAF for close support, partly for reconnaissance and partly for bombing. My plan is different, because I know there's a ford suitable for tanks almost half-way between Parbury and the downstream bridge. I'd use the planes to check the defence, and I'm making the assumption that their main defence will be at Parbury, with a secondary strongpoint at the downstream bridge, and a mobile force as reserve.

'The light tank regiment and a company of infantry will make the first attack towards Parbury, while all the rest will advance to the same spot as Bob's artillery. Then one tank regiment and a company of infantry will attack towards the downstream bridge. The attacks to Parbury and the downstream bridge will be covered by smokescreens, and then we'd put in the main assault across the ford. Once this was gained and consolidated we'd call on the follow-up troops, and assume that the defences at Parbury and the bridge would fall back as soon as they saw they were outflanked.'

It is most unlikely that such a discussion ever took place, but it might have been better if it had. The composition and use of mobile forces were topics for endless debate, but unfortunately very few real life experiments were ever undertaken. It was thus likely that the view of the most opinionated or forceful would prevail, irrespective of whether it was the best.

USE OF TANKS IN THE FIRST WORLD WAR

During the First World War the aeroplane and the tank were used for the first time as weapons of war, and their performance developed and improved rapidly. The aeroplane had been in production before the war, but the tactics of using it as a military weapon had not been thought out in any detail, and had to be developed as the war progressed. Its principal roles were reconnaissance, the support of ground forces, and bombing military and other objectives.

The tank was the second major new weapon of war. The idea of the tank was developed during 1915 and 1916, and its first use was on 15 September 1916, two years after the beginning of the war. The periods of use of the tank can be divided into two, the first being from 15 September 1916 to 20 November 1917. During this first year it was used piecemeal and had all kinds of problems. The problems stemmed partly from the mechanical condition of the tanks which resulted in frequent breakdowns. Secondly, the conditions for the crew inside the tank were such that the fumes from the engine and from the weapons when used created such a poisonous atmosphere within the tank that after a day's fighting the most ardent crews were almost incapable of further action for another twenty-four hours. In addition, there was some doubt in the minds of senior people in the Army as to exactly how the tanks should be used. It was also unclear in the minds of the tank crews themselves. One of the crews who took part in the first battle on 15 September 1916 had this to say in respect of that action: 'Our crew did not have a tank of our own the whole time we were in England. Ours went wrong the day it arrived. We had no reconnaissance or map reading, no practices or lectures on the compass, we had no signalling and no practice in considering orders. We had no knowledge of where to look for information that would be necessary for us as tank commanders, nor did we know what information we should be likely to require.'

Capt Bertram Saxon Beale, MC, G Battalion, Tank Corps, 1916. In this photograph the author's Uncle Bert is wearing the badges of the Heavy Machine Gun Corps.

It is surprising in the light of this lack of training and instruction that the tanks were able to perform at all. But in the period September 1916 to November 1917 they performed quite effectively on a number of occasions, although generally in small numbers. They also performed very ineffectively on a number of occasions, and in so doing discouraged the infantry from having confidence in the help that the tanks might be able to give them.

The second year of their use started on 20 November 1917 with the Battle of Cambrai. This battle showed how effective the tanks could be if they were used en masse and on reasonable going. The lessons of Cambrai generated much greater confidence in the use of tanks by both the people they were supporting and by the army commanders. The result was to accelerate the requirements and the flow of tanks to the armies in France. They performed well in the defensive battles of March, April and May 1918, and at the Battle of Hamel on 4 July 1918 the tanks, in the shape of the 5th Tank Brigade, supported Australian infantry with great success. This battle, which was commanded on the Allied side by the Australian Gen Monash, was very successful in that it was quick, caused few casualties to the Australians and the British, but caused substantial casualties to the Germans and captured the ground that was their objective.

On 8 August 1918 tanks were used in even larger quantities in the commencement of what was the final 100 days of the First World War. Tanks in these last 100 days performed valuable support functions to the infantry and demonstrated their positive and negative points. One positive was in the shape of the use of lighter tanks, or 'whippets' as they were called. A particular Whippet that performed outstandingly was that commanded by Lt C.D. Arnold who was in action from 4.20 a.m. on 8 August until his tank ('Musical Box') was knocked out and set on fire at 3.30 p.m. In the course of this time he had moved extensively through and behind the German lines and had created chaos by shooting up field batteries, destroying transport and killing large numbers of German soldiers. Finally his tank was set on fire, one of his crew was killed and he and his gunner were taken prisoner. When he returned from prison after the war and recounted his tale – which was supported by his senior officer Maj Rycroft and some Australian officers – he was awarded a well-deserved DSO.

The main battle tanks (mainly Mk Vs in 1918) provided the second positive in that they fulfilled the roles they had been designed for: the crushing of wire and the close support of infantry.

The negative aspect of the battles of 8 August and subsequent days was that the tanks available for fighting decreased in numbers very rapidly. From more than 450 on the first day there were about 150 left on the second day and 85 on the third. The casualties were due partly to mechanical breakdown, partly to enemy action and partly to the exhaustion and sickness of the crews. The reason for the sickness of the crews, as stated earlier, was the appalling atmospheric conditions within the tanks.

There was no doubt that the use of tanks over the last two years of the war, and in particular over the last year, contributed considerably to the Allied victory somewhat earlier than had been expected. But it was primarily a victory for the infantry and the artillery, and it was necessary to be careful in making too much of the tanks' contribution.

The lessons in terms of this new weapon were not easy to learn. They were certainly most effective as a means of breaking through barbed-wire defences and crossing trench systems which were impossible for wheeled vehicles and difficult for cavalry. So as a support for infantry they were very valuable. The example of Lt Arnold's tank 'Musical Box' was a pointer in another direction. Light tanks such as the Whippet, if made capable of higher speeds, would be a very potent weapon in exploiting a breakthrough. A force of mobile, quick, light tanks could create all kinds of difficulties for troops behind the front line, once the front line had been broken. One particular aspect of this was the possibility of destroying enemy headquarters and thus, as it were, cutting off the head of the enemy and the brain with it. So there were various lessons to be learned and various ways in which proposals could be drawn up for the use of tanks in subsequent conflicts.

The Medium A Whippet 'Julian's Baby', presumably belonging to J Battalion, Royal Tank Corps; the Whippet was designed as a fast cavalry or pursuit tank to exploit breakthrough opportunities created by the heavy tanks. (Tank Museum, not numbered)

FACTORS AFFECTING TANK TACTICAL DOCTRINE

As a result of their experiences of the war a number of people drew conclusions from the way that tanks could be used; those people can be categorized into three groups: the High Command; senior staff of the Tank Corps; and tank crewmen.

The High Command could see how tanks were available for use to help the infantry to get through heavy defences. In a letter to Sir Douglas Haig on 21 August 1918 the Chief of the Imperial General Staff (CIGS) Sir Henry Wilson wrote, 'The old Boche is learning the art and science of retiring and with more practice he will become perfect. I wish to goodness we had 4,000 or 5,000 more tanks to give you now as we ought to have had if we had looked more into the future.' This was a significant comment from the person who was in effect head of the Army.

The second group of people who could comment on the use of tanks and the lessons to be learned from using them were the senior staff of the Royal Tank Corps (RTC) itself. Col J.F.C. Fuller was one of the staff officers at tank headquarters and his views will be described later. But all the people at that headquarters were in a position to draw lessons from the actions they had commanded or taken part in.

The third group whose views could be significant in determining how tanks could be used – and possibly how they could be made – were the people who actually fought in them. The commanders of the tank battalions, the company commanders, troop commanders and the crew members themselves all would have views as to how tanks could be most effectively used. In addition to these, the people who maintained and supplied the tanks would have views as to the way in which they could be handled tactically and logistically.

There were four major factors to be taken into account in the development of tank tactical doctrine after the First World War. The first was the role for the Army as a whole. It was necessary to decide where the Army would be required to fight in the future in order to determine what type of armoured force would be appropriate. The three roles for the Army were home defence, imperial defence and the provision of the Continental Force. Would the armoured component helping to carry out these three roles need to develop different tactics for each role, and would different types of tank be needed?

The second factor to be considered was the tanks themselves; what tanks were available and what tanks might be available? The lines of development being considered in 1919 included an extension of the Mk Vs into Mk VIIIs and Mk IXs; the Whippet tanks and developments of those; and faster and heavier tanks than the Whippets, designated the medium Cs and medium Ds.

The third factor to be considered was the role of the tank, which of course relates in part to the tanks available. The following roles were considered as potentially appropriate: close support for infantry, providing direct shell and machine-gun fire to complement indirect fire support from artillery; flank guard for infantry and other formations, taking over the role previously discharged by cavalry; anti-tank defence against hostile tank forces; and exploitation, in the sense of a heavy force capable of creating disruption behind enemy lines but equally capable of defending itself should it be attacked by hostile tank forces.

The fourth factor was the integration of tanks with other arms. Tanks need to work at different times with infantry, artillery, engineers, and air support. They must also have satisfactory systems of logistical support, including in particular the provision of supplies and the maintenance of all equipment. The degree to which these different arms should be permanently integrated one with another must be decided, and the appropriate organizational structure set up. It is obviously possible to have a separate tank brigade which operates purely as a tank brigade. But from time to time it will need artillery support, and when it is in the front line it will need infantry support. Thus the organization structure for armoured formations must be designed in conjunction with the policies for the use of tanks.

DEVELOPMENT OF DOCTRINE, 1919–45

BETWEEN THE WARS

Tanks were a new form of weaponry which had only been in existence for two years when the First World War ended, but had been used with considerable success in various ways during those last two years. What was needed now was to bring together the lessons learnt and apply them to probable future needs. As soon as the war was over the Army, naturally, was reduced considerably in size. It was therefore necessary for those who remained with the regular Army to consider first of all how it was to be used and secondly what were the tools that it needed to fulfil its roles. In the early period immediately following the First World War, fundamental questions such as the role of the Army in helping to achieve national objectives were not a topic for immediate consideration; also, at this time there were not many people who were capable of, or had an interest in, attempting to answer such questions.

One person who thought very deeply on these matters, however, was Col J.F.C. Fuller. He was at this time at the War Office, and when his plan for the use of tanks in 1919 was no longer necessary he started to think about the way in which tanks should be used in the future. He and others who had served in the RTC wanted to do all they could to ensure that it continued to exist. There was uncertainty that this new arm would remain, and in other countries, as for example the United States, it was subsumed under the infantry. In Britain the RTC did maintain a continued separate existence which was helped by the patronage of King George V who became its Colonel in Chief. Fuller determined to promote the use of the RTC by showing how tanks could be used effectively in future conflicts. His policies were set out in a paper which he submitted as an entry for the Royal United Service Institute (RUSI) Gold Medal Military Prize Essay for 1919. He described these views in a lecture that he gave to the RUSI on 'the development of sea warfare on land and its influence on future naval operations'. This lecture was given on 11 February 1920 and Fuller was introduced by the chairman as the man 'very largely responsible for getting out the tactics of the tanks'.

Col (later Maj Gen) J.F.C. ('Boney') Fuller, who took a big part (although not as big as he thought himself) in the early development of tank tactics. His attitude and personality were two of the main reasons why many of his excellent ideas were not adopted.

The tone of Fuller's lecture and its content can be judged by some of what he said: 'Let us now become clairvoyant as regards to the future. I see a fleet operating against a fleet, not at sea but on land: cruisers and battleships and destroyers. My astral form follows one side and I notice that it is in difficulty; it cannot see;

there appears an aeroplane and it gives it sight. It says by wireless telegraphy the enemy are yonder. The approach begins. I see a man in one of the aeroplanes, his head is swollen with the future. He is the Commander-in-Chief of the land fleet I am following.'

There were many who thought that it was Fuller's head that was swollen. But it has to be said that his clairvoyant observations were born out of what had happened, and that he did have realistic ideas as to how tanks could be used. There is no record that the War Office or the General Staff decided anything about the way in which tanks should be used in the future. There was, in fact, an analysis put in hand to determine what lessons should be learnt from the First World War. However, the work of this committee was not finalized until the Kirke Report was presented in 1932. Thus the experience of the soldiers and staffs who had managed the arms used by the British Army in the First World War was not consolidated until it had become almost out of date and useless.

Although Fuller was the first to record his thoughts about the use of tanks he was by no means the only person. The next person to consider is George Lindsay. Lindsay had been in the Machine Gun Corps during the war and when the war was over he went to Iraq where he commanded a force of armoured cars. He returned to England in 1923 and became Chief Instructor at the Royal Tank Corps (RTC) Centre for two years. He became Inspector RTC at the War Office in 1925 and remained there until 1929. In 1924 while he was still at the RTC Centre Lindsay began advocating the setting up of a properly organized mechanical force. This would consist of aircraft, armoured cars, fast tanks, motorized artillery, motorized mortars and motorized machine-guns. Such a small but properly proportioned force of this nature was, for that time, an innovative military structure. In 1924, however, the Chief of the Imperial General Staff (CIGS) was Lord Cavan, a somewhat conservative officer, and he did not act on Lindsay's proposal.

Cavan retired as CIGS in 1926 and his successor in February of that year was Gen Sir George Milne. Milne had commanded the British force at Salonika during the last two years of the war. He was known to his troops as 'Uncle George' and was open to new ideas and aware of his difficulties of running the Army with practically no money. He was persuaded (or he decided) to appoint Fuller as his Military Assistant. While the position of Military Assistant is not a highly significant role, he is in constant contact with the CIGS and has every opportunity to present ideas to him. It was therefore an opportunity to present ideas for the use of armoured forces to the highest military person in the Army.

On 15 May 1926 Lindsay submitted to Milne through Fuller some suggestions for making the Army, and the Royal Tank Corps in particular, more suited to the probable requirements of a future war. Because the Army was short of funds it could make a choice between manpower and weapon power. Lindsay recommended that the General Staff set up a mechanical force and carry out experiments to see how it should be most effectively constituted and handled. Milne had some reservations but on balance thought positively about Lindsay's idea.

Col George Lindsay, Inspector Royal Tank Corps at the War Office 1925–9, was an advocate of a properly organized mechanical force (the forerunner of an armoured division). His influenced waned after his perceived lack of success in the 1934 exercises. (Tank Museum 1573/B2)

Within the War Office at this time was a Col Lewin, and he commented on Lindsay's plan with the principal suggestion that some additional arms should be added to the mechanical force, in particular infantry, artillery, engineers and a reconnaissance company on motorcycles. Lindsay was opposed to the transfer of any fighting vehicles to other units, especially cavalry, and wanted no infantry in the mechanical force. This attitude created a problem for other units of the Army. It seemed that Lindsay was all out for the RTC at the expense of every other type of unit, in particular the cavalry. This was not an attitude which was politically sensible, although Milne did endorse the policy of the Royal Tank Corps in an experimental force in June 1926.

It was decided that the Experimental Mechanical Force (EMF), as it was now called, should be established at Tidworth under the control of 3rd Infantry Division commanded by Maj Gen John Burnett-Stuart. On 13 November 1926 the General Staff held a demonstration for the benefit of the cabinet and dominion prime ministers attending an imperial conference. In appalling weather the audience was treated to a demonstration of the older weapons that had been used in the First World War, followed by the more modern tanks and other mechanized forces. The tanks charged towards the spectators and just before reaching them turned sharply to the right to form a column and drove past.

The War Office was clearly doing what it could within its limited budget to develop an acceptance and use of a modern armoured force. On 24 December 1926 Fuller was appointed to command the 7th Infantry Brigade, which included command of the experimental force. This involved the additional duty of being the officer in charge of the local establishment. Fuller considered this matter for some time and after several arguments decided that he would not take on the position of commander, and in March 1927 he presented his resignation. Although several people tried to persuade him to reconsider his decision he remained adamant. He thus gave away an opportunity of developing the EMF and it was felt by many people that he had betrayed the future of the Royal Tank Corps and armoured forces generally.

It was decided that Col Jack Collins should be transferred to the command of the EMF, which was formed on 1 May 1927. After it had gathered itself together it started on collective training on 19 August. On 8 September Milne visited the force and praised the work it was doing, and on 27 September 1927 the culmination of the collective training was a mock battle when the EMF took on the 3rd Infantry Division and a brigade of horsed cavalry. Both forces performed well and many lessons were learnt from the exercise, not only by the British Army but also by other armies.

In the next year, 1928, the Experimental Mechanical Force continued its exercises but when they were over the force was closed down. This was taken to be an indication by the General Staff and the CIGS that they were no longer concerned with the training of this force. However, from statements made later it was clear that the CIGS felt that the exercises had been practical and valuable, but that repetition of the exercises would not provide further value.

In 1929 a book was produced called *Handbook on Mechanized and Armoured Formations*, which was generally called the *Purple Primer* because of the colour of its cover. It was produced by Charles Broad in consultation with George Lindsay. Broad had

Charles Broad (in beret, with map board) on Salisbury Plain, 1931. On his right is the Chief of the Imperial General Staff, Sir George Milne (Uncle George of Salonica). (Tank Museum 884/D5)

served in the First World War in the artillery and after serving as an instructor at the Staff College transferred to the RTC in 1923. He became Commandant of the Tank Gunnery School and in 1925 he succeeded George Lindsay as Chief Instructor at the Royal Tank Corps Centre. Between 1927 and 1931 Broad was serving as deputy Director of Staff Duties at The War Office. He was responsible for producing the *Handbook on Mechanized and Armoured Formations*, as well as an updated version which appeared in 1931 called *Modern Formations*. The *Purple Primer* is an important document in the sense that it is the first statement in any official way regarding the use of armoured troops. The two main sections of the handbook are organization and operations. Various formations are considered which include a cavalry brigade, a light armoured brigade, an infantry brigade, a medium armoured brigade, and divisional and other troops. When these are brought together, however, the infantry are not mentioned in any higher organization. In looking at operations it starts off by saying: 'It is not intended to lay down details of the employment of armoured brigades, since these can be worked out only in actual practice, but rather to indicate the general principles which should be followed. The main principle is that ground is of primary importance and open country is the country suitable for armoured forces whereas enclosed country is favourable to infantry.'

The objectives suitable for an armoured brigade acting independently are listed as: hostile cavalry formations; because cavalry have great speed across country an attacking tank force should make sure that they deny the cavalry entry to any available cover which would be difficult for tanks to enter; hostile infantry formations; in most cases infantry would not expose themselves to tank attack in open country and therefore it would be necessary to influence the infantry to leave cover or attack them before they can reach it; lines of communication; it is suggested that these would normally be provided with elaborate anti-tank protection and therefore surprise is the essence of such an effort; hostile armoured formations, of which it was stated (in 1929) 'such formations do not exist at the moment and because the subject is therefore purely theoretical it will not be further discussed'.

A further section considers the attack in cooperation with other arms and the statement is made here that, 'in allotting tasks to formations, the commander will bear in mind the special characteristics of each arm and use the ground accordingly.'

The information given in this pamphlet is so general as to be of little value. It would seem to be unfortunate that this is the best set of conclusions that could have been made from the exercises of the EMF in 1927 and 1928. Broad did make two comments in his conclusion relating to the sort of people who should be employed as armoured soldiers. He said: 'Morale depends mainly on the confidence a man has in his weapons. A good education is therefore essential if full use is to be made of tanks and their armament.'

Charles Broad in the Medium Command Tank 'Boxcar', Salisbury Plain 1931, commanding the 1st Brigade Royal Tank Corps which contained the 2nd, 3rd, and 5th Battalions. (Tank Museum 884/C5)

'The success of armoured formations will also depend considerably on the technical knowledge of the various commanders from the highest to the lowest. That is to say, unless officers are fully competent mechanically, they will not be able to get the best out of their machines, to judge their limitations, to keep them in action, to prepare them again quickly for renewed effort, or to recommend technical improvements to those whose work it is constantly to improve design.' These precepts would certainly have been of great value had they been learnt and executed by those who soldiered in armoured formations from that time on. The updated version, *Modern Formations*, published in 1931 did include a little more discussion on the use of armour with other arms but once again was not specific enough to provide guidance for those who would actually have to fight with such formations.

In 1931 a tank brigade was established as an experimental formation with Broad in command. In that same year exercises were carried out with the intention of finding an effective means of command using radio. This was done within a fortnight. The tank brigade put on a display of movement in formation which was controlled by Broad's voice on the radio. His words were received in the battalion and company commanders' vehicles and the brigade was able to sustain formation even when passing through a dense fog.

In February 1933 Sir George Milne retired as CIGS after seven years. He was succeeded by Sir Archibald Montgomery-Massingberd who had served in the First World War as Chief of Staff to the commander of the Fourth Army. Montgomery-Massingberd (hereafter called MM) was later given a particularly bad press by military writers such as Basil Liddell Hart. MM was in some ways a traditionalist, but, as many of his actions and writings show, he did his best to progress the modernization of the British Army. In autumn 1933 he established the tank brigade as a permanent formation. He gave the command to Percy Hobart, a dedicated and forceful officer. Hobart had served with distinction in the engineers in the First World War, and transferred to the Royal Tank Corps in 1923. He was a man of firm and fixed views, an excellent trainer of troops and an officer who – for good or bad – had a significant effect on the development of Britain's armoured forces between 1930 and 1945.

Maj Gen P.C.S. (Percy) Hobart, known with reverence and fear by many RTR soldiers as 'Hobo', was a clear thinker and a brilliant trainer; his lack of rapport with the General Staff inhibited wider use of some of his good ideas. (Tank Museum 1573/B6)

After Hobart's appointment as commander of the tank brigade there was some discussion between Lindsay and Hobart as to the relationship of the tank brigade to various other formations. On 17 November 1933 Lindsay wrote to Hobart and suggested that the tank brigade could be incorporated into a mobile division which would consist of the tank brigade, the motorized cavalry brigade, the motorized infantry brigade, mechanized artillery and supporting forces. This was simply an idea at this stage and neither Lindsay nor Hobart had the authority to create a mobile division. However, MM issued a directive for the training of the tank brigade in January of 1934. The directive suggested that the tank brigade could be employed on a strategic or semi-independent mission against some important objective in the enemy's rearward organization. The tank brigade should avoid strength and attack weakness. The directive for the training laid down that the main objectives were 'to test the manoeuvrability of the brigade as a whole, to practise cooperation with the RAF, to try out methods of supply and maintenance, and aim at moving 70 miles a day or 150 miles in three days including an action in each case'.

In spring 1934 the tank brigade assembled on Salisbury Plain. In May a staff exercise was held to develop the techniques to be used in the deployments envisaged in the exercises. In preliminary manoeuvres Hobart normally insisted on a very widely spaced formation for his brigade covering an area 10 miles broad by 10 miles deep. The forces against which he was opposed were generally unmechanized and they were invariably defeated. This imbalance was to be reduced in the main exercises scheduled for November by making the opposing force somewhat stronger, although still conventional. The two respective forces were:

• The tank brigade, commanded by Hobart, the 7th Infantry Brigade, a motorized field artillery brigade, and other supporting units together forming a small mechanized division (known as the Mobile Force) under the command of Lindsay.

• An unmechanized infantry division, a horsed cavalry brigade and two armoured car units. This force was commanded by Maj Gen John Kennedy.

The director of the exercise was John Burnett-Stuart, who was then GOC Southern Command. He felt that the older arms – infantry and cavalry – needed a boost to their morale because of the way that they had been consistently outmanoeuvred by the mechanized forces. He therefore made the exercise particularly demanding for the mechanized forces. The result of the exercise was a win for the conventional forces. There were three reasons for this: Lindsay was not well at the time of the exercise; the opposing force was effectively commanded by Kennedy; the umpiring throughout the exercise was biased against the mobile force.

This outcome was negative for the mechanized forces. It appeared that they could be opposed by conventional forces quite effectively. Lindsay's performance was strongly criticized by Burnett-Stuart, and from that moment on Lindsay's influence in the process of developing tank tactical policies began to weaken. Hobart, whose performance during the exercise had not been totally supportive of Lindsay, was perhaps the gainer from the exercise. His influence was towards an all-tank force, operating in a very dispersed fashion and without formal integration with infantry and artillery units. One positive aspect of the exercise was that after its completion Montgomery-Massingberd decided to form a mobile division to replace the horsed cavalry division. About a year later MM issued a policy paper entitled 'The future reorganization of the British Army'. MM resigned as CIGS about six months later and when he did so he wrote what he called 'Handing Over Notes' for the guidance of his successor, Sir Cyril Deverell. MM stated in the notes that: 'Intervention with the field army on the continent would be essential if a war were to break out with a continental power (the continental power was clearly Germany).'

The Field Force which could be sent to the continent (and the statement claimed that it would be ready to disembark overseas within a fortnight) was to consist of 1 mobile division, 4 infantry divisions and 2 air defence brigades. The infantry divisions were to be supported by one infantry tank battalion for each division.

He also recommended that eight regiments of cavalry should be mechanized, one in 1936 and the remainder by the end of 1938.

Another event in 1936 of importance to the development of British tanks and tank tactics was the visit by Maj Gen A.P. Wavell (later FM Lord Wavell) and the Assistant Director of Mechanization, Giffard Martel, to observe manoeuvres in Russia. The quantity of tanks possessed by the Russians impressed them greatly. They were also impressed by tanks using the suspension developed by J. Walter Christie in the United States. Martel thought this was so important that he decided to import a model of this tank from the United States to see how it could be used in the development of British tanks. (This development is described in a subsequent chapter.) But this type of tank had an effect on tactical doctrine in that it was seen to provide an additional type of tank which was called a 'cruiser'. Thus there were at this time about to be four different types of tanks in the British Army – light, medium, cruiser and infantry. The tactical use of these different types of vehicles was something which had not been clearly thought out.

In May 1937 Neville Chamberlain became Prime Minister. As Chancellor of the Exchequer, in charge of the Treasury, from 1932 he had been a major constraint on the development of weapons for the British Army. In his terms he was quite justified in that he had to consider the economic stability of Britain as well as its security. However, he was not by nature a person who supported a strong defensive posture, believing as he did that peace could be obtained more by diplomatic than by military means. He decided to appoint Leslie Hore-Belisha as Secretary of State for War. Hore-Belisha had performed well as the Minister for Transport and his name is immortalized in London by Belisha beacons. Although he had had military service in the First World War, he was not, nor pretended to be, a military thinker. It was suggested to him that he could benefit from military advice from Basil Liddell Hart. The two men found that they could work together and indeed their relationship was sometimes called 'the Partnership'. This meant that Liddell Hart's ideas about the use of the Army in general and the use of tanks in particular were fed into the ear of the man who had the greatest influence – except the Prime Minister and the Treasury – on military doctrine and resources.

In September 1937 the mobile division was effectively established and there was considerable discussion about the appointment of its commander. There were recommendations for a cavalry officer or alternatively, a Royal Tank Corps officer. In the end the command was given to Maj Gen Alan Brooke, an artillery officer. He was a most effective commander, although it could have been queried whether his previous experience was appropriate for a position as head of a new type of formation. He stated that one of the major problems of his command was to determine the correct policies for use of his formation. He said: 'There was on the one hand the necessity to evolve correct doctrine for the employment of armoured forces in the field of battle, and on the other hand some bridge must be found to span the large gap that existed in the relations betweens the extremists of the Tank Corps and the cavalry. There was no love lost between the two. The cavalry naturally resented deeply losing their horses, giving up their mounted role and becoming dungaree mechanics.' Thus at this point there was no clear doctrine as to how armoured forces should be used.

In December 1937 Hore-Belisha sacked Sir Cyril Deverell and appointed Lord Gort as CIGS. In January 1938 the new Army policy gave emphasis to home and imperial defence with the Continental Force as the lowest priority. This was, in part, due to Liddell-Hart's conviction that the continental role was the least important task of the Army. This he conveyed to Hore-Belisha, and the resulting economies in not having to provide a Continental Force were warmly welcomed by the Treasury.

In November 1938 the General Staff decided to form a second mobile division in Egypt, and Hobart was sent to command it. The 1st Mobile Division was renamed the 1st Armoured Division in February 1939 and was somewhat reduced in size. In the same month the cabinet acknowledged that the British Field Force must be brought up to continental standards. All of these changes in strategic policy made it difficult for the commanders at lower levels to determine exactly how they should employ the troops they commanded, and thus how to set up appropriate training programmes. It has to be said, however, and it was acknowledged many times, that the crew and collective training carried out by Hobart in Egypt made the forces that fought there in later years very capable of carrying out their operational duties.

TANK TACTICS AFTER 1939

Up to 1939 there had been little opportunity for any tank forces to gain experience of the effectiveness of their tank tactics in combat. There had been some opportunity for the forces who had taken part in the Spanish Civil War to see how their tanks operated and how they should work, both on their own and with other forces. But the numbers employed and the difficulties of terrain were not such as to give useful or correct information to those who were trying to draw lessons from those operations. In Britain the only opportunity to test out tactics was in the exercises that we have described. These were so restricted and infrequent that they were much too small a sample from which to draw valid conclusions.

The first armoured troops to gain useful experience of combat were the Germans fighting in Poland. The campaign was a brief one, but it certainly allowed the Germans to try out various techniques – in most cases extremely successfully. These involved the integrated use of tanks, mobile infantry and aircraft, and adopted the general principle of bypassing points of resistance and striking at rear areas to cause demoralization of their opponents. These operations were observed, in so far as they could be, by other military forces. Whether they learnt lessons from them is difficult to say. The problem for Britain was that they still had very small and poorly armed tank forces. The rate of supply of weapons was also very slow. When the fighting in France began on 10 May 1940 the British armoured forces consisted of the reconnaissance cavalry units attached to the infantry divisions, the 1st Army Tank Brigade and the First Armoured Division which was still in England. These were used in action in very piecemeal attacks. The only really organised attack was that on 21st May 1940 by the 1st Tank Brigade in conjunction with the 50th Infantry Division at Arras. This created some concern to the German forces, but the British were soon forced to come to a halt because of the very small numbers of tanks available to support the infantry. The First Armoured Division landed in the west of France and advanced as quickly as possible towards the Germans; once again the tanks were thrown in piecemeal and were forced to retire at high speed. Almost all the British tanks were left behind in France. Fortunately, a very large number of the crews were able to find their way back to England and thus form the nucleus of the armoured forces that would now have to be created almost from scratch.

In terms of tactics what did they learn from the experience of these few weeks fighting in May and early June of 1940? One person who was able to draw lessons from the fighting in France in 1940 was Brig Vyvyan Pope who acted as advisor on armoured vehicles to the C-in-C, Lord Gort. Pope had been involved in most of the tank fighting in France and was able to see many deficiencies, both in tactics and in equipment. He was asked to present his views to a committee which was reviewing the lessons to be learnt from the French campaign. He presented himself to this committee on 17 June 1940 and was asked what was the smallest number of tanks that he would consider decentralizing under the command of another formation; he replied: 'an armoured division'. There was some discussion from which Pope obtained the impression that the committee was abandoning the task of studying the lessons learned and was devoting itself to the task of the defence of England. Some members of the committee were anxious to form small packets of brigade groups containing all arms and tanks and to scatter them freely around England. Pope made it very clear that he could not subscribe to any doctrine of that kind, and that the experience in France had shown that the dissipation of armoured forces had led to its defeat in detail. In defence, armoured troops should be held concentrated in reserve, ready to strike when required. Pope was also extremely critical about the quality and quantity of tanks supplied to Britain's armoured forces in France. This deficiency will be discussed in a later section of this book.

The next time that British tank troops were in action to any significant degree was in the Western Desert in December 1940. After trying some preliminary pushes against the opposing Italian forces, the formation trained by Hobart, now named the 7th Armoured

Division, decided to push westwards along the coast of North Africa. Using the open desert and the mobility of tanks, and brilliantly commanded by Lt Gen Richard O'Connor, they succeeded triumphantly. Although they were subsequently pushed back by Rommel and the German forces they had achieved a very significant victory and one which heartened the politicians and the people of Britain. One unfortunate result of this victory, however, was that it appeared that tanks on their own could achieve victories. This reinforced the prewar teaching of Hobart, and the 'tank only' policy gave rise to many of the calamities which occurred in the Western Desert in the next two years.

In terms of tactical doctrine, no record has been located showing what the policies should be for handling armoured forces, until, that is, Army Training Instruction No. 3 'Handling of an Armoured Division' was published in 1941. This document provides a structure for the division which at that time contained the following: an armoured car regiment, two armoured brigades and a support group. The support group contained 1 lorried infantry battalion, 3 field batteries of artillery, and 3 batteries of anti-tank guns and the light anti-aircraft batteries. Two interesting points are included in the details of this instruction. First, the tactics for the engagement of enemy armoured formations include the possible use of anti-tank guns supporting the armoured forces. Second, it makes a very clear statement that 'fire from stationary positions will always be more accurate than from a moving platform'. This second statement is in complete contradiction to the policies of firing on the move which were so strongly advocated and taught by Hobart and other tank officers before the war.

In July 1943 the War Office produced another document called 'The Tactical Handling of Armoured Divisions'. This expressed a rather different set of policies and organizational structure to those which had been put forward in 1941. The composition had changed and now consisted of an armoured regiment, an armoured brigade, an infantry brigade, supporting engineers and artillery. The artillery consisted of two field regiments, one of them equipped with self-propelled guns, and one regiment each of anti-tank guns and anti-aircraft guns. Thus the emphasis was tilted away from armour towards infantry, making a more balanced division. It must be remembered that by July 1943 the British forces had had significant success in North Africa. One of the main policy items was that: 'An armoured division is a formation consisting of all arms. Tanks by themselves cannot win battles and the unarmoured units of the armoured division are indispensable while the administrative services play roles no less vital and equally dangerous in maintaining supplies of all kinds.'

The roles of an armoured division were described in the July 1943 document as:

- The cooperation with the main Army and the air forces in effecting the complete destruction of the enemy, usually by envelopment or by deep penetration through his defences after a gap has been made in his main position by other formations.
- Pursuit.
- Cooperation with other arms in defence, usually by counter-attack.
- To threaten the enemy and so force him to alter or disclose his dispositions.

It can be seen that the lessons of Alamein and subsequent desert battles were those which were documented in this training pamphlet. Whether these methods would be appropriate in other theatres of combat such as Sicily, Italy, Normandy and north-west Europe remains to be seen.

The last document to be considered setting out the tactical handling of armoured forces is that produced by FM Montgomery in December 1944. This is set out in his brisk style and summarizes very well the lessons that had been learnt in all of the war up to this point. The predominant theme is one of flexibility.

'Monty' makes a number of points, the main ones of which are:

All commanders must be well versed in the employment of armour. This obviously means that Army and corps commanders should be capable of making the best possible use of armoured formations at their disposal.

The armoured division is particularly suited for employment in the fast-moving and fluid battle. The aim of planning should be to create opportunities to use the armoured division in this role: if suitable opportunities can be created, then the action of the armoured division is likely to be decisive.

An armoured division can also carry out many of the tasks that are normally given to an infantry division: but it is a different kind of weapon and the job has therefore to be tackled in a different way.

The main characteristics of an armoured division are:

- Its armour
- Its firepower
- Its mobility

No plan for the employment of the division will be sound which does not exploit these characteristics to the full.

The armour is most effective when employed concentrated: a mass of armour, particularly in the enemy's rear, has a moral effect.

Monty also says that the armoured division can be grouped in a variety of different ways. The grouping adopted in any particular case must depend on the problem; there is no normal grouping, and any rigidity in this respect is to be deprecated.

This is completely borne out by the comments of Maj Gen Pip Roberts who said: 'Throughout the war the tactics used within an armoured division and its organization were continually changing. It was not until our third battle in Normandy that we got it right, and that was an organization of complete flexibility. At the shortest notice the organization could be altered from an armoured brigade and an infantry brigade to two mixed brigades, each of two armoured regiments and two infantry battalions and artillery as required. All units were entirely interchangeable.'

Roberts was probably the best armoured divisional commander in the north-west

Europe campaign, commanding as he did the 11th Armoured, or Charging Bull, Division. There seems at last to have been agreement at all levels of the military command on the way in which armoured forces should be used. But those people who were participants in armoured battles in the five years up till then were certainly at the mercy of commanders handling them in a sub-optimal way.

As a postscript to this section and a link with the next section which deals with the tanks that Britain's armoured forces had to use during the Second World War, comments by Alan Jolly are very appropriate. Jolly commanded the 144th Regiment RAC in the north-west Europe campaign. This unit was converted to the 4th Royal Tank Regiment before the end of the war to replace that which had been captured in Tobruk; Jolly himself had a distinguished military career and ended up as a general. In the epilogue to his book *Blue Flash* he reflects on some of the observations he had made and lessons he had learned during the course of his military career. In discussing the use of tanks he says: 'There are two basic purposes for which tanks exist and for which at present [1952] there are no substitutes. The first of these is to provide direct fire support for infantry as opposed to the indirect fire of artillery. Artillery provides a greater weight of fire but can only deal with an area target and must therefore cease during the last 150 yards of the infantry's advance to their objectives. This is where they usually suffer the bulk of their casualties from small arms fire, and it is here that the tank must fill in the gap by shooting with weapons of pin point accuracy up to the moment that the infantry close with their enemy.

'The second basic purpose for which the tank exists is to provide the hard core of the mobile portion of an army. This faster portion which provides the decisive action in battle is composed of armoured divisions, the tanks of which provide a concentration of mobile fire power which can disrupt, disorganize and pursue an enemy whose front has been broken or cracked by the slower infantry divisions and their supporting armour and artillery. The tank has one other significant purpose and that is to fight other tanks. However, the two fundamental purposes are to provide direct fire support of a nature which cannot be produced by artillery and to form the hard core of the mobile portion of an army.'

These thoughts of Alan Jolly's are a crystallization of much experience, and influenced the development and design of armour from that time on. The way in which tanks were developed in the years between the two wars and during the Second World War itself is discussed in the next chapter.

CHAPTER 3

A Sad Tale: British Tank Development, 1919–45

Scene: 14 September 1942, Alam Halfa Ridge, Egypt

Two of the armoured corps officers wore Royal Tank Regiment badges and the third that of the 8th Hussars. All were captains, and had the unmistakable aura of experience in war. Brigade headquarters pennants fluttered outside the tent a few yards from where they stood.

'What does the old man want, I wonder?'

'Perhaps we've got a special posting back to England and then on to America. I hear that's what's happening to Michael Halstead.'

'Fat chance. Anyway Mike was badly wounded at Gazala. It's more likely Burma for us to give them special instruction on fighting desert warfare in the jungle.'

Brig Charles Eastwood came out of his tent. 'Ah, there you are gentlemen. Thank you for being so prompt. Would you come in here, please.'

In the tent the brigadier waved them to three chairs, and sat down himself.

'First, I'll tell you why I want to talk to you. It starts with something that happened to me ten years ago. My CO was Charlie Whitehouse, and he called three of us subalterns together to discuss with him ideas for the proper handling of tanks. He took all our ideas on board, and eventually some of them were used. But the point was, he was willing to listen to others, to let them have their say. And as you know, he's now one of our better armour generals. What I want to do now is the same sort of thing, but on a different topic – the sort of tanks that we need in the British Army. You've all had a lot of experience out here in the desert, and I know you've fought in a wide range of tanks between you. I gave you a short brief in the note I sent you, so you've had time to think about it. You first, Tom.'

'My first thought, Sir, is that we should limit the number of tanks we use. We've got light tanks, cruisers, I-Tanks and in-betweens like the Valentine. As different makes we've Vickers lights, Honeys, Crusaders, Valentines, still a few A9s and A10s, Matildas, Grants, and I understand that the first Shermans will be up with us very soon. All this variety must be a terrible problem for tech stores and maintenance, and as we all know none of them are perfect and some are bloody awful. I think we should have one light tank and one other tank to serve all the other purposes. We could call it a main battle tank and use it for the heavy tank brigades as well as the armoured brigades. Bigger than the Valentine and faster, wouldn't need to be as fast as the Crusader, but with a decent all-purpose gun.'

'That's a good start, Tom. What are your thoughts about the gun, Peter?'

'I agree with Tom about one type of main battle tank, Sir. I think the tank should be designed to take the best all-purpose gun we can make so that we've got a fair chance – preferably better than fair – against whatever the Jerries can throw at us. We need a heavier anti-tank weapon. The two-pounder has been a good gun, and still is, but some of theirs are beginning to outrange us quite a bit. We need at least a six-pounder like they're issuing to the anti-tank gunners, but I believe that hasn't got much of an HE shell – which is what we need to get the Jerry anti-tank guns, especially the 88s. I always wondered why they didn't convert our 3.7 anti-aircraft gun, like the Jerries did with their 88s.'

'I agree with you, Peter. I do believe there are one or two mad gunners who have used our 3.7s against tanks, and very successfully. But the Royal Artillery powers that be weren't at all amused, and evidently they're so jealous that they won't entertain even any experimental work with the 3.7s. So what you're saying, Peter, is that we need a good gun that can throw a decent HE shell, and at the same time deal with any German tanks we're likely to meet over the next two to three years. And we will probably need purpose-built tanks to carry this gun. That about it?'

'Yes. Sir.'

'Fine. So on to you, Mark.'

'Agreed with all so far, Sir. A good all-purpose gun for a single main battle tank is definitely the way to go. But there are at least three more points I'd like to add. First, the tank must be reliable. These Crusaders we've had are dreadful, and they tell me the Churchills they've issued to quite a few units in England are not much better. Grants and Honeys are marvellous compared with all the British tanks I've had anything to do with. The second thing is that the crew must have a reasonable chance to operate properly. Any two-man turret crew means that the commander is completely overloaded, and if he's the troop or squadron commander he might as well throw the gun away for all the good he can do with it. And last, we should have the ability to upgrade the tank. This means that the suspension needs to be strong enough to take the extra weight of a heavier gun or heavier armour, and the turret needs to be able to cope with the bigger gun.'

The discussion recorded above is imaginary, but there were plenty of people in the Royal Armoured Corps who were very concerned at the pathetic quality of British tanks. What was even more exasperating was that the views of the users were transmitted upwards in various ways, but no observable action ever took place. This is not to say that there was no action, because there was plenty, as this chapter records. The main reasons for action being ineffective and much too late were: the delay in providing money for rearming the Army, as described in Chapter 1; the inability of anyone to crystallize the specification for a tank gun, a tank to carry that gun, and a chain for development to meet new threats and new opportunities; and, very importantly, the lead time required for design and manufacture.

Pages 68–74 describe what should be considered in the specification for an Armoured Fighting Vehicle (AFV), and pages 74–82 show the factors in determining the lead time to develop and manufacture an operational AFV. The rest of this chapter describes what actually happened in the development of British tanks.

PREAMBLE

The story of British tank development between 1919 and 1945 is an extremely depressing story. Britain had evolved the idea of the tank and large quantities had been manufactured in Britain in the last years of the First World War. In the 1920s British military theorists had developed tank tactics along novel and potentially effective lines. Yet tactically, technically and quantitatively the British Army's tank forces in 1939 compared unfavourably with those of Germany even though the equipping of the Wehrmacht had started almost from scratch in 1933. This sad situation in 1939 was not greatly improved during the first years of the Second World War, and Britain was compelled to redress the balance in the old world by calling in the resources of the new. It was certainly ironic that during the last two years of the Second World War the British developed a superb tank, the Centurion, which was delivered to field forces a few days after the fighting stopped. There are many reasons for the sterility of the armoured re-equipment policy, in particular during the period 1930–39. The reasons include:

- Disarmament pledges prevented the construction of tanks heavier than 16 tons.
- Notable industrial designers had died.
- Financial resources for design and production were very tight.
- The national commitments of the Army varied.
- The organization and employment of armoured forces, as we have seen, was a matter for debate.
- The regular soldier was not machine-minded.

Even though all these reasons had an effect, they do not constitute an effective explanation of the muddle and mismanagement of tank development. The disarmament limitations on tonnage were restrictive but they did not have to be crippling. A country which depends on three or four designers of outstanding skill is in a bad state. Financial restrictions hampered all services, but the Royal Navy and the RAF developed new and effective equipment, and the artillery arm of the Army developed the very effective twenty-five-pounder field gun, the 3.7 in anti-aircraft gun, and the 4.5 in and 5.5 in medium guns. The commitments of all the services were subject to variation, the RAF in particular being uncertain as to its defensive or attacking role. The regular soldier certainly had an interest in equestrian pursuits, but most of the regimental histories record that they took to their new machines with dedication if not overwhelming enthusiasm.

All of the above listed difficulties were certainly real, but the basic need that was not met was a definition of the function which tanks would be called upon to fulfil. One major error was the attempt to link the functional definition to a strategic commitment and to assume that each locality needed its own type of vehicle. This created the situation where a change in overall strategy required a change in equipment to deal with that strategy. As it turned out it made very little difference as to where a tank was required to fight. The Valentine, for example, functioned effectively both in the desert and in the northern winters of 1944 and 1945. The Churchill tank functioned effectively in Tunis and in north-west Europe. The German tanks fought in even more extreme climates, including the desert and the snows of Russia.

In terms of tank design and production one very important factor is the volume of tanks that are to be produced. A manufacturing organization can set up a production line with much greater efficiency if it knows that the number of units of a particular type that it is going to produce is quite substantial. One of the problems for British tank manufacturers was that up until 1938 the volumes required by the War Office were generally both small and variable. Not only were the quantities variable but the specification changed frequently. Thus to achieve output that was prompt and of the required quality was extremely difficult. The time required for the design, development and production process can be 3 to 4 years. But much preliminary planning can be done if the functional requirements and specification are developed early to allow the process of manufacture to be embarked on as soon as output becomes urgent. Britain's great problem was that the slowdown in development and the lack of direction in the years from 1919 to 1939 meant that when war became much more likely there was not time for the full development process to take place. This resulted in several tanks being issued to forces in the field in an unproven condition, which meant that the elimination of faults had to be done in the field units themselves. If they were actually fighting they had more casualties from breakdown than they did from enemy action. This was certainly so with the Crusader in the desert. In the case of the Churchill it was perhaps fortunate that the field units to which it was issued were in England during the period needed to eliminate most of the bugs from its system.

TYPES AND NOMENCLATURE

The British tanks had a complicated naming system. Each specification that was issued by the General Staff had a number which was prefixed with an 'A' for tanks. The first prototype was given the identification 'E1'; thus the first prototype of the first tank specified by the General Staff was A1E1. This was in fact the 'Independent'. If another prototype had been developed it would have been called A1E2. The tanks developed during the period up to 1945 went to A43.

The tanks were further divided into different types: light, medium, cruiser, assault, infantry and heavy tanks are the various categories under which British tanks were required, and in some cases produced. They can be grouped into three major groups. The first group are the light tanks which developed over the complete period and which performed reconnaissance functions. The second group were the medium and cruiser tanks; these were intended to provide the hitting force in an armoured formation, and their main requirement was speed coupled with effective armament. The third group were the slower moving tanks which were expected to work with infantry and to be capable of fighting against substantial defences; the three categories here are the assault tanks, the infantry tanks and the heavy tanks. Assault tanks were designed but never produced, and heavy tanks were produced only in prototype. But the infantry tank was produced in substantial numbers and performed effectively in the function for which it had been designed.

The descriptions of British tanks were further complicated by being given numbers in the various categories. For example, there were medium tanks called medium 1, medium 2 and medium 3. The cruiser tanks were numbered from Mk I to Mk VIII. But as well as having the identification as Cruiser 1, Cruiser 2, etc. they also had 'A' numbers. The Figure 3.1 shows the complete relationship (for cruiser tanks) between the 'A' numbers and, in some cases, an actual title for a tank. The table shows that cruiser Mk I was the A9. This had no name given to it as some of the others in the table did; Mk II was the A10, Mk III was the A13. But the A13 came in Marks I, 2 and 3 which related to the Cruiser Mk III, IV and Mk V. Cruiser Mk V, the A13, Mk III was also given the name 'Covenanter'. Mk VI was the A15 which was given the name Crusader. The Crusader was produced in Mks I to III. The differences between these were in the type of armament that they possessed and in the shape of the turret. Mk VII Cruiser was the A24 and given the name Cavalier. This was an extremely bad vehicle and was not modified from its original production. Mk VIII came in two versions: the A27L (for Liberty engine) which was called the Centaur, and A27M (for Meteor engine) which was called the Cromwell. The Centaur came in Mks I to IV and the Cromwell in Marks I to VIII. In the case of the Cromwell the differences are shown in Figure 3.2. This table shows that the differences were generally related to the armament but could include the armour and modification to the track.

The Medium Tank A7 E3 (experimental version 3) was designed by the Chief Superintendent of Design and built by the Royal Ordnance Factory at Woolwich. It never went into production, but had considerable influence on the design of subsequent tanks.

FIGURE 3.1: IDENTIFICATION OF CRUISER TANKS

Mark	General Staff Specification No.	Name (when given)
I	A9	
II	A10	
III	A13 Mark I	
IV	A13 Mark II	
V	A13 Mark III	Covenanter
VI	A15	Crusader (Mks 1 to III)
VII	A24	Cavalier
VIII	{A27L*	Centaur (MKs I to IV)
	{A27M*	Cromwell (MKs 1 to VIII)

* A27L was powered by a Liberty engine and A27M by a Meteor engine (made by Rolls-Royce).

FIGURE 3.2: TYPES AND MARKS OF CROMWELL TANK

Changes to a tank as originally designed were made in response to user criticism or request or improvements developed by designers or manufacturers. The Cromwell developments were classified as Types and Marks, both of which are shown below. No tank of one Type could change into another

Type A: the earliest Cavaliers, Centaurs and Cromwells as built.
Type B: Centaurs and Cromwells fitted with the front gunner's escape hatch.
Type C: Centaurs and Cromwells with 25mm rear hull top plates and a revised pattern of air intake.
Type D: Centaurs and Cromwells with a revised layout of engine compartment cover plates.
Type E: Late model Cromwells with modified final drive gear ratios to reduce top speed.
Type F: Late model Cromwells with a matching side escape hatch for the driver.

The 'Marks' of the Cromwell tank were:
I: The original version with a 6-pdr gun.
II: A reworked tank with the hull gunner and his weapon removed, running on wider 15½ in tracks.
III: A Centaur I re-engined with a Meteor engine.
IV: A re-engined Centaur I or III with a 75mm gun, or a newly built model with this configuration.
V: A reworked Cromwell I with a 75mm gun.
Vw: A newly built Cromwell using welded construction and mounting a 75mm gun.
VI: A reworked Centaur I or IV or a newly built Cromwell with a 95mm howitzer.
VII: A reworked Cromwell IV with 101mm frontal armour and 15½ in tracks.
VIIw: A reworked Cromwell Vw with thicker frontal armour and wider tracks, or newly built to the same standard.
VIII: A reworked Cromwell IV with thicker frontal armour, wider tracks, and a 95mm howitzer.

The same type of complicated naming applied to the infantry tanks and to the light tanks; it is therefore sometimes quite difficult to understand exactly what vehicle is being discussed. In what follows we have used all means possible to identify clearly the vehicle that is being discussed.

DEVELOPMENT OF TANKS

The development of British tanks is shown in diagrammatic form in figure 3.3, 'Lineage of British Tanks'. These diagrams show a number of chains of development, and these will be discussed separately. The linkage between one vehicle and another is sometimes quite close and sometimes rather more tenuous. However, there is in each chain influence from the previous designs to the one under consideration.

The different chains are:

- Independent: This was a development on its own, although it did have a significant influence on later designs.
- Light tanks: This is a chain of development which gave rise to a number of tanks that were used between the wars and in the early part of the Second World War.
- Medium and cruiser tanks: This is one of the major areas where development took place. It includes the mediums, the various types of cruiser, and also the light cruiser tanks A17 and A25.
- Assault tanks: These were a special group which never resulted in a tank that was used in action.
- Infantry tanks, of which the most significant were the Matilda and the Churchill; the Valentine was designated the Infantry Tank Mark III, but was used in cruiser type roles rather than as an infantry-support tank.
- Heavy tanks TOG 1, 2 and 3: TOG stands for 'The Old Gang' who were a group of designers who had been very important in tank production in the First World War. These were never operational.

Each chain in the diagrams will be dealt with separately, and the three that never resulted in a tank that was assigned to field forces will be dealt with first. These are the Independent, the assault tanks and the TOG tanks. We will then look at the development of light tanks, next medium/ cruiser tanks, and, finally, the infantry tanks.

DEVELOPMENT CHAIN I: TANKS NEVER USED

The first tank to consider is the A1 or Independent. In December 1922 the War Office wrote to Vickers and invited it to consider designing a heavy tank. The functional requirements were:

- Speed, 7 miles per hour (mph).
- climbing ability 30° slope
- Trench crossing 9 ft
- Ground clearance 18 in
- Armament: one three-pounder and two .303 in machine-guns
- Ground pressure 12 pounds per square inch (psi)

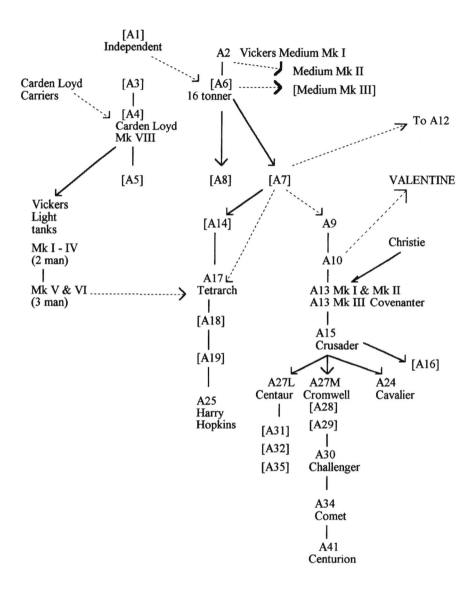

FIGURE 3.3: LINEAGE OF BRITISH TANKS: DIAGRAM I

1: 'A' numbers were assigned progressively to specifications issued by the General Staff.
2: 'A' numbers in square brackets relate to models that never became production tanks; their development stopped at the drawing board stage or at the prototype stage.

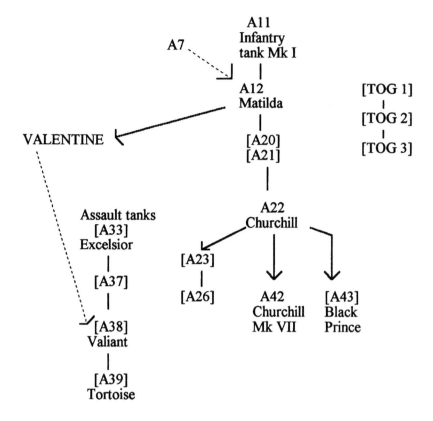

LINEAGE OF BRITISH TANKS: DIAGRAM 2

The War Office specified the configuration of the track and also required that the highest point of the vehicle should be the cover for the driver's head. The engine compartment was to be at the rear and the tank generally was required have as low a profile as possible.

Vickers was asked to submit drawings to indicate the general configuration of the vehicle, and not to produce any detailed drawings at this stage. This they did by March 1923. They also provided an alternative design which was reasonably close to the War Office specification, but added features which they thought would be desirable; in particular their design incorporated a turret with all-round traverse for the main armament. This added to the height of the vehicle and to the weight; in Vickers' opinion, however, the advantages greatly outweighed the disadvantages. In 1924 the War Office allocated £40,000 to the construction of a prototype which was to be made to the Vickers' design. This prototype was completed in 1926 and the vehicle underwent its first trials. Various problems were encountered, particularly the final drive. This was replaced by a new design by Walter Wilson. The Independent was tested intermittently until 1933 during which time many modifications had been made. By this time the engine was worn out and work on the Independent was stopped altogether. A number of features that were incorporated in the Independent, in particular the provision of a rotating turret floor and co-axial machine-gun, were incorporated in most of the tanks developed after that time.

The next group of never-used tanks to be considered are the assault tanks. The purpose of these tanks was apparently so that they could enter into an area being shelled by their own artillery. In this way they would be able to destroy any anti-tank guns in that area, because the crews of those guns would not be manning the guns while under shell fire. This meant that the assault tanks should be particularly heavily armoured and should have weapons capable of destroying the enemy anti-tank guns. The first one on the diagram, the A33, apparently named Excelsior, was to weigh about 40 tons, mount a 75mm gun and have 6 in of armour on the front. The English Electric Company undertook this work in 1942 and three pilot models were built by late 1943. These were tested with a 1,000-mile run, during which, while travelling across country, they managed to pick up two tonnes of mud. The first pilot was described as reliable, but a second 1,000-mile trial virtually wrote it off. This project was as good as dead by early 1944.

A37 was a heavier version of A33 with an extra suspension bogie per side, a longer hull and a seventeen-pounder gun. This was designed by English Electric and Rolls-Royce and weighed 52 tons. It never got beyond the paper stage.

The A38 was called Valiant. There were two models: the Valiant I, A38G, with a GMC engine and an AEC gearbox, weighed 27 tons and was built as a pilot by Ruston Hornsby. Valiant II, A38M, had a Meteor engine and a Rolls-Royce gearbox and was also designed by Ruston Hornsby. When it was tested, the Valiant was found to be extremely difficult, from the human point of view, to drive and since the tests took place in late 1944 this design was not proceeded with.

The last vehicle in the assault tank chain is the A39 or Tortoise. This was not really a descendant of the Valiant, although its genesis was in the War Office specification for the Valiant. Nuffield Mechanisation and Aero in Birmingham received the Valiant specification and submitted a number of designs, each bigger and heavier than the last. The proposal that was in fact accepted by the War Office was for the A39 Tortoise, which was much larger than anything that had gone before. There was no limitation put on weight or width and the tank, as finally produced in pilot form, weighed 78 tons and had a gun which could fire a 32-lb round. Its pilot trials proved that it was extremely difficult to transport anywhere, although it was reliable and provided an excellent gun platform. Since it was delivered in September 1945 it was not required to go into production for field units.

As can be seen from the description of this chain of development much time was spent on the design and pilot production of vehicles which were of no value to the British Army. Particularly in respect of the later models, it is extraordinary that while resources were being expended on work in relation to the assault tanks, resources were also being spent on the development of the highly successful A41 or Centurion. The question needs to be asked as to whether a diversion of resources from these assault tanks to the A41 would have meant that at least some tank units were provided with a respectable combat vehicle before the war ended.

The third chain of never-used tanks to be considered is that of the TOG tanks. They have some similarities with the A39 or Tortoise in that they were extremely heavy. Like the assault tanks the TOGs also diverted resources away from the production of usable tanks. TOG as stated earlier stood for 'The Old Gang'. This 'gang' was led by Sir Albert Stern who had been the secretary of the First World War landships committee. He was a man of much strength and drive who had been instrumental in ensuring that British tanks were developed in the First World War. Some of the people that worked with him in the First World War were Walter Wilson, William Tritton, Harry Ricardo, Ernest Swinton, Eustace Tennyson D'eyncourt and others. Stern managed to persuade these people with whom he had worked twenty-five years previously to group together again and provide Britain with the tanks that it needed. It appeared that they were given no specification by the War Office but developed their own. What they wanted to do was to produce a tank that would meet the trench war conditions of 1916–18. They developed TOG I which was a 73-ton giant. Modifications were made to the first TOG tank and work proceeded on the various TOG models for nearly three years. The end result was no useful vehicle and not much of value that could be transferred to other designs. Once again the very unfortunate thing was that the undoubted skills and drive of the 'gang' were not properly harnessed to a tank that would be of value for the Second World War.

We now look at tank development in the three categories where useful tanks, in the sense that they were issued to field units, were developed. These are the light tanks, the medium/cruiser tanks, and the infantry tanks.

DEVELOPMENT CHAIN 2: LIGHT TANKS

Light tanks were developed in the early 1920s and many of them were used in the early years of the Second World War. The first one to be developed was the A3 which was a three-man tank produced by the Royal Ordnance Factory. It was a low-profile design, carried three-men and two machine-guns, and was nearly 18 ft long. It was tested at the Mechanical Warfare Experimental Establishment (MWEE) in spring 1926 but it very soon passed from view. It was not until 1928 that a light tank was developed that would be of value to the tank forces. This tank was the A4 which was based on the development of the Carden-Loyd carriers produced by Vickers. Development from the A4 led in two directions, the first to the A5. This was a three-man light tank weighing 5 tons. It was probably designed in 1928, one pilot was built and tested, but it was finally scrapped in 1934. The other chain of development led to the Vickers light tanks. These were produced by Vickers and did not have general staff 'A' numbers. The first four marks had a crew of two, a speed of 30 mph, a range of 150 miles, and were armed with one Vickers machine-gun. The thickness of armour varied, but otherwise the only change was to the engine which was, progressively, made more powerful.

A two-man tank requires that many duties must be carried out by the crew member who is not driving. This was clearly recognized by the War Office when in October 1932 the Master General of Ordnance said: 'Apart from many criticisms of the design of the Light Tank Mk IV, one particularly serious criticism has been strenuously expressed. This is the difficulty experienced in fighting in this vehicle. The crew of every armoured fighting vehicle has these duties to perform in battle:

- Driving.
- Aiming and shooting the tank's armament.
- Internal control, i.e., movement of the tank, maintaining direction, and maintaining position; this will include reading a map.
- External controls, i.e., the tactical handling of sub-units.
- Observation and information; this will include sending reports back to higher formations, which will require the use of a wireless set if such is fitted to that tank.
- Operation of the wireless set, making sure that it is functioning correctly and tuned to the right frequency.
- Loading the ammunition into the tank's gun, and remedying any breakdowns of the armament.'

With a crew of two, one of whom is fully occupied with driving, it is clear that the remaining duties cannot be performed adequately by one man. It is equally impossible for the driver to carry out any of the other duties effectively, even though some vehicles were fitted with guns that were supposed to be operated by the driver. The solution to this problem was clearly to have three men in the tank, two of whom were in the turret; even then the commander was likely to be overloaded, but it was a great deal better than being on his own in the turret. A provisional specification for a three-man tank was issued on 7 November 1932. On 16 December 1932 Sir John Carden presented drawings of a three-man light tank to the War Office. Some modifications were requested but the Light Tank Mk V then entered production. Twelve prototype Mk Vs were sent to the 1st Battalion RTC in 1934. They were accompanied by a team of Vickers Armstrong engineers during the trials. This innovation greatly reduced the time needed for the vehicle to be brought into service and also created much goodwill between the manufacturer and the user. The users were able to make suggestions and requests at first hand and these could be discussed directly with the people responsible for making the tank. The Mk V was followed by the Mk VI which had a similar layout but increased armour thickness. The Mk VI was further modified to VI A and VI B, again with minor modifications only. The Mk VI B was the most widely used British light tank of the Second World War.

The last part of the light tank chain is the series that stems in part from the A7 and in part from the Vickers light tanks. This begins with the A17 or Tetrarch. The pilot vehicle was developed in 1938 by Vickers as a private venture. Vickers intended to offer the tank to the War Office, but if it was not accepted to place it on the export market. It was intended to fulfil the function of light cavalry, which by this time had been converted to light tanks. The Tetrarch, as finally completed, was fitted with the two-pounder gun. It also incorporated a new system of steering. The four equal-sized road wheels could be tilted and turned in a curve, warping the tracks so that in the higher gears the tank could be driven round less sharp bends using car-type steering. Skid steering was used for sharp corners and when travelling in the lower gears. Tetrarch was not produced in any great volume, and was used by British tank forces only in the invasion of Madagascar.

Tetrarch was succeeded by the A18 which was a projected cruiser tank based on the A17 design. It was abandoned before reaching the pilot stage. The A19 was another projected cruiser tank, also based on the A17 but also abandoned in 1939.

The only vehicle in this chain that was produced in any quantity was the A25 or Light Tank Mk VIII, which was called the Harry Hopkins. It had a similar Meadows flat 12-cylinder engine and the track-warping system of steering used in the A17. Development started in 1941 and in 1942 the first models were entering production. In the end ninety-two tanks were made, the last being produced in 1944. This marked the end of the light tank chain which had begun in 1929.

DEVELOPMENT CHAIN 3: MEDIUM/CRUISER TANKS

The next chain of tank development to be considered is that which comprises the medium tanks and the cruiser tanks. As we shall see there is some linkage between this chain and those of the light tanks as well as those of the infantry tanks. However, the general chain of design is for a tank with a good turn of speed, a reasonable gun and a range of 150 to 200 miles.

The chain starts with the Vickers medium Mk I, also given the General Staff classification A2. Deliveries of the medium Mk I began in 1923. It had all-round traverse for the turret and geared elevation for the main armament. The main armament was a three-pounder gun and in addition there were four machine-guns in the turret and two in the hull. There was a crew of five. It had a 90 horsepower (hp) Armstrong Siddeley engine and a speed of 18 mph. The armour was 6.5 mm thick. This was, for many years, the tank on issue to tank regiments. Its successor, the Medium Mk II, was slightly up-armoured to 8 mm but down-gunned to have one co-axial machine-gun in the turret with the same two machine-guns in the hull. The engine, crew and speed were the same as for the Mk I. It was issued to field forces in 1925. The Mk II was generally similar in appearance to the Mk I except that the tracks were now protected by armoured skirting plates.

In 1926 the War Office announced that it wanted a tank to replace the existing medium tanks in service. The requirement was outlined in a preliminary specification, the main features of which were:

- Two independent machine-gun turrets were desirable.
- The weight of the tank should be limited to just under 16 tons, and the width should be within the railway loading gauge.

- The main armament of the tank should be able to penetrate a similar machine at a range of at least 1,000 yd.
- The tank should have heavy armour in front for protection when crossing a crest.
- The fuel tanks should be outside the main hull.
- Silence was a most desirable feature from a tactical point of view.

Vickers produced a statement of the method and specification for the tank that it was going to produce – Vickers having been chosen to build the first tanks to the War Office's specification. Its comments were:

'The tank is generally on the lines of the Independent tank, the fighting chamber being at the front and the engine and transmission at the rear, isolated from the fighting chamber by a transverse bulkhead. The nose of the machine is brought forward to be level with the front idler wheels and is well-rounded and made of 13 mm plate.

The fighting chamber is fitted with a central main turret, similar to the independent tank, 63 in in diameter, fitted with a three-pounder gun, with all-round traverse.

There are two machine-gun turrets in front of the main turret as in the Independent tank, each fitted with single- or twin-machine-guns.

There is a similar turret at the rear end in the transmission chamber in which a man kneels on a large soft pad to operate the gun.

- Engine: the tank will be fitted with a 120 hp engine, which at normal engine speed provides a tank speed of 14 mph.
- Weight: in running order is 14 tons 7 cwt; armour is to be between 6.5 mm and 13 mm thick.
- Armament: the three-pounder in the main turret has all-round traverse, 30° elevation and 10° depression except over the front turrets where maximum depression is 3°.'

Vickers made two mild-steel prototypes which were ready for trial in just under a year. A third mild-steel prototype was built in 1930 but the whole A6 (widely known as the 16-tonner) project was then terminated, partly because of non-uniformity of the guns and their firing gear, but also because the cost of the 16-tonner was well beyond what the War Office felt it was able to afford.

It can be seen from Vickers specification that the A6 used many features which had been originally developed on the A1 or Independent. The chain of development from the A6 led in three directions. The first derivative was the Medium Mk III, which had a larger crew and a more powerful engine. Only three units of this tank were made and that chain of development came to a halt. The next chain of development was to the A8. This was an experimental medium tank ordered from Vickers. It had two Rolls-Royce Phantom engines and was to weigh 17.5 tons. The pilot was never completed, although there was development during the years from 1934 to 1937.

The other vehicle which was influenced by the A6 was the A7. This was an experimental medium tank designed by the Chief Superintendent of Design and was built by the Royal Ordnance Factory at Woolwich. Development of the A7 took place in parallel with that of the A6. There were three experimental versions of the A7: E1, E2 and E3. These were worked on for several years and a number of changes were made, particularly to the transmission and the suspension. The engines chosen for the A7E3 were the AEC engines developed for London buses. These replaced the Armstrong Siddeley engines which had been used in E1 and E2. Work on the three models of the A7 took place over the period from 1929 to 1937.

Although the A7 never went into production it provided several ideas for incorporation in the four chains of development which are shown in Figure 3.3. It influenced both the Matilda (A12) and the Valentine; it was also a predecessor in various aspects to the chain starting with A9, the chain starting with A17 and the one-off A14. The contribution to the A17 has already been considered in the section on light tanks; the contribution to the A12 (Matilda) is discussed in the section on infantry tanks. We look here at the chains beginning with A14 and A9.

The A14 was a development along the line of medium tanks and work began on this in June 1937. The tank was to have a crew of six, a two-pounder gun and armour 30 mm thick. It was to have a new form of steering developed by Wilson which provided a range of geared turning circles. This was efficient in that it did not waste power when turning, but was inefficient because it meant a considerable increase in weight. Work on this tank was given to the London Midland & Scottish (LMS) Railway company in March 1938 and the first prototype was running by June 1939. It was found to weigh 29 tons, 4 tons more than the specification allowed. Work continued on a second pilot in an attempt to

The A9 specification was placed with Vickers Armstrong in June 1934. In November the specification was modified to include fitting the two-pounder gun, and the tank became known as the Cruiser Mk I. It gave reasonable service in its day, both in France in 1940 and in the desert.

Medium Tank A10

The A10 was a heavier version of the A9; it went into production in 1939, and saw service in France in 1940 and in the desert.

bring the weight down to 25 tons. In the end this project was abandoned with the first prototype nearly complete.

The second chain of development, and the most significant one, was the one that started with A9. The General Staff specification for A9 required a tank having the same firepower and armour protection as the Medium Mk III – which was a direct derivative of the A6. It was intended to be cheaper than the A7 or the A8, which seemed a difficult specification to meet. The specification was placed with Vickers Armstrong in June 1934 and the tank was designated the Medium Mk IV. Sir John Carden was responsible for the design of this tank. In November 1934 the War Office modified the specification to include fitting the two-pounder gun. Because of this modification, and a change in the concept of the role of tanks, the A9 became known as the Cruiser Tank Mk I. When the first prototype was developed it was found to be over its specified weight by 3 tons. When it was tried out it revealed problems with the suspension and a tendency to throw off its tracks. Vickers Armstrong worked on modifications for another twelve months and finally produced a vehicle which was, for its day, a good tank. The engine and transmission were reliable and it had an exceptionally fine anti-tank capability in its two-pounder gun. In 1937 an order was placed with the Vickers Tank Department at Elswick for fifty of these tanks. Deliveries began in 1939, and the tank was used as a fighting vehicle in both France in 1940 and in the desert.

At the same time as the A9 was specified by the War Office, they also considered the need for a heavier vehicle. Three months after the beginning of the A9 project, work

The Medium Tank A11 was subsequently known as the Infantry Tank Mk I. It was intended to be heavily armoured, which it was, and committed to close support of infantry. It was armed only with machine-guns, and the two-man crew placed an impossible burden on the turret member of that crew.

Medium Tank A13 E2; this was the first British tank to use the Christie suspension, designed to allow high cross-country speeds. Its main problems were a tendency to throw its tracks, and a turret not designed to allow effective fighting.

started on the A10 in September 1934. It was originally intended as an infantry version of the A9, achieving this by having thicker armour of 30 mm. Various changes were made to the design and the tank finally went into production in 1939. The A10 was classified as the Cruiser Mk II and also saw service in France in 1940 and in the desert. The total production of the various models of A10 was 170 tanks.

The next tank in this chain is the A13. As the diagram shows, this was influenced by both the A10 and also the Christie tank. The source of information regarding the Christie tank came from a visit made by Wavell and Martel to manoeuvres carried out by the Russian Army in 1936. They were surprised by several features of the manoeuvres. First the quantity of tanks in service with the Russian Army was much greater than they had expected. But of even greater interest was the quality of the tanks, particularly those which had a type of suspension they had not seen before. This suspension consisted of four large road wheels with the track running round the edges of these four wheels. The particularly impressive thing about this suspension was the way that the wheels adjusted to the ground over which they travelled. These tanks were able to move at high speed over rough country, and, from Wavell's and Martel's observations, had few or no mechanical problems.

Martel in particular was very eager to obtain a sample of this type of tank suspension so that its possible incorporation into British tanks could be evaluated. He found that the suspension was not a Russian invention, but an American one. The inventor of the system was J. Walter Christie. He was, in appearance, one might say, a typical inventor with white hair, a lean build and a general frontiersman appearance. He was concerned mainly with speed. In 1932 he had built a tank-type vehicle which was capable of 65 mph on its tracks.

Martel's difficulty was to obtain a sample of this tank so that it could be tried out on the testing grounds in Britain. It was clearly not possible to obtain one from Russia, and it was even found quite difficult, in view of export restrictions, to obtain one from its country of origin. However, by using various subterfuges a sample of the Christie tank arrived in Britain on 17 November 1936.

When it arrived at the Mechanization Experimental Establishment (MEE) at Farnborough it was examined for its good points and points that might need modification. The suspension was, of course, found to be excellent. It was also found that the power unit was very good. It was an American Liberty V12, an aero engine developed in 1917 capable of developing 350 bhp at 1,800 rpm. It was also possible to push up the revs to 2,500 without damage to the engine. The gearbox was impressive, being clearly made specifically to suit the engine and hull. The transmission to the drive sprockets was also ingenious.

The first point that needed attention was the tracks. These were large square flat plates and they gave trouble in the excessive battering to the front idler and the pins linking the tracks. The other major modification was the complete redesign of the turret. This was converted to a three-man turret incorporating a two-pounder main armament and a co-axially mounted machine-gun. The first production machines came two years after the work had started, being delivered in December 1938. Development of the Cruiser Mk III

The Covenanter, or A13 Mk III, was one of the worst tanks ever produced, and represented an enormous waste of human, material and financial resources. It looked sleek and powerful but was a mechanical disaster and never saw fighting service in any theatre of war. (Tank Museum 1832/B4)

(A13) was carried out by Nuffield Mechanisation and Aero combined with the Mechanization Board. In the end sixty-five units of the Cruiser Mk III were produced.

The next tank in this chain of development was the Cruiser Mk IV. This was an improved version of the Mk III and was also produced by Nuffield Mechanisation and Aero. After various designs had been considered, a model was accepted which incorporated a reduced Liberty engine, five bogies to a side instead of four, and an auxiliary hull turret mounting a Besa machine-gun beside the driver. A mock-up was viewed and orders were placed in January 1939. Some 270 units of the Cruiser Mk IV were produced, and in service they gave difficulty with cooling and steering.

The next tank in the medium/cruiser chain is the A13 Mk III or Cruiser Mk V, also called the Covenanter. This was a vehicle which looked excellent from the outside but was a mechanical horror when in field use. It was not a problem of hurried design, because work had begun on it well before the war. The design was put in the hands of the LMS Railway company who kept in close touch with the Mechanization Board. It had the Christie suspension and a three-man turret with a two-pounder main gun and a co-axial Besa machine-gun. It had a Meadows 12-cylinder engine which developed 300 bhp. This engine was horizontally opposed and kept the whole profile low. The turret was also low and, coupled with the speed of the vehicle, it looked sleek and effective. It had a rather unusual hatch to the turret which was similar to a sliding roof; it could be hinged back over the back of the turret and held in the open position by a catch. Unfortunately the catch did not always hold and there were many cases of people with significant head injuries and broken teeth when the catch let go and the hatch lid came forward forcibly on the back of the commander's or loader's head.

In addition to this relatively minor problem it had a major problem with the cooling system. The radiators were located at the front of the tank and were thus some distance from the engine mounted at the back of the tank, which they were supposed to cool. The tank, when running well, was fast over ground, but initially had a very heavy steering mechanism. Various modifications were made and eventually contracts were placed in April 1939. Deliveries began in summer 1940 and it was found immediately that these tanks were quite unbattleworthy in the state in which they were delivered. The faults in the mechanical systems of the Covenanter were such that they would take many months to correct. The decision should have been taken immediately to stop production of these tanks altogether and allow the production facilities to be used for better tanks. However, the policy of producing anything that could move and provide firepower was followed to such an extent that almost 2,000 of these machines were made and manufacture continued until the middle of 1942. The Covenanter was just adequate as a training machine, but never saw fighting service in any theatre of war.

The Crusader (A15) followed in the chain of development from the A13. It was capable of bearing a greater load, either in armour or armament, but mechanically had a similar – and deserved – reputation for unreliability. This particular tank is believed to have belonged to the 9th Australian Cavalry Division. (Tank Museum 1836/E6)

The next vehicle in the cruiser chain is the A15 or Crusader. This was designed by Nuffield Mechanisation and Aero. The design was based on existing A13 technology with the Christie suspension and the Liberty engine. It had a similar turret to the Covenanter but at the insistence of the General Staff it had a hull machine-gun in addition to the co-axial machine-gun in the turret. The radiators were now moved back to the engine compartment and the tank was made longer by the addition of an extra bogie on each side. This gave the tank a greater load-bearing capacity and allowed the opportunity for an increase in the weight at a later stage, which could be used to accommodate a heavier gun or thicker armour. This was made use of in the Crusader Mk II in which the armour was increased in the front from 40 mm to 49 mm. Production of the Crusader started in 1940 under the parentage of Nuffield Mechanisation and Aero. Seven other companies built Crusaders and over 5,000 were produced until it was taken out of service.

The first time that the Crusaders saw action was in the middle of 1941 in the Western Desert. The particular operation in which they made their debut was called Battleaxe. This was not a particularly impressive debut because they were found to be mechanically unreliable, and it was difficult to use their speed over the rocky ground where the fighting took place. The Crusader fought with the 7th Armoured Brigade for the next few months and then in November 1941 took part in the operation which had its own name 'Crusader'. This battle was considered to be a moderate victory as far as the British troops were concerned. The Crusader by now was beginning to show up as a most unreliable machine. The specific problems related to the radiator fan drive and the water pump; they stemmed partly from lack of care in shipping the tanks from Britain to the desert, and were compounded by the lack of urgency in any effort to correct the problems that were found. At this point the Crusader had obtained a reputation for unreliability that it never threw off. Thus when American Grant tanks, followed later by Sherman tanks, were delivered to the British tank forces they felt that they never wanted to use British tanks again.

The next stage in the development of cruiser tanks goes back to July 1940. Work was proceeding with the A13 and A15, which in due course were delivered to tank users. It was felt, however, that designers should look ahead to the next generation of tanks and on this occasion they required that the tanks developed should be capable of mounting the six-pounder tank gun. The diagram shows that after the Crusader there were three tanks in parallel that eventually went into production, and the A16 that did not. A pilot model of the A16 was submitted for trials, but was then abandoned. The three models that eventually reached field or training units were the A24, the A27L and the A27M. The first of these to be specified was the A24. This required a tank with between 64 mm and 75 mm of frontal armour, a 60 in turret ring and a six-pounder main gun. The crew remained at five, the suspension was Christie and the engine an up-rated Liberty. There was to be a four-speed gearbox and a Wilson type steering system. The required top speed was 24 mph. The proposals to meet this specification were considered by the Tank Board on 17 January 1941. The board stressed that the new tank must be in production within just over a year and therefore it was necessary to base the design on existing types, so there would be no need for pilot models. Some members of the Tank Board insisted that doing without pilots was a recipe for disaster, but the decision went against them. The order was placed with Nuffield Mechanisation and Aero on 29 January 1941 for six tanks.

During this time another set of circumstances occurred which had a very significant influence on the development of the A24 and the associated models. The firm of Rolls-Royce had been producing aircraft engines since the early part of the war and had obviously dropped the manufacture of the Rolls-Royce car. Rolls-Royce had a design team of highly skilled engineers under the leadership of W.A. (Roy) Robotham. In October 1940 Robotham met Henry Spurrier who was general manager of Leyland Motors. Leyland was then building engines for the Matilda tank and was proposing to build complete tanks such as the A13 and the Covenanter. Spurrier was particularly concerned that the engine being used for the tanks was of a relatively low horsepower. This was the American Liberty Aero engine which had first seen the light of day in 1916. It was a fine engine but developed only 350 bhp which was not nearly enough for the heavier tanks that were now required. Robotham was surprised to find that the plans were being pushed ahead for the large-scale manufacture of Liberty engines in new factories. He saw an opportunity to show that Rolls-Royce could produce the engine that the British tank industry required.

There were two main engines that could be considered, the Kestrel and the Merlin. Bench tests of the Kestrel showed that it could produce considerably more power than the Liberty but still substantially less than the 600 bhp required by the long-term policy of tank design. The important ratio here was that the engine should be capable of producing 20 bhp for each ton of the tank's weight. The Kestrel was not capable of reaching this power, so the Merlin was considered instead. The Merlin proved very suitable right from the start. It was more compact than the Liberty, although both engines had the same cubic capacity and would be readily interchangeable. This was important because most British tanks in existence and being planned at that time were designed to use the Liberty. The latest tanks in production were the Crusaders and the first step was to install a Merlin in one of them and give it a trial. The supercharger was removed and the Zenith carburettor fitted instead of the type normally used in the aircraft application.

The first test of this configuration (a Merlin engine in a Crusader tank) took place under military supervision at Aldershot. The tank had to run over a half-mile course, at the end of which was a sharp bend. The driver was required to go as fast as possible and be timed while so doing. Robotham suggested that if the tank was driven flat out it would not be able to negotiate the bend at the end of the course; the officer in charge, however, accustomed to slower vehicles, assured Robotham that this would not be a problem. The Army driver obeyed orders and drove as fast as he could down the track. He was unable to turn the corner at the bottom and the tank went straight on, knocked down a telegraph pole and plunged into a wood. Fortunately the driver was not injured and the tank finally came to rest. The recorder in the tank registered its maximum reading of 50 mph.

Further tests, amounting to 3,600 miles in all, revealed that the Crusader could not withstand the strain of being propelled by such a powerful engine. Its transmission and suspension were not able to stand up to the increased power, and it was found difficult to fit the radiators into the space available. It was clear that the tank needed much more improvement than the engine, so the government asked Rolls-Royce to set up a small experimental establishment to make a vehicle which was completely battleworthy. This involved developing the unsupercharged Merlin as a tank engine and modifying the steering, transmission and suspension as well as the electrical, hydraulic and pneumatic ancillaries. It was also required to look at the accommodation for the crew and the storage of the ammunition. Robotham and his team of engineers installed themselves in an old iron foundry at Belper, just outside Derby, doing work that they were very well suited for.

It should be noted that at this stage Robotham and his team were concerned with the powertrain of the tank as their major task. Leyland Motors were then building tanks as previously noted, and it was suggested that they should include the Merlin, now named Meteor, in the tank that they were going to produce to meet the heavy cruiser specification. At some point in these discussions Leyland decided that it would not use the Meteor but would use the Liberty in what became specification A27L, subsequently named Centaur. Thus two trains of development took place along the paths shown in Figure 3.3. The Centaur built by Leyland was based upon the Rolls-Royce designs but had the Liberty engine. Leyland commenced design on this in November 1941 and had the first pilot run in July 1942. This pilot run and subsequent trials showed that the Liberty engine had an unsuitably short life expectancy for the requirements of the tank. The Centaur did however, go into production, but as a report of late 1943 told: 'The Centaur with its Liberty engine proved so unreliable when handled by units at home that as a gun tank it had been condemned. The Liberty engine is to go out of production, but in order not to break up manufacturers' organizations, production will have to continue long after condemnation as a gun tank engine.' In fact the Centaur did see active service in the role of close-support tank of the Royal Marines Armoured Support Group. These tanks were armed with 95mm howitzers.

Development of the A27M (the A27, Meteor engine, designated 'Cromwell') commenced after a meeting between Robotham and Harry Moyses of the Birmingham Railway Carriage and Wagon Company. Robotham suggested that they should work together to produce a tank specifically using the Meteor engine and meeting the general specification outlined for the A24. This was agreed and Moyses' company was made the parent for the A27M. The meeting between Robotham and Moyses was in September 1941 and by January 1942 they had a pilot model running. In February and March of 1942 this model was tested at Farnborough and found to be exceptionally good.

There were, of course, faults, but these were modified and in August 1942 the first pre-production models came off the line. In January 1943 production started to come off the main production lines and in due course the Cromwells were issued to field units. It has to be said, however, that the report produced at the end of 1943 states: 'The

Cromwell had up to the end of 1943 not proved in quality to be a vehicle of sufficiently reliable performance to be used in battle. Its production in quantity fell far short of that programmed. As a result it was considered necessary to change the parentage for Cromwell production in May of 1943. It was in fact Leyland Motors who took over responsibility for the Cromwell from the middle of 1943, even though they were still producing Centaurs at that time.'

Figure 3.3 shows that after the A27L and the A27M there were a number of projected tanks before the A30 and the A34 reached production and were issued to field units. Dealing with all of these, although chronologically some of them come later than the A30, the first chain is the A31, A32 and A35.

The A31 was a Rolls-Royce design for a Cromwell with heavier armour. It weighed 32 tons and was abandoned at the paper stage. A32 was also a Rolls-Royce design with the armour increased to the standard of the A22 or Churchill. It had a new suspension in order to meet the weight of the vehicle, which was now 34.5 tons. This design was also abandoned at the paper stage.

The A35 was, again, a heavier type of Cromwell with increased armour and stronger suspension. The design was by LMS Railway and Rolls-Royce. This model weighed 36 tons and was not progressed beyond the paper stage.

Cromwell on test in the UK. The Cromwell was first issued to field units in 1943. It was fast across country, and reasonably reliable. However, it could not accept a larger gun in the turret than the medium velocity 75mm. (Tank Museum 313/C4)

The first modification of the A27M was the A28. This was designed mostly by Rolls-Royce and was a Cromwell with increased armour and skirting plates to protect the suspension. It weighed 28 tons and was abandoned at the paper stage.

The A29 was considerably larger. This was also a Rolls-Royce design and was for a large cruiser to carry a seventeen-pounder gun. It weighed 45 tons and was abandoned at the paper stage in favour of the A30.

There is some uncertainty about the development of the A30, which was given the name Challenger. The building of the pilots and the design were under the same parentage as the Cromwell, the Birmingham Railway Carriage and Wagon Company and Rolls-Royce. The period of development was from late 1941 to the beginning of 1943. The prime requirement of this vehicle was to be able to mount a seventeen-pounder gun. This it did, but with some difficulties. The turret had to be made rather high, and the armour of the turret had to be reduced so that the suspension could carry the total fighting weight of the tank. Three pilot models of the A30 were being built at Birmingham in May 1942 and they were inspected as they were progressively produced in August 1942 and January 1943. The tank was accepted as being an excellent anti-tank vehicle in so far as armament was concerned but there was a feeling by at least one observer that the A30 was a white elephant and should not be proceeded with. However,

Comets of B Squadron 4th RTR on transporters at Trieste for the Victory Parade on 2 May 1946. The Comet was a good tank, purpose-designed to accept the high-velocity 77mm tank gun.

in February 1943 200 were ordered and in due course these were issued to those field units whose main tank was the Cromwell.

The A34 or Comet was designed to take the high-velocity 75mm tank gun designed by Vickers. This gun was essentially a seventeen-pounder with a shorter barrel and lighter weight. It became known as the 77mm tank gun in order to distinguish it from the 75mm medium-velocity gun and the seventeen-pounder. It was designed as a powerful anti-tank weapon, and it performed successfully in this role, although for only the last two months of the Second World War. When the gun had been developed it was realized that it was necessary to develop a new tank to accommodate it. The Comet was a heavy cruiser of 33 tons with frontal armour of 100 mm. It was entirely based on the Cromwell suspension, engine and transmission, suitably upgraded where necessary to meet the increased weight. The really significant thing about the Comet was that it was a complete design in itself, and was based upon its capability to mount a specific gun. Its design and production parentage was that of Leyland Motors and in spite of a number of changes to specification the company was able to meet the agreed delivery schedule in January 1945. They were issued to the 29th Armoured Brigade, who were able to use them from the crossing of the Rhine until the end of the war in north-west Europe. They were well thought of by their crews and were proved to be both mechanically sound and effective as a tank weapon.

DEVELOPMENT CHAIN 4: INFANTRY TANKS

Figure 3.3 shows one tank which is between the cruiser chain and the infantry tank chain. This is the Valentine. The Valentine has no 'A' number, because it was not made to a General Staff specification. It was based upon a medium tank, but it was designated as an infantry tank. It therefore occupies a central position between these two groups of tanks.

In January 1938 Vickers was invited to make either a Matilda II or an infantry tank based upon the A10, which had been its own original infantry tank design. The latter was preferred and a rough design was put forward by Vickers in the following month. One of the explanations for its name, Valentine, is that the design was delivered close to St Valentine's Day in 1938. An alternative explanation for the name relates to Sir John Carden, who was Vickers' chief designer until he was killed in an air crash in December 1935. His middle name was Valentine and it has been suggested that the tank was named in his honour. The tank, as designed, was based on the A10 and had a two-man turret crew. It had 60 mm of armour and its main armament was the two-pounder. The requirement of the General Staff was for a three-man turret and 70 mm of armour, and the tank was therefore rejected at that time. Vickers responded with a three-man turret version but with only 50 mm of armour. In April 1938 the War Office categorically refused the four-man Valentine on the following grounds:

The Valentine was derived from the A10 and had an uncertain identity. It was too slow for a cruiser tank and too lightly armoured for an infantry tank. Initial marks also had room in the turret for two men only, thus limiting its fighting capability. It was, however, very reliable and saw long service in many different roles. (Tank Museum 1787/B5)

- Only 50 mm of armour.
- No cupola for the commander.
- No protection for the suspension.
- Petrol engine.

By April 1939 requirements for tanks had become much more urgent. Sir Harold Brown wrote to Cdr Micklem of Vickers: 'Providing you can give us reasonable deliveries it is probable that we can place an order with you for about 100 of the three-man Valentine. This decision has been obtained against considerable opposition. It has been agreed to only for the reason that we can get additional infantry tanks in this way quicker than in any other.'

The three-man Valentine was accepted in that month and in May 1940 the first production machine was undergoing trials at Farnborough. In the course of its life, which lasted until 1945, it was found to be an extremely reliable vehicle. It was modified in many ways and in all there were eleven marks of the Valentine. The total production was 8,275, the last tank leaving Vickers' factories in April 1944. It was a tank which was always reliable but very rarely a match for its opposition.

Infantry tanks made to War Office specifications start with the A11 or Infantry Tank Mk I. In the early 1930s there began to be a demand for heavily armoured tanks designed for, and committed to, intimate support of the infantry. In April 1934 outline specifications were produced for two types of infantry tank, both with at least one inch of armour all around and a speed of 10 mph:

1. A small tank, mounting a machine-gun, inconspicuous and available in large numbers to act as mobile machine-gun posts.
2. A heavy tank mounting a two-pounder anti-tank gun to deal with enemy tanks.

In relation to the small tank, Sir John Carden of Vickers said that he could produce a small infantry tank for about £5,000 if he were given a free hand. This offer was quickly accepted and in October 1935 the project to produce the Vickers Mk I Infantry tank was commenced. The pilot model appeared in September 1936. This had 65 mm of armour at the front and 60 mm on the side. It weighed 11 tons and had a top speed of 8 mph. It had a two-man crew and mounted a .303 in Vickers machine-gun in the turret. The tank was cheap and was mechanically very reliable but obviously it was very unsatisfactory with only a two-man crew and such poor fighting capability. The A11 was produced as an interim measure and a total of 140 units were built. These were eventually to form the greater part of the two infantry tank battalions in France in 1940.

These Mk Is clearly had to be replaced by a more powerful vehicle. The tank to meet the second specification described earlier was the one which the infantry tank units needed and this was designated the A12. The design was undertaken by the Mechanization Board in conjunction with the Vulcan Foundry. It was found that it was not practical to develop the A11 and the design of the A12 was based on the A7. The tank was to mount a two-pounder and the mock-up for the A12 was ready by April 1937. Various engine layouts were considered and the AEC diesel engine was chosen as a satisfactory solution. As mentioned earlier, this was already manufactured to meet the requirements of London buses. The Wilson epicyclic gearbox was used and the suspension was developed from the Vickers 'Japanese-type' design. This was to accommodate the weight which was now 24 tons with 70 mm of armour. The first pilot was ready in April 1938 but an order was given in December 1937 for work to start at once on a batch of sixty-five tanks. In May 1938 this was increased to 135.

One of the problems with the A12 or Matilda was that it was constructed from a number of large castings bolted together. This gave great strength but demanded many man hours of specialist skill in manufacture. The result of this was that the rate of production was extremely slow and when the war broke out there were only two Matildas in service. But in France in May 1940 it proved to be an exceptionally good tank for its time. It was even given the title of 'Queen of the Battlefield'. The few Matildas that were used in France in 1940 were all left behind. This allowed the Germans to examine the armour and to conclude that they would need to develop a more powerful anti-tank gun. This they did, with the result that in a few months the Matilda was no longer the queen of the battlefield. For the first few months in North Africa the Matilda was still paramount against the Italian tanks that were available, and was highly regarded by all the crews who fought in her. Two things were against the Matilda however:

- The impossibility of increasing the strength of the main armament due to the small turret.
- The very slow process of manufacture.

In spite of this a total of 2,987 Matildas were built until production ceased in August 1943.

The next tank in the infantry tank chain is the A20. This was a tank designed for a very specific purpose. In 1937 and 1938 it became apparent that because of the defences being put up by the French, in the shape of the Maginot Line, and the Germans, in the shape of the Siegfried Line, it was quite possible that there might be conflict similar to that experienced in the First World War. This would require a tank similar to those developed and used very successfully in the years 1916–18. It was therefore decided that a tank capable of moving over muddy and cratered land was required. In September 1939 the specification for the A20 had been drawn up. It was to be capable of leading a direct assault on enemy positions and able to operate over very soft ground. It had to withstand the current German anti-tank gun and had to be able to travel at 10 mph. In the initial specification it was also required to employ an unditching beam.

The specification was modified in various ways and finally the main features were that the A20 should be armoured to 60 mm, equipped with the turret and armament of the A12 Matilda and incorporate the engine and transmission of the new A13 Cruiser Mk III.

By the end of October 1939 outline drawings were nearly complete and the Belfast company of Harland and Wolff was approached to manufacture the A20. By January 1940 it was decided that the first two models should be completed in mild steel, but it was considered that production could not be completed before 1941. Various changes were made to the layout of the armament and in the end it was agreed that a 3in howitzer would be used.

Early in 1940 Vauxhall Motors were approached for their assistance in the production programme. They were invited to propose an alternative engine to the Meadows flat 12-cylinder engine that had been developed for the A13. They were supported by the Ministry of Supply in providing equipment for a new factory, and they very soon developed a flat 12-cylinder engine based on their own Bedford engines which were used for trucks. The development of the A20 proceeded and finally a pilot model was ready for trials in the middle of 1940. It weighed 40 tons and carried a crew of seven. The pilot trials were not particularly successful and this, combined with the substantial weight of the tank, decided the War Office to terminate this development. A subsequent development of the A20 was the A21. This never got beyond the stage of schematic drawings.

In June 1940, after Britain's defeat in France, there was very little equipment left with which to arm tank forces. The decision was taken to manufacture tanks as soon as possible, concentrating first on those which were already in production. This was done in spite of any deficiencies the tanks might have had, or any lack of ability to combat the German Army.

One decision that was taken in June 1940 was to look for manufacturing capacity in industries suited for the manufacture of tanks. Most such companies were already engaged in the output of military hardware, but one company which did have spare capacity was Vauxhall Motors which had already had some involvement with an engine for the A20. This project had been abandoned, but the facilities for producing the Bedford flat 12-cylinder engine were still in existence. In June 1940 a revised specification for a heavy tank, the A22, was prepared. This tank was to carry 102 mm of armour, to mount a 3in howitzer in the hull, and to have a turret containing a two-pounder and a co-axial Besa. It was further specified that the turret should be able to mount a six-pounder gun as soon as that was available. Winston Churchill took a special interest in this tank – which shortly afterwards was named the Churchill – and demanded that 500 should be completed by March 1941. It was July 1940 and a nine-month gestation period for a new tank was almost impossible. It was decided that the 500 would be produced for issue to field units, doing away with any consideration of prototypes or pilot models. For the unfortunate units that eventually received these first tanks they proved to be prototypes rather than production models.

It was soon found that they had faults in almost everything, including the tracks, suspension, gearbox and engine, as well as some of the armour plate and castings that were used. Vauxhall was well aware of these problems as soon as it started to test the tanks itself, and it issued a notice which was incorporated in all the Churchill user handbooks. In this leaflet it acknowledged the problems, gave the reasons for some of them and reassured the users that, in time, all would be well. It said, in part: 'The defects exist solely because of the inadequate time that has been available for comprehensive testing. They are the teething troubles inseparable from a new design. In normal times every one of them would have been eliminated before the vehicle was released for production. Times, however, are not normal. Fighting vehicles are urgently required and instructions have been received to proceed with the vehicle as it is rather than hold up production. All those things which we know are not as they should be will be put right. Please do not draw the wrong conclusion from this statement of defects. This tank is a good vehicle. The troubles which have emerged from recent tests are not in any way abnormal. The only abnormal factor is that we have not been in a position to put them right before production begins.'

For the people that had to use them, for example 9th RTR and 10th RTR of 31st Tank Brigade, the initial Churchills were a nightmare. Tanks would go out on manoeuvres and perhaps 25 per cent would be able to return to camp at the end of the day. The remainder would be scattered around the Yorkshire Moors, with their crews either sleeping beside them for the night or helping the squadron fitters to put them right in a night-long exercise. The Churchill programme had to be supported by a programme of rework. This meant that when the appropriate modifications had been determined the tanks had to be withdrawn from the units for those modifications to be carried out. This not only withdrew the tanks from training, but also took up resources which were required for the production of new tanks. The proving period for the Churchill was something like two years, and took place to a large extent within field units. Although this was a gross wastage of resources it also made the Churchill crews adept at detecting and curing problems, and led to them becoming quite attached to these temperamental vehicles. In

A Mk II Churchill, armed only with a two-pounder gun in the turret. It was capable of taking a six-pounder on a 75mm gun, but these were not available in the early years of the war. These tanks were on an exercise in the UK in January 1942. (IWM H16965)

the end they became a reliable tank and served very usefully in campaigns in North Africa, Italy and north-west Europe. The Churchill chassis was used for many special vehicles and was one of the best tanks for hill-climbing and for moving over soft ground.

The Churchill had the problem of most British tanks that it could not readily be up-gunned. It was able to accept the six-pounder and the 75mm medium-velocity gun. A number of models were also fitted with the 95mm howitzer. A further improvement was made by increasing the thickness of the armour to 152 mm in the front. This was called either the Churchill Mk VII or the A42. There were a number of proposed developments from the Churchill, which were:

- The A23 which was a projected lighter version of the A22 but never proceeded beyond the sketch stage.
- The A26 which, again, was a lighter and faster version of the A22 but never proceeded beyond the sketch stage.
- The A43: a draft specification was issued for this in December 1943 and required an infantry tank mounting the seventeen-pounder gun. Its estimated weight was 50 tons. In May 1944 six prototypes were ordered with varying types of armament. A mock-up was prepared in August 1944 and the first prototype was completed in January 1945. The A43 was now known as Black Prince and was clearly a Churchill

Churchills training in 1942. The tank in the foreground is a Mk I, armed with a two-pounder gun in the turret and a 3in howitzer in the hull. At this stage the Churchill was so unreliable mechanically that the training area would by nightfall be littered with broken-down tanks, most of them not recoverable until the next morning. (IWM H16959)

brought up to date. However, it was not sufficiently brought up to date and in the end the six prototypes were the only units produced. It had in fact been overtaken by the much more effective A41, or Centurion, of which prototypes were sent to field units in May 1945.

The infantry tank was no longer required after the Second World War because its function was taken over by 'universal' tanks such as the Centurion. They were able to perform the functions required both in armoured brigades working in an armoured division and armoured brigades working to support infantry divisions. The Churchill had become an extremely good platform on which to mount all kinds of weaponry and other facilities required on a battlefield. It did in fact remain in use for many years after the Second World War and certainly held a special place in the hearts of those who fought in it.

BRITISH TANK DEVELOPMENT, 1919–45: COMMENTS

Analysis of Figure 3.3 'Lineage of British Tanks' shows that British tank development from 1919 to 1945 had two main characteristics: a large amount of effort was spent in projects that resulted in nothing useful; and of the tanks that were delivered to field units something like 75 per cent were useless as battle tanks at the time they were delivered.

The only British tanks that could be called useful were: Matilda (for a very limited period), Valentine (but always undergunned) and Churchill (but always undergunned), Cromwell (always undergunned); Comet was a good competitive tank, but saw only two months' action in very limited quantities.

This is an appalling outcome for a country that had developed the original tank concept, had skilled and innovative designers and engineers, and had the manufacturing infrastructure with the potential for precision-built engineering products. This chapter has described what happened in tank development. In the last chapter of this book we will attempt to find some reasons for failure.

WHAT TANK TO BUILD?

Before preparing a specification for an Armoured Fighting Vehicle (AFV), decisions must be made on three main items and those decisions must then be communicated to the specification writer. The three items are: the function of the tank as a whole, the function of the tank's armament, and the hostile actions that the tank will have to contend with.

FUNCTIONS AND OPERATING CONDITIONS

Functions of the tank as a whole

The function of the tank as a whole is determined by the role it is required to play; five possible roles are:

- It could be used purely as a reconnaissance vehicle where its role was to find out what was happening on the other side of the hill and come back to report. In a case like that the desirable features of the vehicle would be speed and a low profile. The amount of firepower required would be minimal.
- If the tank was required to carry out a role such as guarding a flank, one of the roles of the cavalry in previous years, the tank would need to be able to protect itself while it was making contact but would also need to be able to move rapidly back to the better-armed main body of the force whose flank it was protecting.
- The third role is that of the main strike arm of a fast-moving attacking body. In this case it would need to be reasonably fast, reasonably well armed and to have reasonable protection. The 'reasonable' requirements would have to be quantified as the specification became more precise and complete.
- The fourth type of role that a tank could play would be that of direct infantry support in the fashion mentioned by Alan Jolly. To do this it was likely that the tank would have to approach heavily defended localities. It would thus require heavy enough armour that it could take substantial punishment while it was closing in on those localities. If these included anti-tank defences, then the designers would need

to have some idea of the strength and type of that anti-tank weaponry. The three most common anti-tank weapons in the Second World War were anti-tank guns, hostile tanks and self-propelled anti-tank guns.

- The previous role leads to that of self-protection, in which role it must be able to eliminate the items particularly hostile to it, namely enemy tanks and anti-tank guns.

FUNCTION OF A TANK GUN

The second item to be defined in the tank's function is the role of the gun itself. It will have one of two main purposes: first to provide direct firepower to assist infantry in their assault on enemy positions. The most likely method for success in doing this is a high-explosive (HE) shell, assuming that the opposition consists of items which are not completely protected, particularly from the air. The second main purpose of the tank principal armament is to combat other tanks. This requires an anti-tank capability which normally requires high-velocity fire to provide a flat projectory, and the use of solid shot. A third but subsidiary role for a tank gun is to provide smoke.

CONDITIONS OF OPERATION

The third thing to be considered in the specification is the conditions under which the tank will be required to operate. This will include such considerations as an ability to move along roads, an ability to travel across country and an ability to climb. The ability to travel across country will be further sub-divided into various types of going. The tank may be required to cross sandy ground or ground where very low track pressure is required, such as the conditions experienced in Holland in 1944, or conditions where the going is broken under the tank tracks. The ability to climb is also very useful in that it allows an enemy to be surprised by the appearance of tanks where they were not expected.

OPPOSITION

The next general requirement to be considered is the sort of opposition that the tank may encounter. Opposition can include: anti-tank guns, either tank-mounted or ground-mounted; weapons held by infantry; mines; and attack from the air. Anti-tank guns, whether ground-mounted or tank-mounted, are generally considered the most significant opposition against which a tank should be able to defend itself. It is likely that as the protection of a tank becomes better, so the enemy will increase the capability to penetrate that armour. This is done in one of three ways: first by increasing the size of the projectile, second by increasing the muzzle velocity of the projectile and third by using special types of shot which increase penetration of the armour.

QUANTITATIVE PARAMETERS

The next step in specifying an AFV is to consider quantitative parameters that the user would like to define.

- **Armament**: The person defining the function of a tank may want to say that the attack performance of the main armament is such that it will penetrate a certain thickness of armour at a given range. The users may also define that they want the main armament to be able not only to fulfil that defined anti-tank role but also to provide support to other arms in the form of a high-explosive capability. This capability would also be extremely valuable to the tanks themselves in dealing with ground-mounted anti-tank guns.
- **Mobility**: The user may define that the tank should be able to move at a certain minimum speed along the road and another minimum speed across country.
- **Suspension**: The user may define that the suspension of the tank is such that it will give its crew a reasonably comfortable ride over a defined roughness of country, but more importantly that it will provide a reasonable platform from which to fire on the move. It must be noted that this requirement for firing on the move was something that the users between the wars insisted upon. Whether firing on the move was in fact effective is very much open to question. Almost all tank crews during the Second World War found it much more effective to fire when stationary. However, if this was a user requirement then it had to be met in some way.
- **Protection**: The protection of the tank and its crew depended on the expected opposition. As the opposing anti-tank capability became stronger, so the thickness of armour had to become greater. There were various other possibilities in providing adequate protection, i.e. by modifying the type of armour to make it more resistant and thus, for a given protective performance, lighter. A further need for protection came from the use of infantry anti-tank weapons such as the German *Panzerfaust*. These could be, in part, combated by additional skins or some form of additional protection outside the main armour.
- **Fighting capability**: This covers several things, the first of which is the accommodation for the crew. If a fighting compartment is too crowded or a position is too cramped or uncomfortable, it clearly reduces the efficiency of the tank crews and makes it difficult for them to respond rapidly to the demands of the battlefield.

   The second item in fighting capability is the workload for crew members. When a two-man tank was built it required one person to drive it and one person to do everything else. The second crew member had to load the gun, fire the gun, operate the wireless set, give directions to the driver and maintain communication with his troop or squadron commander. This was clearly quite impossible. Even with a turret crew of two the duties were such that either one or both of the people in the turret were overworked to the point where they were inefficient. In the two-man turret one split of the turret duties was for the wireless operator to load the gun and for the commander to fire it. Quite clearly, when firing the gun the commander cannot effectively command the tank and in most British tanks the three-man turret crew was the normal requirement for effective operating.

- The third item in fighting capability is the amount of ammunition that can be carried. The more ammunition that can be carried the longer the tank can remain in action without having to retire to forward rally to stock up with more ammunition.

  The fourth item in fighting capability is the system for sighting the main armament. It is obviously highly desirable that the gunner is able to knock out opposition at the first shot. This is likely not only to preserve the life of all the people in the tank by destroying the opposition immediately, but also to preserve the necessarily limited supply of ammunition carried in the tank. Good optical systems made a very substantial contribution to fighting capability.

- **Ease of maintenance and repair**: A real problem for tank and maintenance crews was that they had to spend a great deal of time in accessing items and carrying out tasks that presented unnecessary difficulty. Some of the earlier tanks were not user-friendly in respect of maintenance. For example, in the Churchill if there was a leak in the petrol tank – and in the early models this happened very frequently – the complete tank engine had to be removed before the petrol tank could be repaired; obviously this took up an enormous amount of maintenance resource, quite disproportionate to the severity of the fault.

- **Capability for accepting upgrades**: A really important feature of tank function is that it should be able to be upgraded without fundamental changes being made. For example, if it may be necessary to mount a larger gun in the foreseeable future then the turret must be of such a size that the larger gun can be incorporated without having to change the turret in any significant way. Many of the British designs were such that it was extremely difficult to up-gun the tanks from the original model. Attempts were made with the Valentine and the Crusader, but with the larger guns they became difficult for the crew to use.

  The second item to be designed with the capacity for upgrading was the suspension. If the suspension was built in such a way that it could only just take the weight of the tank as initially designed, then any increase in weight would overload the suspension. This would mean constant suspension breakdowns and thus an unreliable tank. One of the main features of the German Mk III and Mk IV tanks was that they were able to accept significant increases in firepower and weight without having to make radical changes either to the suspension or to the turret. Another item that required modification, generally increasing the weight, was the tank's protection against anti-tank fire. Unless a new type of protective armour was developed, then it would be necessary simply to make the existing armour thicker, thus obviously increasing the weight.

- **Range of operation without refuelling**: This would clearly depend upon the efficiency of the engine and the available volume for petrol storage. First World War tanks had extremely small 'circuits', as they were called. In a mobile force it is clearly desirable to have a substantial range of operation, because a tank can only be refuelled from its own logistical supply (unless it is fortunate enough to find local supplies of petrol, either civilian or military). Thus the range of a tank unit was determined both by the capabilities of the tank itself and by the systems put in place to refuel the tanks.

- **Reliability**: It is difficult to quantify reliability, but is certainly a very real factor in a tank's performance. The tanks produced by Britain during the early years of the Second World War were notoriously unreliable, in particular the Covenanter, the Crusader and the Churchill. The last of these was eventually made reliable enough that mechanical breakdowns were relatively rare, but the first two obtained such a reputation for unreliability that in spite of other good qualities they were rejected by the tank crews as soon as there was any possibility of a replacement. One of the outstanding qualities of the German Mk IIIs and Mk IVs was their mechanical reliability. When the Mk V (Panther) and the Mk VI (Tiger) were brought into service they were found to be not so mechanically reliable as their predecessors. However, their firepower was such that their unreliability was certainly not immediately apparent to the crews that opposed them.

Some of the functions required by tanks were well expressed by Montgomery in December 1944 in his instruction 'The armoured division in battle'. He wrote a few notes about tanks in his usual crisp style and made the following points:

- A tank is an armoured vehicle designed to carry about firepower: this definition, once understood, simplifies the problem of the employment of armour on the battlefield.
- The tank must have a really good gun (dual purpose), and mechanical reliability is a necessity.
- It is our policy to have only two types of tank – the capital tank to fight, the light tank to reconnoitre.

    The term capital tank means a dual-purpose tank, suitable for working with infantry and also for operating in an armoured division.
- The aim is to have all armoured brigades equipped with the capital tank; then the commander can reinforce any part of his command with a standard type of tank. It is undesirable to have special function tanks, e.g. close-support tanks, because these can only be used for special purposes at intermittent stages of a battle.
- The weight of any tank should not exceed about 45 tons. Having selected the best possible gun as a primary weapon and designed an engine with sufficient horsepower to give the required speed, then armour should be fitted up to the maximum weight allowed.

These comments by Monty are clear and give a good guide to anyone who has to produce a detailed specification for a tank.

PHYSICAL CONSTRAINTS: INTERNAL

There are certain relationships or ratios between some of the parameters mentioned in the previous section which provide constraints to the tank designer. These should be taken account of in preparing a detailed specification. Some of these are classified as internal constraints and some as external. The internal constraints integrate the size of the tank gun, the size of the turret, the width of the tank and the length of the tank, as follows.

It is generally accepted that the required firepower is the primary function of a tank. As Monty said in his description of tank function, the tank must have a really good dual-purpose gun. The size of the gun will determine the size of the turret. There must be room for safe recoil of the gun, there must be sufficient room for the loader to load shells into the main armament and there must be sufficient space to store as much ammunition as possible. The turret must also be sufficiently large for the crew to be able to function effectively and continuously. As stated earlier, it is extremely desirable to have three people in a turret: one to fire the main and co-axial armament, the second to load the guns and to operate the wireless set, and the third to command the tank. Any crew fewer than three provides a substantial overload to one person or the other, and it becomes extremely difficult to use a tank to the limit of its capabilities.

Given a certain turret size, as determined by the factors mentioned above, then the turret ring must be of an appropriate diameter. This turret ring size will determine the width of the hull. The width of the hull will determine the spacing between the centre lines of the two tracks. For effective steering the ratio between the amount of track on the ground to the distance between the centre lines of the tracks should be approximately 2:1. This means that the turret size determines the width of the hull which in turn determines the approximate length of the hull. Thus there is a clear connection between the armament required and the main dimensions of the complete tank.

The gun may need to be depressed or elevated to give it the capability of firing downwards from a dominating position or upwards when attacking higher ground. There is therefore a need to depress or elevate the main gun to some determined degree. This will determine the height of the turret, because the tank gun breech mechanism must clearly have sufficient room between it, at maximum depression, and the roof of the tank turret. Another item which determines the space required in the turret is the recoil system for the main gun. Some very innovative methods were used at different stages of the Second World War, in particular the way in which the seventeen-pounder tank gun was fitted to the Sherman tank.

EXTERNAL CONSTRAINTS

During the first part of the Second World War there were a number of external constraints on the dimensions or other parameters of a tank. The first two external constraints concerned the width of the tank: there was a definite limitation caused by the

Loading tanks on to rail flats was a time-consuming and occasionally dangerous job, often made frustrating by the varying and uncertain demands of different railway systems. (IWM H16295)

British rail gauge and the requirements of the people operating the rail systems; the second dimensional constraint was provided by the width of the Royal Engineers' bridging systems, particularly the Bailey Bridge. This width limitation caused a number of arrangements to be made to reduce the width for special purposes, i.e., being transported by rail flats. Churchill tank air intakes were external projections to the main body of the hull. When a Churchill travelled by rail the air louvres had to be unbolted and placed on top of the tank; when the journey was over and the tanks had been unloaded from the rail flats, the air louvres had to be bolted on again. This was a time-consuming and particularly heavy job for the tank crews. Another external limitation was, in some cases, the track pressure. If it was expected or required as a general function that tanks should be capable of keeping going on soft ground, then it was necessary to limit the track pressure. This meant that the track width or length had to be increased so that the weight of the tank was spread over a greater area in contact with the ground. Some tanks had substantially better qualities for keeping going over soft ground than others. Tanks mounted on the Churchill chassis kept going particularly well in muddy conditions, such as those of the Reichswald battle in February 1945.

Another external constraint was the total weight of the tank. This was to ensure that tanks could move over most of the civilian bridges that existed, and could also move over the Royal Engineers' bridges such as the Bailey Bridge.

STEPS IN PRODUCING A TANK

The process of designing and producing a tank is a long and involved process which involves many different stages and the contributions of many different people. The start point is when the user or General Staff have decided that a new tank is needed to match or outmatch the potential opposition. We will assume in this case that the main armament has already been agreed and is available in production quantities. The finish point of this project of producing a new tank is taken to be the moment when the tank is delivered in quantity to field units and the tank and maintenance crews have been trained in the operation and maintenance, respectively, of the new tank.

As has just been said, the start point is when the General Staff representing the user have produced a requirement which they want to be satisfied. As an example we can take the 16-ton tank (A6) which was requested in July 1926. The outline specification gave the following points:

- There should be two independent machine-gun turrets.
- The weight of the tank should be limited to 15.5 tons because of the limits [at that time] of bridging equipment; the length should be increased as much as was compatible with this limitation and the width should be within the railway loading gauge.
- All parts of the vehicle should be accessible and the design should be as simple as possible.
- The lubricating oil range should be as great as that of the petrol.
- A wireless set should be installed.
- Anti-aircraft protection must be included and the vehicle must be highly gas-proof.
- The main armament of the tank should be able to penetrate a similar machine at a range of at least 1,000 yd.
- The tank should have heavy belly armour in front for protection when crossing a crest.
- The fuel tank should be outside the main hull.
- From a tactical point of view, silence was a most desirable feature.

That was an outline specification outline in 1926. In 1943 we can see another specification where the General Staff put forward the idea of a new heavy cruiser tank. This they suggested should have 4 in of frontal armour and mount a seventeen-pounder gun, which they considered was likely to be superior to any weapon that the enemy could mount in a tank. The particular purpose of this was that they would not just be catching up with the Germans, they would be going beyond what they could expect the Germans to produce in the next year or two.

After the specification for a new tank has been drawn up and agreed there are three main stages that must take place before the tank is operational in the hands of field units. The three stages are:

1. A pilot model is designed, made, tested and modified. After iterative modification as necessary, the pilot model is approved and production can go ahead on a large scale.
2 After that approval, all manufacturing facilities for the new tank are acquired. Materials are purchased, components and assemblies are made or purchased, and the tank is assembled as a complete unit.
3. The production model tank is proved, modified as necessary and issued to field units. Tank maintenance crews are trained for the new tank.

CODE	DESCRIPTION	DURATION (MONTHS)
A	Prepare specification and obtain approval	3
B	Prepare mock-up and approve	4
C	Obtain and train design staff	5
D	Design pilot	2
E	Prepare production facilities for pilot	2
F	Build pilot	4
G	Test pilot; modify; approve	4
H	Write detailed manufacturing specification	3
I	Design/specify machine tools	4
J	Manufacture/procure machine tools	6
K	Prepare detailed manufacturing drawings	3
L	Make manufacturing tooling/jigs	6
M	Design manufacturing facilities	3
N	Build manufacturing facilities	6
O	Procure materials	3
P	Procure bought-out components and assemblies	4
Q	Specify labour resources for manufacture	1
R	Obtain labour resources	2
S	Train labour resources	2
T	Manufacture components	5
U	Assemble tank	4
V	Prove tank	5
W	Modify and issue tank	6
X	Prepare training instructions for tank crews	2
Y	Train tank crews	3
Z	Write maintenance procedures	3
AA	Train maintenance crews	3

FIGURE 3.4: NEW TANK PROJECT; ACTIVITY LIST

Start point: General Staff decide that a new tank is needed to match/outmatch potential opposition: main armament has already been agreed and is available in production quantities. Finish point: Tank delivered in quantity to operational units; tank and maintenance crews have been trained in the operation and maintenance of the new tank.

Those three main stages are broken down into a series of activities. A typical listing of activities is shown in Figure 3.4. The first activity is to prepare specifications and obtain approval. The second one, coded B, is to prepare a mock-up for approval. The mock-up is normally in the form of a timber frame with plywood to indicate the size, silhouette and general shape of the tank, and also to give some idea of the sizes of the compartments: the transmission compartment, the engine compartment, the fighting compartment and the driver's compartment.

The mock-up is shown to the sponsor of the project, who would normally be General Staff or representatives of the General Staff. At the same time as that happens, staff must be trained to act as designers. It may be that there are already enough design staff to carry out the design of the pilot and the production models later on, but one of the problems for British tank production, particularly in the early years of the Second World War, was the shortage of trained design staff.

Having obtained or trained people to act as designers, then the pilot model can be designed, based on the approved mock-up. At the same time as the pilot is being designed, arrangements must be made for its production. The organization responsible for the design may have production facilities which can be made available; in many cases, however, it would be necessary to find production facilities outside, either sub-contractors with knowledge of vehicle design and production or engineering organizations which could be trained to build pilot models. One of the major problems during the early years of the Second World War was the difficulty of finding suitable facilities for the work that was required to produce components and assemblies to the tolerances required.

Having obtained the production facilities for the pilot and having designed the pilot, it can be built and then tested. This test should involve cross-country trials, road trials and gunnery trials. The extent of the trials should be as wide as possible, and the number of vehicles or units of pilot production tried out should be as large as possible.

Having gone through a testing programme, which may take some weeks or even months, it will become apparent that modifications are needed. Those modifications should be made, the units retested and, after what may be a lengthy iterative process, the pilot and its modifications are approved. In Figure 3.5, which is titled Stage 1: Design, Build and Test Pilot, there is a decision point after 'Test, modify and approve pilot'. At this point the sponsor will decide whether, in the light of the tests that have been carried out and the comments from people who have carried out the tests, the tank should be built as an operational tank. This decision point is of course the most significant milestone in the whole chain of the process, because after this point large sums of money will have to be spent to enter into full production.

Having decided to build the operational tank the first step is to write a detailed manufacturing specification. This will break down the pilot design into all the various components and assemblies which go into the tank. The production engineering function of the organization that is building the tank will then work out the way in which each of the components and assemblies of the tank should be made. They can decide whether certain items should be made internally or whether they should either be purchased as a complete assembly or made by a sub-contractor.

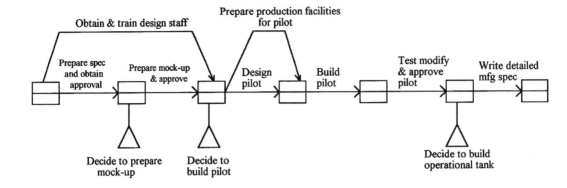

FIGURE 3.5 STAGE 1: DESIGN, BUILD AND TEST PILOT

Whatever method they decide for the production of each of the component parts, they must be sure that all the components fit with each other to the appropriate tolerances. One of the problems that British tank-makers had in the Second World War was that they used craftsmanship rather than mass production methods; this meant that almost every time a component was fitted to its assembly some hand work was needed to make it to fit. American production methods set close tolerances for their components and insisted on the achievement of those tolerances; they never expected to see anybody filing a component so that it would fit into its assembly. This process of ensuring that all parts fit with each other is now called configuration control. If changes are made to one part, the effect on other parts which are associated with that part are examined to see whether they too need to be changed in some way. The amount of work that was necessary to modify individual components in British factories in the early years of the Second World War was very extensive and wasteful.

The end result of the detailed manufacturing specification is a complete list of all the items that are required, a statement of where they will be obtained from or how they will be made, and clear statements as to the tolerances and other quality aspects required in those components. The manufacturing specification will also show what types of machines are required on which to make the parts and whether any special tooling or jigs are required to make those parts or to fit them to other parts; and will reveal to all the people concerned exactly what part they should play in the manufacture.

When that manufacturing specification has been prepared there are six things that can be done. These are set out in the network which is titled Stage 2: Produce Operational Tank (Figure 3.6). Let us deal with each of the chains of activity on that diagram in turn, starting from the top: the first line includes the activities 'design machine tools' and 'manufacture machine tools'. If the machine tools on which the components are going to be made are themselves to be made within the factory making the tank, then the machine tools themselves will have to be designed. Alternatively, they can be procured from outside; in that case the activity would be 'specify machine tools'.

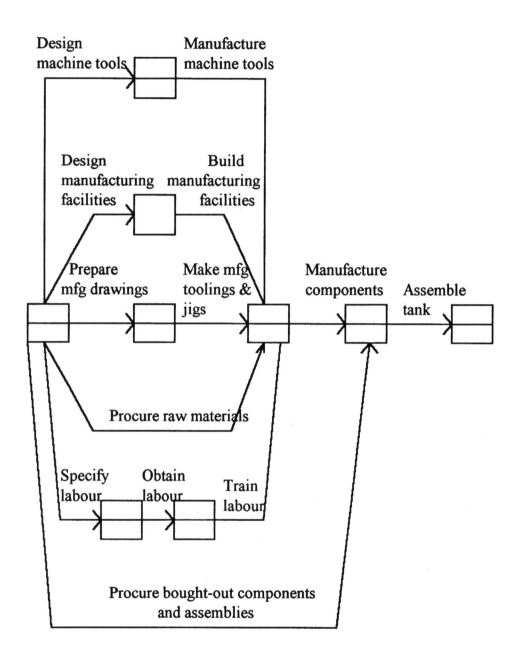

FIGURE 3.6 STAGE 2: PRODUCE OPERATIONAL TANK

The machine tools having been either designed or specified, they must then either be manufactured or bought from outside. Depending on the nature of the machine tools, these two processes can be very time consuming. It may, of course, be that the particular factory making the tank already has the required machine tools for the components that it is going to have to manufacture; obviously this is a highly desirable way to design the components, i.e. design them so that they can be made on existing machines.

The second chain of activities in Stage 2 is to design and build the manufacturing facilities. This could require the building of a complete factory in which the tank production is going to take place, with all the services and facilities that are required in a factory of that type. If the factory already existed, it could mean modifying it to include appropriate methods for handling materials through the processes of manufacture. A typical example would be a flow line for assembling tank hulls, each hull moving progressively through a series of workstations. There may be a number of other manufacturing facilities which are required, and it is the duty of the factory management to ensure that all necessary manufacturing facilities are identified, checked to see whether they are available, and supplied as necessary.

The next chain consists of the preparation of detailed manufacturing drawings. These drawings are the ones that will be used by the supervisors and operators within the manufacturing departments to make the various components and assemblies which are going to be made within the factory itself. The working drawings for the components having been done, it may then become apparent that tooling or jigs may have to be made in order to make those components on the machines that are available.

The fourth chain consists of the one item 'procure raw materials'. These should be identified in the detailed manufacturing specification, and would include materials such as steel, rubber, cable and all items which could be bought from external suppliers as stock items.

The next chain considers the operators who will be required to produce the components in the tank manufacturing factory. The three steps are: to specify what labour is required; to obtain that labour from the labour market; and to train that labour. In training the labour obviously it will be necessary to have some training programme. That has not been included in the network but could form an additional chain of activities.

The last chain is the procurement of components and assemblies bought outside. These are items which can be procured from specialist suppliers; for example, electric motors, traverse gear, gearboxes, and possibly suppliers of complete power units. It will also include the main armament which will be provided by some other ordnance factory.

Once all the manufacturing facilities, tools, raw materials and labour have been obtained and are ready to operate, then the components can be manufactured. At this point we have the components manufactured by the factory workforce and we have all the components and assemblies which have been procured from external suppliers. Having got all of these together, then the tank as a whole can be assembled.

The last stage in this process is the proving of the production tank (Figure 3.7). In the proving process the tank is put through a series of tests and trials which will simulate the

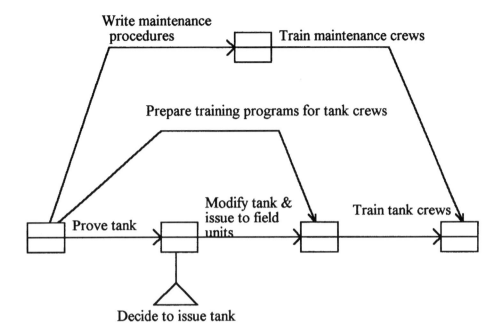

FIGURE 3.7 STAGE 3: PROVE TANK AND ISSUE; TRAIN CREWS

type of battle situation in which it will find itself later on. Under some circumstances it is possible to take the pilot models and put them into action in real combat. This may not be very cheerful for the tank crews, as the Canadians discovered in their Churchills at Dieppe in August 1942.

Having put the production model of the tank through its proving trials, then there would almost certainly be modifications to be made. At this point it should be possible to decide whether the modifications were sufficiently minor that the tank could be issued with reasonable confidence, or whether so many changes were still needed that the tank should be abandoned. Assuming that the first case applies, once those modifications had been made then the tank could be issued to field units. At the same time as the tank is proved, then the training programmes could be prepared for the tank crews and for the maintenance crews. Then, having prepared those training programmes, both of the types of crew – i.e. maintenance and tank crew – could be trained using the training material that has been prepared. At the end of this project we would have a tank and crews ready to operate in the field.

Figure 3.4 gives estimates of durations for the activities needed to execute the New Tank Project. The durations are based on experience in heavy engineering, but are obviously subject to substantial variations depending on what skills and facilities are already available; whether the design is based on previous designs proved in the field; whether some components are common with those used in previous models, etc. It must also be said that most estimates of activity durations are optimistic and make no allowance for the unexpected setbacks that always occur in real life.

Using the estimated activity durations listed, the project duration is calculated using the methods of critical path analysis. It is assumed that resources are available to carry out a number of chains of activities simultaneously (as indicated in the arrow diagrams of Figures 3.5, 3.6 and 3.7). The time required from commencing preparation of the specification to the production tank being manned by trained crews is fifty-three months, just under four and a half years. This project duration is exaggerated by the assumption that most facilities were not available at the start of the project, and that the design was not firmly based on previous work. It would seem realistic, however, to make an estimate of three and a half years as the minimum duration for a project to produce a piece of operational hardware of such complexity as a tank. And for the tank to be fully operational the project must include the training of tank and maintenance crews.

CHAPTER 4

Without a Gun the Battle was Lost

TANK GUNS AND DEFINITIONS

Several times in the course of this book it has been said that a tank should be designed around the gun it has to carry. The function of the gun depends on the role that armoured forces, or different parts of them, are required to play. Because that role varied in a number of ways over the period from 1919 to 1945 the requirement for the gun also varied. In this chapter we look at those varying roles, the guns that were developed to help achieve those roles and the problems in matching the guns to the tanks. In this first section we identify the guns that are to be considered, and some definitions and terms relating to the guns and to the ammunition they use.

A tank can carry a wide range of armament, including: the main tank gun; machine-guns, mounted co-axially with the main gun, as a hull gun, or in separate turrets; a hull gun, either intended for anti-tank use or for firing high-explosive shells at suitable targets; mortars, often mounted in the tank turret to fire smoke or HE; machine-guns mounted on the top of the turret as anti-aircraft protection.

All of these are important, but the most important is the main tank gun, generally mounted in the turret; it is the main tank gun only that will be considered in this chapter. The main tank guns to be considered will be further restricted to those used in the period 1933–45 in British tanks.

They are listed here, showing their main characteristics:

Description	Calibre(mm)	Projectile weight (lb)	Muzzle velocity (feet per second/fps)
two-pounder	39	2.4	2,600
six-pounder	57	6.3	2,800
75mm (MV)	75	14.9	2,030
77mm (HV)	76.2	17.0	2,750
seventeen-pounder	76.2	17.0	2,900
95mm	95	25.0	1,485

The length of the gun barrel can be expressed as a multiple of the calibre; a 50mm gun with a length of 50 calibres would have a barrel length of 2.5 m.

If the gun is intended to be a weapon to destroy enemy tanks it can be made more effective in three principal ways: increasing the weight of the projectile; increasing the muzzle velocity; or making modifications to the projectile. The first can be achieved by increasing the calibre of the gun. The second can be achieved by increasing the charge, lengthening the barrel, or tapering the barrel so that the projectile is squeezed as it moves towards the point of discharge. Modifications to the projectile, the third method, are listed here.

AP shell: This was a high-explosive shell fitted with an armour-piercing (AP) nose or plug, and was used until 1938 in two-pounder ammunition.

AP shot: The projectile was solid shot in order to increase penetrative performance, and was adopted in 1938.

APC: Armour-piercing capped; this was designed to prevent the break-up of the projectile when hitting face-hardened armour plate.

APCBC: Armour-piercing capped ballistic capped; this added a streamlining cap to the APC shot and increased the velocity of the projectile.

APDS: Armour-piercing discarding sabot – almost always referred to simply as a 'sabot'. The sabot (shoe) acted as a jacket to a smaller and lighter shot, thus allowing a relatively greater charge to be applied to the shot and resulting in a higher muzzle velocity.

In some of the tables and text in this chapter, reference will be made to German equipment. The principal abbreviations used in respect of guns are:

Flak: *FliegerabwehrKanone*: anti-aircraft gun
Kwk: *Kampfwagen Kanone*: tank gun
Pak: *PanzerabwehrKanone*: anti-tank gun

FUNCTIONS OF TANK GUNS

It will be assumed here that the main gun in the tank is the weapon that will carry out all primary functions. Other weapons may be used for specialist functions, e.g. smoke projection and anti-aircraft protection; or for complementary functions, e.g. machine-guns for engagement of soft-skinned targets. But the main gun will carry out the major requirements of offence and defence that the tank as a military unit has to perform.

The functions to be performed by the main tank gun in attack or defence are: to knock out enemy tanks or self-propelled anti-tank guns; eliminate ground-mounted anti-tank guns; destroy soft-skinned targets, e.g. enemy infantry, transport, stores dumps, field and other artillery; assist infantry in the assault of strong points by providing direct fire.

Some of these functions must be provided by direct fire, especially knocking out enemy tanks. The best gun to do this is one which fires with a flat trajectory at a high muzzle velocity. Other functions are best achieved by lobbing or indirect fire, especially when using HE shells. This also applies to the use of smoke, which can be an extremely valuable capability under many different battlefield situations.

What the tank gun has to do will depend on the tactical doctrine of the time, and will also depend on the changing offensive and defensive capabilities of the enemy. Both of these changed over the period that we are reviewing, and we will follow the way in which the designers and producers of main tank guns were able to meet the changes – or not, as the case might be.

One further general point to be considered is the desirability of having multi-purpose main guns as opposed to single-purpose main guns. The two main purposes, as we have seen, are: knocking out enemy tanks by the use of high-velocity flat trajectory solid shot (or variations); and eliminating soft-skinned targets at substantial ranges (or close range, if needed) by low-velocity lobbing trajectory high-explosive shells. (To be of any significant value HE shells should weigh 10 lb or more.)

The advantages of essentially single-purpose tank guns are obviously that they can perform a given task well. In their day, and against contemporary opposition, the two- and six-pounder tank guns performed well. The seventeen-pounder performed particularly well in the anti-tank role and had an effective explosive HE capability. Its high muzzle velocity, however, made it less than ideal in its HE role.

The single-purpose HE gun was the 95mm howitzer mounted in various British tanks, including the Churchill Mks V and VIII. There were two of these tanks in each squadron of Churchills in some regiments, and they were normally commanded by the squadron leader and his second-in-command. That they were particularly useful in this role is shown by two quotations from the history of the 9th Royal Tank Regiment.

The 95mm howitzer tank 'Ich dien', commanded by Capt Sidney Link, C Squadron 9th RTR. The short barrel demanded the enormous counter-weight shown. (Peter Boden)

Tpr Jack Woods, July 1944: 'On Hill 112 all the tanks were lined up as if ready for attack, no camouflage, and shelling and mortaring morning, noon and night. C Squadron HQ Troop had Maj Holden's and Capt Link's 95mm howitzers. Capt Kidd, who was my officer, had a scout car and a tank. Once I drove the scout car with Tpr Patchett towards the German lines and hid behind a knocked-out tank. Capt Kidd then crawled out with field glasses and intercom and sent messages to Patchett; Maj Holden's tank would fire a shot, two adjustments, then Capt Kidd crawled back. Get out quick, he said.

We used the gun next day to support an infantry patrol. A Spandau machine-gun opened up on them, Maj Holden was in communications with the officer and three shots put the Spandau out.'

Maj Ronnie Holden, DSO, MC, also figures in the next episode demonstrating very effective use of the 95mm. This was in Holland on 22 October 1944, and was recorded by Sgt Trevor Greenwood:

'At one point of our journey (an armed reconnaissance by the squadron headquarters and three tank troops) the major had a narrow escape. A carefully concealed German 75mm anti-tank gun opened up at 50 yd – and hit the rim of his 95 gun muzzle. Luckily the major saw the gun, and his own gun was suitably traversed. Before the enemy could fire a second shot, the major had fired a 95HE – a direct hit and the Jerry gun went up in bits; two more 95s were pumped in just to make sure.'

Later that afternoon: 'Dicky (Sgt Dicky Hall) discovered another gun, this time a 50mm, and shot it up. He also used HE on the fleeing crew – no prisoners.'

The gun in Dicky Hall's tank was a 75mm, and his prompt action in destroying the anti-tank gun and its crew suggests very strongly that he was obeying the injunction: 'if in any doubt, HE up the spout'.

The 75mm tank gun was the first genuine dual-purpose gun to be mounted in British tanks. Its performance against German tanks in the desert – when it was mounted in American and not British tanks – was satisfactory against its current opposition. In Normandy, however, it was at a very substantial disadvantage in the anti-tank role; although, as shown above, tank crews were quite happy with its HE performance.

The disadvantage of the single-purpose gun, and the corresponding advantage of the multi-purpose gun, is clearly stated by Montgomery, then C-in-C 21st Army Group. In a letter to the Deputy Chief of the Imperial Staff, Gen Sir Ronald Adam, dated 1 April 1944, he wrote:

My Dear Ronnie,

Many thanks for your letter of 29 March regarding the 105mm Sherman tanks.

Now that the armoured divisions are provided with self-propelled (SP) artillery regiments, I cannot see any advantage in adding the 105mm gun to the equipment of an armoured regiment, and there are a number of grave disadvantages. The SP artillery provides, with the necessary degree of concentration and control, and with the very minimum of delay, the gun howitzer support required.

I do not think it sound to add the complication of an additional weapon to squadron headquarters. The squadron leader will not be able to control the 105mm efficiently in addition to his other duties; the squadron will also lose flexibility because the squadron headquarters tanks are often used to reinforce a troop which has suffered casualties.

I consider that the 75mm shell is adequate for its purpose and that if the filling of the 75mm smoke shell were improved, this would also be all that is required.

Yours ever,

B.L. Montgomery

Monty makes the point very clearly that it is much better operationally for all the tanks within a squadron, and perhaps even within a regiment, to be the same. This was reinforced by a statement from 21st Army Group to the Director, Royal Armoured Corps (at the War Office) on 19 May 1944, that: 'The long-term policy is that all gun tanks (including 95mm) in Churchill regiments should be 75mm, but 95mms will be accepted in lieu of 75mm to the tune of six per regiment until such time as the 95mm production can be turned over to 75mm.'

Various other configurations of tank issue presented substantial logistical problems. Perhaps the worst was the tank establishment for armoured regiments of the 7th Armoured Division, which for the invasion of Normandy was: 43 75mm Cromwells, 12 seventeen-pounder Shermans and 6 95mm Cromwells.

A Cromwell in Normandy mounting a 75mm medium-velocity tank gun. Because it could fire a good weight of HE many crews approved of it, but it was not competitive against the German tanks it met in Normandy. (Tank Museum 4546/C4)

Two different tanks to maintain and repair, and three different types of ammunition to take forward to the fighting squadrons. Not a way to make life easy for the quartermaster!

To this point we have considered the basic functions that must be addressed in determining a policy for tank guns. In summary: the tank gun may have to deliver high-velocity projectiles at flat trajectories against armoured targets; the tank gun may have to deliver lobbing high-explosive (or smoke) low-velocity projectiles against soft targets; these two somewhat conflicting requirements can be met either by a multiple-purpose gun or two or more single-purpose guns.

We consider now how this was actually done, looking first at the vacillating policies and then at the dilatory ways in which those policies were implemented by the provision of the tank gun hardware.

POLICIES AFFECTING DEVELOPMENT OF TANK GUNS

As we have seen in earlier chapters, the policy for employment of tanks generally was not clearly defined for almost all of the period from 1919 to 1943. In the earlier years of this period this was due to uncertainty regarding the role of the Army generally. The uncertainty was to some degree resolved when Britain declared war on Hitler, because it became clear that a Continental Force had to be provided. The Continental Force would also have to have equal priority with home defence, and defence or control of the empire had to be maintained.

The role of Britain's armoured forces as part of the Army remained unclear throughout most of the period, and no definitive policy statements came from the War Office. There was, in general, a positive feeling about the possibilities for tanks, but it was certainly difficult to produce equipment to meet loosely defined and conflicting purposes – with the added and major constraint of a shortage of money.

It is useful to summarize the general tank situation in October 1936, roughly at the start of the rearmament process. This statement by the Secretary of State for War has been referred to before, but it is here evaluated for its significance in relation to the policy for tank guns. The statement is important for what it does not say, as well as for what it does:

> Until about 1933 the only tank formation contemplated for the Army, apart from light tank units in Egypt and in India, was the tank brigade. This consisted of one battalion of light tanks and three mixed battalions of medium and light tanks. For this purpose it was considered that only two types of tank were needed:
>
> a.) A light tank for reconnaissance, protection and intercommunication. These tanks were required to be speedy, with a good cross-country performance and with sufficient armour to afford protection against the smaller type of anti-tank weapons; and only the lighter types of armament were considered necessary, i.e., machine-guns.
>
> b.) A medium tank of heavier weight, with a crew of at least five men, carrying several machine-guns and an anti-tank weapon firing shells.

The change in the situation in Europe in 1935 and 1936 accentuated the need for rearmament. In this context the evolution of an infantry tank, for close cooperation with the infantry in the assault, had to be considered. Such a tank had to possess different characteristics to the light and medium tanks mentioned above. It would have to face a concentration of anti-tank weapons and obstacles, and by reason of its role could not in all circumstances rely on speed to the same extent as the tanks in the tank brigade.

A further development has taken place over the last two years, when it has been decided to form a mobile division which should include brigades of mechanized cavalry and infantry. The cavalry units in this mobile division are to be equipped with light tanks.

After some discussion on the tanks currently (1936) available the document goes on:

There has been a remarkable development throughout the world in anti-tank weapons. We have ourselves in the last twelve months produced two entirely new weapons, one a shoulder type rifle and the other a small gun, which are vastly superior to any other armour-piercing weapons formerly designed.

The rifle was the Boyes anti-tank rifle and the small gun was the two-pounder. The document continues:

The cruiser tank: what appears to be needed for the cruiser tank role in the tank brigade is a tank of the Christie type (which has been adopted with success by the Russians), having: an excellent cross-country performance; a considerably higher speed than our present light tank; slightly more armour; and an anti-tank gun firing a shell.

In terms of specifying what is required in a tank gun – let alone tanks – this is a disturbing document. It makes no clear statement as to what might be required in terms of function, except to say that the cruiser tank should have an anti-tank gun firing a shell. The infantry tank mentioned would have to face a concentration of anti-tank weapons, but nothing was said about how it should do that. The implication is – particularly in view of the heavily armoured Infantry Tank Mk I, armed only with a machine-gun – that the purpose of the tank was to absorb anti-tank punishment rather than to destroy that threat. All other tanks were armed only with machine-guns, and thus could take offensive action against soft targets only.

This document has been discussed in some detail, because it articulated the view of those at the highest level of the British Army in 1936. Because it is at that high level, it might be said that there was no reason for it to address the details of military equipment. But as we have seen, the tank gun is central to the tank and without a broad indication of its purpose it is impossible to develop useful designs or even a statement of needs.

At the time of its introduction in 1935 the two-pounder tank gun was very competitive. It was mounted in the A9, A10, Matilda, A13, Covenanter, Crusader and Churchill, and is here shown in Valentines. Its anti-tank performance was good, but its HE performance poor. (Tank Museum 352/E2)

An evaluation of the performance of British tanks in the Mediterranean Theatre was written by Lt Col F.W.S. Gordon-Hall in 1945. In his comments about tank guns he says:

> The British conception of a tank action before the war envisaged short-range battles on the move. The idea of performance of the tank gun at long range was hardly ever considered. Thus it came to be thought that provided the tank gun was capable of penetrating enemy armour at 500 yd or so, nothing else was required. This idea persisted and made the British Army slow to anticipate the need for a larger tank gun.
>
> In addition, the earlier British tank guns were designed solely for their armour-piercing qualities, and although high-explosive shells were provided, they were a very secondary consideration.

Thus on the outbreak of war the policy in respect of tank armament was to have a main gun – if mounted at all – which could take on enemy armour at short range. And the two-pounder tank gun was very competitive against the German or Italian opponents it was likely to meet in 1939 and 1940. The opportunity to show this competitiveness was short-lived in France during the sojourn of Britain's Expeditionary Force. For eight months from September 1939 to May 1940 there was no significant contact with the German Army, and during these eight months the tank forces' equipment edged only painfully slowly in the direction of becoming complete. Thus, neither was equipment complete nor were realistic tactical doctrines taught to the armoured forces before the German assault began on 10 May 1940.

The tank units fought as valiantly as they were able with the equipment they had. The two-pounders in the very few Matilda II tanks available certain startled Rommel at Arras, and other people elsewhere. But what were the lessons for tank gun policy? The nature of the battles suggested that the two-pounder was excellent, and had there been enough of them mounted in the well-armoured Matildas they might easily have held the German onslaught and given the French and British armies a chance to regroup on a stabilized front. Shortage of ammunition and inferior optics in the Matilda had been additional disadvantages beside the lack of tank numbers.

One of the more percipient participants in the retreat to Dunkirk was the one-armed Brig Vyvyan Pope, DSO, MC. He was the adviser to Lord Gort, C-in-C of the BEF, on the use of tanks. He was able to take effective executive action during the battles, but just as importantly was able to take an objective view of what was happening and to draw lessons from his observations. Although he saw that the two-pounder was effective at the time, he wrote: 'Every tank must carry a cannon. The two-pounder is good enough now, but only just. We must mount something better.' As we shall see later, the 'something better' was already available in the shape of the six-pounder gun. It was nearly two years before the six-pounder was mounted in tanks issued to armoured units.

Bobby Stewart cleans a six-pounder mounted in a Churchill Mk IV. Capt Roger Long looks into the turret to watch the operation. (IWM H32696)

The results of Dunkirk, in terms of immediate and future tank gun policy, were two. First, the destruction or abandonment of all warlike stores in France meant that Britain had to take immediate steps to replace the lost items, including tanks as very important items. It was decided – an immensely difficult decision, and one taken by Churchill himself – that in order to provide weaponry to defend Britain the manufacturers would have to continue making exactly the same weapons they had been making before the fall of France; no modifications, no new equipment. Thus the two-pounder continued in production. The major exception to this fiat was the authorization to produce the A22, or Churchill Infantry Tank, as quickly as possible. Second, the Matildas which the Germans had found very hard to knock out had all been left behind in France. The German technicians could see exactly what they were up against and could proceed, as they did, to develop an anti-tank gun capable of destroying a Matilda at a reasonable range.

Along the coastal deserts of North Africa the British were facing the Italians in the second half of 1940. In September 1940 the Italian forces advanced into Egypt. From December 1940 to February 1941 the British, Indian and Australian forces advanced under the audacious and highly skilled leadership of Lt Gen Richard O'Connor until they had destroyed a large part of the Italian Army in North Africa. In doing this they found their two-pounder guns completely capable of knocking out the Italian tanks opposed to them.

An Italian 90/53 multi-purpose (anti-tank and anti-aircraft) gun captured by 8th RTR in Tobruk. While not as formidable as the German 88mm, it could still make attacking tanks very uncomfortable. (P.N. Veale)

German 50mm anti-tank guns and German-used Russian 76.2mm anti-tank guns captured in Tobruk. (P.N. Veale)

This Italian disaster resulted in the dispatch of German forces under Rommel to North Africa to bolster the Italian forces that remained and to drive the Allied Army back to the east. Rommel succeeded promptly and brilliantly, and the British were driven back to the Libyan-Egyptian border. During the battles that followed over the next fifteen months the general British policy was to treat their tanks as attackers of German tanks, and to consider soft targets as secondary but important objectives. In the British Army cooperation between arms was not well taught or executed. Regiments of tanks tended to act on their own, without effective integration with infantry, field artillery, anti-tank artillery or air. The troops were not taught the skills of cooperation, and higher commands did not enforce them.

German tactics emphasized cooperation. In particular, in relation to tank warfare, they achieved good integration and understanding between the tanks and the anti-tank units. The anti-tank units began to be armed with a long-barrelled 50mm gun, and the 88mm anti-aircraft gun was brought into use as a most effective anti-tank weapon. The effective range of both of these weapons, especially the 88s, was much greater than that of the two-pounder, still the only gun mounted on British tanks.

The History of the 10th Royal Hussars describes how the Germans and the British guns matched – or did not match – at the Battle of Sawunnu in January 1941, when they were chased back by Rommel from El Agheila.

Russian 76.2mm all-purpose guns captured in Tobruk; in spite of their relative lack of protection for their crews, these guns were very effective against tanks and aircraft, and could, if necessary, be used in a field role.
(P.N. Veale)

We would stress at this point that the fire of our two-pounder and 37mm tank guns was effective against German tanks only at very short range, say 500 yd. On the other hand the fire of the German 50mm guns in their Mark III tanks was effective against us at 1,000 yd or more. We thus had to close the range over those 500 yd while their fire was effective and ours was not. It was similar to destroyers closing in a naval action against heavier ships.

The main German tactic was a combination of fire and movement between tanks and anti-tank guns. Tanks advanced to a certain point and anti-tank guns came up to position themselves on the ground that had been taken; the tanks advanced further, until they bumped a British position. If the German assault on British tanks failed, they would retreat to the area of their anti-tank guns. The British tanks, many of their leaders and crews unthinkingly heroic in the style of fox-hunting cavalry, would charge the retreating Germans to destroy them. Then they met the anti-tank guns.

Besides being substantially outranged by the German anti-tank guns, they had no suitable weapon to destroy the ground-mounted guns. Armour-piercing shot was not the right tool to use, and the two-pounder high-explosive shell was so small as to be useless. Yet the general policy in respect of the tank gun was that its primary purpose was the destruction of other tanks.

In early 1942 shipments of the American Grant tanks reached the British troops in the desert. In American tank production terminology this was the M3, and its colloquial name in the US Army was General Lee and in the British Army the General Grant – hopefully not implying any conflict between the two! The differences between the two were not very significant, although the British version had thicker armour. The armament was identical, and this was what was really important.

The Grant had two main guns, a 75mm hull gun and a 37mm gun mounted in the fully rotatable turret. The hull gun had very limited traverse, and the tank had to be substantially exposed before the gun could be fired. But it was a dual-purpose weapon which fired a respectable armour-piercing shot (14.4 lb weight at 1,850 fps [feet per second] muzzle velocity for the Mark II, 2,030 fps for the Mark III) and an effective high-explosive shell.

The tank experts in Britain viewed the Grant and were unhappy with many of its features. They did not like the hull-mounted gun which meant substantial exposure of the tank when firing, neither did they like rubber-block tracks nor the stowage systems. But the tanks were sent to North Africa, accompanied by a team of US Army instructors. Although they had teething troubles in the desert environment these were soon overcome, and they became as popular with the troops who used them as they had been unpopular with the experts in Britain – who in the course of the two and a half years of war had not been able to supply them with anything better.

An American Grant tank in desert camouflage, 1942. The 75mm hull gun was what really delighted the British tank crews, because it would throw 14 lb of high explosive at ground-mounted anti-tank guns, and could make a nasty dent in attacking enemy tanks. (P.N. Veale)

The great advantage of the Grant was the 75mm gun. This enabled tank crews to engage enemy ground targets, especially anti-tank guns, at long range. And the 75mm was reasonably competitive against many of the tanks the enemy could put against it.

The success of the 75mm in the Grant was reinforced in September 1942 by the generous reallocation of 300 M4A1 Shermans. With the authority of President Roosevelt, the Chief of Staff Gen George Marshall offered to mobilize the US 2nd Armoured Division under Gen George Patton and send it to North Africa. In autumn 1942 it seemed that this might take too long, so the tanks went on their own for issue to the British tank crews. The Sherman was more effective than the Grant in several ways; it also had a similar 75mm gun, but in this case it was mounted in a fully rotatable turret. The demand for dual-purpose guns in British tanks became more insistent.

A tank regiment officer, Lt Col George Witheridge, DSO, relates how he was able to use the 75mm and a special feature of the American 75mm ammunition. He was able to develop a form of airburst at a height of some 30 ft above the target:

'This was done by setting the M48 fuse on delay, rather than on point detonation. When the shell struck the ground it rose into the air and burst above the target with devastating effect. I have fired three loads of 75mm HE shell in one action. I have killed an 88mm anti-tank gun at more than 4,000 yd with HE. This method is equally effective against enemy in trenches or slits. HE is invaluable for ranging, being observable amid the dust and confusion of battle.'

Small wonder there was enthusiasm for a dual-purpose gun such as the 75mm. But was this enthusiasm communicated in such a way that it was translated into policy?

In October 1942 it was stated (AFV Liaison Meeting, 27 October 1942) that while the long-barrelled six-pounder would be fitted in existing tanks, a new design would have an eight-pounder projectile. This was a 75mm dual-purpose gun to fit into the six-pounder mounting.

At this time, when the General Staff were encouraging these dual-purpose proposals, the old tactical requirement of armour penetration still held first place. As late as September 1942 the first comprehensive statement of General Staff policy on tanks specified: 'The tank gun must be an efficient weapon against enemy armour and must therefore be a first-class anti-tank weapon of the six-pounder or heavier type modernized to its highest performance, and one which can outclass enemy tanks we are likely to meet. In addition the tank gun should be as efficient a weapon as possible against personnel and lorries.'

That is, a dual-purpose gun with armour penetration as its main role. By early January 1943, however, only four months on, policy was completely reversed. The specification now reads, 'Gun. Fulfilment of their normal role necessitates that the main armament of the greater proportion of tanks of the medium class should be an effective high-explosive weapon; and at the same time, as effective a weapon as possible against enemy armour of the type so far encountered in this war'.

Could this reversal have been due to a message from Gen Montgomery in November 1942? Montgomery had successfully fought and defeated Rommel and his German and Italian forces in the second Battle of El Alamein from 23 October to 4 November 1942.

During the days after El Alamein the War Office received a cable under Monty's signature reading: 'The 75mm gun is all we require'. The cable was drafted by Col Willie Blagden, a technical observer from the Tank Board. Being Britain's only victorious general in two years of war – since O'Connor's victory in North Africa and those in East Africa – Monty's prestige was enormous. His requirement was regarded by the General Staff as, in effect, a command, and was passed to the Director General of Artillery at the Ministry of Supply for action.

The War Office commentary on this reversal of policy, caused by whatever stimulus, stated: 'In view of the evidence to date that the 75mm tank gun in use in American medium tanks is the best dual-purpose tank weapon yet produced, and also in view of the advantages of standardization, the 75mm tank gun should be adopted as soon as practicable as the main armament of the majority of British tanks.' In order to achieve this the War Office were willing to go to great lengths: 'If necessary, the adoption in the UK of American medium tank design.'

A proportion of future British design of tanks mounting a seventeen-pounder was asked for (December 1942), and pending a successful outcome of that design the six-pounder was accepted as an anti-tank gun for use on tanks. Infantry support was to be provided by a 95mm howitzer mounted on a proportion of Churchill and Cromwell tanks. These decisions were embodied in the tank production and design programme of February 1943.

This revolution in tank gun policy had no sooner been achieved than its wisdom was questioned at the highest level. Two successive cabinet meetings (April and May 1943) heard arguments advanced that reliance placed on the 75mm was dangerous. The opposition, however, was divided on the question of alternatives. Lord Cherwell, (formerly Prof Frederick Lindemann, and Churchill's principal scientific adviser) favoured the adoption of the 95mm howitzer as the common purpose gun, firing hollow-charge ammunition in the anti-tank role. The Director General of Artillery, Gen Campbell Clarke, advocated a flat trajectory high-velocity weapon (such as the seventeen-pounder). The CIGS and other War Office representatives adhered to the original proportions of 75mm, six-pounder and 95mm.

The prime minister suspended judgment, but said that the policy regarding tank guns should be reviewed immediately. On this basis of further investigation, he gave the following provisional ruling (May 1943):

a. Pending the development of the high-velocity 75mm gun (subsequently called the 77mm to avoid ambiguity), only 30 per cent of British tanks should be fitted with the medium-velocity 75mm gun (either identical or similar to that mounted in the American Grant and Sherman tanks).

b. The proportion of tanks fitted with the 95mm howitzer should be increased from 10 per cent to 20 per cent.

c. The balance of 50 per cent should continue to mount the six-pounder until the high-velocity 75mm becomes available; at that point the proportion of six-pounder tanks can be greatly reduced [relative percentages were not stated].

The 77mm high-velocity gun was designed by Vickers, and had a better performance than the contemporary American 76mm high-velocity gun which had been designed to up-gun the Sherman. Despite the superiority of the 77mm its adoption was not decided upon lightly, because it involved alterations in manufacturing capacity of a serious nature. Conversely, acceptance of the American 76mm high-velocity gun would have eased problems both of production and field supply.

In September 1943 the Director Royal Armoured Corps (DRAC) officially rejected the US 76mm and adopted the 77mm. The calibre of the 77mm was altered to allow it to accept seventeen-pounder projectiles. Further developments were the conversion of the American Sherman tank to take the British seventeen-pounder, and plans to mount the gun on the Challenger (A30), Comet (A34) and Churchill (A43). The Sherman mounting the seventeen-pounder was named the Firefly and was issued to armoured regiments destined for Normandy and north-west Europe; the seventeen-pounder was much appreciated and was very successful. The Challenger (A30) mounted a seventeen-pounder: some 200 were produced and achieved moderate success. The Comet had a 77mm and performed well in the battles from March to May 1945. The A43, or Black Prince, was built as a prototype but never advanced beyond that stage.

The policy regarding tank guns was stated by the War Office in April 1944 by percentages of types, thus (DRAC Report No. 9): 65 per cent best dual-purpose weapon, firing an effective HE shell; 25 per cent best armour-piercing weapon; 10 per cent best close-support weapon. DRAC Report No. 9 stated further:

> The basis on which these proportions were decided is that recent operational experience has proved that the majority of targets engaged by armour demand the use of HE shell. The anti-tank gun in particular, which forms the most frequently encountered target for tank guns, can most effectively be destroyed by this type of weapon and shell. At the same time it is essential that every armoured unit should possess within its own resources a proportion of weapons capable of dealing with the most heavily armoured tanks which the enemy can put into the field.

This policy is fully endorsed by Gen Montgomery, C-in-C of 21st Army Group, with one exception. He does not see the need, in operations in western Europe, for the close-support howitzers. He has therefore requested that if possible these weapons should be omitted and the proportion of dual-purpose weapons raised from 65 per cent to 75 per cent.'

This was, in effect, the final statement of British tank gun policy in the Second World War. It is interesting to consider the effect of the expanding use by the Germans of self-propelled anti-tank equipment, probably a more suitable target for armour-piercing shot rather than high-explosive shell. Two comments from tank crews are worth recording.

Arthur Reddish was a hull gunner in a fighting squadron of the Sherwood Rangers Yeomanry. In his book *Normandy 1944 from the hull of a Sherman* he writes:

> Reviewing the military situation at the end of July 1944 several of us crewmen came to the conclusion that our quick firing 75mm gun (medium velocity) was preferable to the

seventeen-pounder when fighting in close country. The 75mm had a very good HE shell and this was the ammunition most in use in that type of fighting. We considered that the present mix – one seventeen-pounder tank in each troop – was the best we could have. The infantry had a towed seventeen-pounder, which could be quickly in action.

Sgt Tom Tomney commanded the Churchill tank named 'Independent' in 13 Troop of the 9th Royal Tank Regiment. In Holland in October 1944 9th RTR were taking part in an armoured thrust consisting of three regiments from 34th Armoured Brigade. The thrust was commanded by the Brigadier in person, taking with him one of the regiments while the other two provided support. Tom Tomney records:

> 'We had just moved through Nispen when Brigadier Clarke came on the air asking if anyone could see the German self-propelled gun (SP) up on the hill some 1,000 yd away. I was the only one who said I saw it, and the Brigadier replied: "I don't care what you do but empty your entire stock of ammo if you must and put it out of action; it's blowing our battalion to pieces." We did just that and set it on fire.'

Tom did not record whether he used HE or AP, but he was certainly armed with the 75mm medium-velocity gun, thus proving its value against the enemy's armoured vehicles.

Shortly before the invasion of Normandy figures were made available on certain aspects of the performance of British and German anti-tank weapons (which could be either tank-mounted or field-mounted). That information is reproduced in part in Table 4.1; the response to a request for its wider dissemination is also reproduced.

A German Panther in Paris in June 1945 for the De Gaulle Parade. Its long-barrelled 75mm KwK 42 is clearly seen as a formidable weapon. (Peter Boden)

TABLE 4.1: GERMAN AND BRITISH TANK AND ANTI-TANK GUNS

German (PAK: anti-tank gun; KwK: tank gun)

Calibre	Designation	Type of Ammunition	Weight of projectile	Muzzle velocity feet/sec
128mm	PAK44	APCBC	62.5 lb	3030
	(Fortunately not used in Normandy)			
88mm	KwK43	APCBC	22.4 lb	3280
	(Field mounted and in Tiger)			
75mm	Kwk42	APCBC	15 lb	3068
British:				
40mm	2-pdr	APCBC	2.4 lb	2600
57mm	6-pdr	APCBC	7 lb	2725
75mm	(75mm mv)	APCM61	15 lb	2300
76.2mm	77mm	APCBC	15 lb	2575
76.2mm	17-pdr	AFCBC	17 lb	2900

Response to request for this information to be disseminated (from the Deputy Director of Artillery):

> The reluctance of the Director General of Artillery to release performance of tank guns to the hands of troops is not so much a matter of security. There are so many conditioning circumstances to the successful attack of a tank that the authorities are naturally afraid less tactics contrary to authorized teaching should result from the technical possibilities taken by themselves. I feel that the user has come to think from past experience that the tactically desirable range from which to hit successfully is greater than the technical power of his weapon. The present performance of weapons and ammunition is the reverse of this.

For the amount of helpful information contained in this it seems likely that the DD of A, Col A.J. Cole, had a successful career in politics after the war.

FIRING ON THE MOVE

A central belief in British armoured doctrine between the two wars was that tanks should be able to fire accurately while on the move. The main implications of this were:

- That the tank suspension should provide a reasonably stable platform from which to fire the gun.

- That the gunner should be able to respond rapidly to the changing position of the gun in relation to the target; this meant the ability to elevate, depress and traverse rapidly.
- That the gunner needed intensive and continuous training to obtain the necessary facility in controlling and moving the gun position.

The policy of firing on the move was set in stone – until it became obvious from practical experience in battle that it was merely a waste of ammunition – and woe betide anyone who questioned it. Brig Percy Hobart was a Royal Tank Corps officer with progressive ideas on the use of tanks and of outstanding ability as a leader and a trainer; he also had a strong personality and an abrasive manner. In September 1936 he wrote to the military thinker Basil Liddell Hart about the views of a recently appointed Director of Military training (DMT, a senior appointment at the War Office under the CIGS): 'I hear the new DMT thinks tanks ought to halt to shoot! God! I thought we had killed and disproved that heresy ten years ago'.

To make firing on the move a reasonable proposition for the tank gunner it was essential, as stated above, to be able to move the gun up and down rapidly and to traverse it rapidly. Free elevation using a shoulder pad (as opposed to a geared elevating mechanism) allowed very rapid response in elevation, even if accuracy depended on the steadiness of the gunner's shoulder. Quick response in traversing was best achieved by a power traverse, and the British did develop very effective hydraulic traversing gear. This was, in fact, one of the few advantages British tanks had over the German Panther and Tiger tanks, whose turrets could traverse only slowly. Training in firing on the move was simulated using RYPAs. The acronym stood for 'Roll, Yaw and Pitch Apparatus', and the apparatus could simulate very effectively all the movements of a ship at sea. Trainees were taught assiduously on the RYPAs, and their construction, establishment and use must have consumed many thousands of soldier-hours and substantial sums of money to very little practical purpose.

The report on Armoured Fighting Vehicles in the Mediterranean Theatre by Lt Col Gordon-Hall had a number of interesting comments relating to firing on the move. In the section on control of the tank gun he says:

> Early British mountings were all of the free elevation type because guns were small and shooting on the move was expected and practised. To a certain extent this proved a disadvantage because such a gun must be balanced about the trunnions. This makes for a greater inboard length and consequently reduces the size of gun which can be accommodated in a given turret. German mountings were fitted with geared elevation from the start, and their superior accuracy in long-range shooting soon became apparent'.

He comments that the British traversing gear, as we said above, started and remained well ahead of the German mechanisms. He then goes on to discuss the development of stabilizers in 1943–4.

A very interesting innovation was the introduction of the Westinghouse stabilizer for elevation. This was a highly complicated and delicate piece of apparatus which was intended to make shooting on the move easier. In practice it arrived at a time when stationary shooting was almost invariably practised, and the stabilizer was not therefore considered of much importance. In addition, adjustment was a matter for specialists, and the performance of the gear in user hands fell far short of expectations.

Comments on firing on the move looked at from the German side are taken from interrogation notes by the Australian war correspondent Chester Wilmot. A prisoner of war who had been a member of a Tiger battalion, said: 'Fire with our main armament is opened at 1,600 m range where possible, and it is considered that the second shot should be a hit on a target 2 m high. Fire is never opened on the move. Even if attacked, Tigers normally move on to a firing position preferably hull-down before replying (except with machine-guns).'

CHRONOLOGICAL DEVELOPMENT OF TANK GUNS

The tank guns to be considered in this section are: two-pounder, six-pounder, 75mm medium-velocity (MV), seventeen-pounder, 95mm howitzer and 75mm high-velocity (HV), alternatively designated 77mm. The development of each will be separately recorded, but from time to time there was substantial interaction between the different guns. The interaction was largely expressed as a conflict related to allocation of scarce resources such as design capacity, raw materials and manufacturing facilities.

TWO-POUNDER

The two-pounder design was commenced in 1932–3. It was designed to replace the three-pounder mounted in the current medium tanks, which had a muzzle velocity of 1,850 fps. The intention of the two-pounder design was to provide a substantially higher muzzle velocity – which it did at 2,700 fps – thus giving the gun projectile a much flatter trajectory and the gunner a less complicated sighting system.

The two-pounder was also adopted as a ground-mounted anti-tank gun when the War Office realized in 1934 that all continental armies were deciding to provide light guns firing shells for anti-tank defence. A CIGS meeting of October 1934 recorded:

The Director of Artillery said that the new two-pounder for tanks appeared to be suitable as an anti-tank gun, and if the same weapon could be used for tank and anti-tank units it would be a great advantage from the manufacturing point of view. The two-pounder had been tried against 25mm of high quality plate at 900 yd and had just failed. They were now trying a slightly heavier shell (2.4 lb) which he thought should easily penetrate 25mm at 1,000 yd, considerably more than the requirements of the draft specification.

There was by no means unanimity on the question, but it was not the essential function of penetration that was questioned. The CIGS felt that a 2 lb shell was too heavy, but the reply was that any smaller projectile would have an inadequate bursting charge. At this stage shot had not superseded shell and tank ammunition was armour-piercing shell fitted with an armour-piercing nose or plug.

The two-pounder was mounted in most British tanks designed and produced from 1935 to 1942, including the A9, A10, Matilda, A13, Covenanter, Crusader, Cavalier, Valentine, and the first Churchill. In 1941 there were thus six cruiser and three infantry tanks mounting a gun that had definitely passed its use-by date.

It must be remembered, however, that up to the end of 1940 it had been competitive against most of its enemies, certainly in armour penetration. But a replacement was delayed for various reasons, as we shall see when considering the six-pounder. A really regrettable situation was that in December 1941 units of the two-pounder were still on order, and their production, distribution and use would, of necessity, be spread over the years 1942 and 1943. An alternative action would be to make them and scrap them – an appalling waste of scarce resources.

SIX-POUNDER

During the period when the two-pounder was being developed and mounted in tanks (as well as being used for ground-mounted anti-tank equipment), the thickness of armour on all tanks was rising steadily. There was clearly a case for a heavier gun. Col Campbell Clarke was Deputy Chairman of the Ordnance Board in 1937, and he had urged the then Director of Artillery, Maj Gen H.A. Lewis, to order a tank gun which could deal with tanks armoured to the 78mm standard of the Matilda. Lewis said that the General Staff did not consider it necessary. On 1 April 1938 Campbell Clarke succeeded Lewis as the Director of Artillery, and on handing over Lewis said to Clarke, 'Now you can get on with your gun'. Clarke proceeded to do just that.

The prime cause of this work was the field anti-tank gun rather than the tank gun; but from the start the possible future use of the gun in tanks was allowed for. Clarke called for general exploratory work on a six-pounder anti-tank gun in April 1938 'following generally the specification which governs the production of the two-pounder'. This request was made to the Design Department; but that department was understaffed and busy with other guns, and Clarke could not get General Staff priority.

Because of the shortage of design resources and the priorities given to them, designs for the six-pounder were not available until autumn 1939. The attention of the Director of Mechanization, Maj Gen A.E. Davidson, responsible for the provision of tanks to the armoured forces, was drawn to the new gun at an early stage. But he was even less interested in a six-pounder tank gun than a six-pounder anti-tank gun; thus when a gun was available for trial in April 1940, and was approved, subject to testing, as a tank and anti-tank gun, it was not specifically adopted for use in tanks.

In June 1940 the six-pounder passed its tests at Shoeburyness. In July 1940 the Ministry of Supply was asked to make fourteen pilot models, and in October they increased this to 50. At about this time Clarke read in an Ordnance Board minute that the Churchill tank (A22) currently being rushed through the design and manufacturing process was still to mount the two-pounder. Clarke protested vigorously to the Assistant Chief of the Imperial General Staff (ACIGS), Sir G.N. Macready and to his own boss, the Director General of Munitions Production (DGMP), Sir Harold Brown. Clarke had already pointed out that the Germans, having investigated the Matildas left behind at Dunkirk, were very likely to increase the strength of both the armour and the armament on their tanks – which they did.

Clarke also pressed the Director of Mechanization to adopt the six-pounder in his tanks. Maj Gen Davidson pointed out that there was no General Staff requirement for a more powerful gun on tanks, and that 'it was no part of the Director of Mechanization's duties to dictate to the General Staff when they had already decided their policies; the new Churchill tanks were designed to mount the two-pounder; and the size of the six-pounder would involve radical enlargement of the hull and turret'.

Macleod Ross records that: 'On Clarke's remonstrance Adm Sir Harold Brown (the DGMP) immediately ordered 2,000 six-pounder anti-tank guns and 2,000 six-pounder tank guns. Unlike the D of M he did not care whether the General Staff approved or not, action which might be termed "the Nelson touch".'

The facts, as recorded in Command Paper 6865, have different but comparable figures for the ordering of six-pounder equipment, as follows:

December 1940: Order placed for 500. There seems to have been at this time no clear instructions from the War Office whether these were to be for field mountings or to mount on tanks. A different breech ring is required for the latter; but because a gun made with the breech ring suitable for tanks can be used for the field mounting – but not vice versa – the Ministry of Supply ordered half and half.

January 1941: Design finally fixed for a production basis.

February 1941: First volume order placed for 7,000.

May 1941: Order increased to 14,000.

December 1941: Order increased to 38,750 and planned rate of production increased to 2,000 per month. The Army authorities were apparently still unclear as to how many were required for tanks and field mountings respectively. The Ministry of Supply divided the bulk orders into 60 per cent for tanks (because that type of gun was interchangeable) and 40 per cent for field mounting.

The orders were there, but was the manufacturing capacity? Production was allowed to start only in a new factory at Radcliffe near Bolton because of War Office insistence that production of two-pounders in existing factories should not be compromised. Even the new factory at Radcliffe was affected. In the expectation of getting at least 600 six-pounders by the end of 1941 the CIGS agreed that the new factory should tool up for six-pounders. But in February 1941 the Ministry of Supply pointed out that, in respect of those guns, 'even suppose we change only half the plant over to six-pounders the diversion of effort and plant in the preparatory stages would be such that we should lose some 600 two-pounders this year only to get some 100 six-pounders.'

This presents an interesting problem in decision-making, in that the two-pounders were obsolescent or obsolete in terms of their opposition, and the six-pounders were unproven in battle.

Deliveries made available from the production facilities resulted in 300 guns being delivered in December 1941. These were all made as tank guns, but no suitable mountings in any tanks were ready for mounting them. But field mountings were available and the guns were therefore mounted on them, with some of the complete anti-tank assemblies sent to North Africa.

This section is concerned with the development of tank guns rather than complete tanks. But to follow up the statement that tanks were not ready to take the six-pounders – as a matter of interest and concern – the history unrolled thus. The two types of tank in which six-pounders were planned to be mounted first were the Crusader and the Churchill. The Crusader was the more important of the two, because it was currently fighting in North Africa.

The decision to produce a mock-up for a six-pounder turret for the Crusader was taken in March 1941, some three months after the decision to produce the six-pounder had been taken. This was not discussed with the Crusader manufacturers, Nuffield Mechanization and Aero, until September 1941. They found the mock-up design unacceptable, produced one of their own, and had completed successful trials at Lulworth by December 1941. In May 1942 the first six-pounder Crusader was delivered, and by the middle of July the total delivered was forty-four. Some of these were sent to North Africa, and about 100 took part in the Second Battle of Alamein in October 1942.

It was thus from April 1938 to October 1942 before a requirement recognized by some as being essential was achieved – four and a half years, during three of which Britain had been at war. The story with the Churchill is similar. In April 1941 the decision to mount a six-pounder in a Churchill was taken; in February 1942 the first six-pounder Churchill Mk III was accepted, and by July 1942 output was running at forty per week. These replaced the two-pounder Churchills Mk I and II progressively during late 1942 and early 1943. In January 1943 the 21st and the 25th tank brigades arrived in Tunisia armed with Churchills Mks I, II and III. By the end of the Tunisian campaign tank soldiers on the spot were happy with the armour-piercing capability of the six-pounder, but considered the six-pounder HE almost useless.

75MM MEDIUM VELOCITY (MV)

As described in the section on tank gun policy, the experience of tank crews with the 75mm MV in the American Grant and Sherman in North Africa was very positive. Monty's cable 'the 75mm is all we need' was quoted earlier. In December 1942 the General Staff indicated that they would be happy to see the American 75mm adopted as the main armament for the majority of British tanks. Well before this, however, requests or suggestions had been put forward regarding the provision of an effective dual-purpose tank gun. A report to the Secretary of State for War from the ACIGS in September 1943 lists the chronological sequence:

1942

30 June:	Director Armoured Fighting Vehicles (DAFV) asked the Controller General of Research and Development (CGRD) to consider the possibility of fitting the 75mm MV into the Cromwell.
6 July:	CGRD replies that this project would involve 'the designing of new mountings throughout and a host of other changes'. It was suggested that a weapon interchangeable with the six-pounder should be adopted.
18 November:	DAFV again asked the Chairman, Armoured Fighting Vehicles Division (of the Ministry of Supply) to clarify whether the 75mm MV gun could or could not be mounted in the Cromwell. The Middle East confirmed on this date, in response to a query by the War Office, that the 75mm was better than the six-pounder – Monty's cable.
3 December:	It was decided at the AFV liaison meeting that the AFV Division of the Ministry of Supply should investigate mounting a gun at least equivalent to a 75mm.
23 December:	Vickers presents an outline design for converting the six-pounder to take 75mm ammunition; drawings of the American 75mm to be supplied to Vickers.

1943

23 January:	Vickers proves the gun to be satisfactory; several difficulties exist with the mounting which will require a substantial amount of work to correct.
3 July:	Chairman, Armoured Fighting Vehicles Division agrees that six-pounder mounting will take 75mm as designed and produced subject to defined modifications.
10 July:	Modifications specified to Ministry of Supply.
11 October:	First tank mounting for the British 75mm MV gun delivered.

The 75mm was mounted to Cromwells and Churchills. In the case of the Churchill it was mounted during the course of manufacture in the Churchill Mk VI. It could also form the subject of a conversion of a Churchill Mk IV, which could be done either in the factory or in the field. An example of the latter method is described here, taking place in May 1944 at the same time as the tank was being waterproofed for the Normandy landing: 'We took out the six-pounder gun and put a 75mm in its place. This meant that all turret and hull ammunition racks had to be taken out and replaced, plus the tricky job of hauling the old gun out and fitting the larger calibre gun in its place.' This was done by the crew of Sgt Dicky Hall's tank in C Squadron 9th RTR, presumably guided and aided by the regiment's armourer specialists.

The eighteen months or so taken to make what appears to be a relatively simple substitution is excessive. It was fortunate that only a relatively small part of Britain's tank forces were in action at that time, and that many of the others had time to make the change to the 75mm tank gun before the Normandy D-Day. Irrespective of that, there were lessons to learn from the slow and problem-ridden process of conversion. The Select Committee on National Expenditure commented (as recorded in Command Paper 6865):

It was sought to accomplish the task of carrying the 75mm gun in British tanks with a mounting which was less robust than that used for the equivalent gun in the Sherman. To use a less robust mounting was to take a risk which could only be guarded against by special care in the design and materials used; this care does not seem to have been taken.

Trials were carried out in artificial conditions and with mountings of a design different from that first selected for production; passing these artificial trials led to acceptance for production.

The arrangements for manufacture seem to have been such that parts were made of faulty material improperly treated and finished. It is extremely disturbing that manufacturers capable of such work should have been selected for making vitally important parts of war weapons, and that such faults should not have been detected on inspection.

SEVENTEEN-POUNDER

In September 1940 intelligence reports were received by the War Office which indicated that German tank armour of a thickness between 100 and 150 mm might be met in the future. As a result of discussions between the War Office and the Ministry of Supply, and after considering the implications of this possible development, a meeting was called by the Director of Artillery in April 1941 to consider the design of a future tank and anti-tank weapon. As a result of this meeting a specification was agreed for an anti-tank weapon of 3in calibre firing a 17 lb shot. The muzzle velocity was to be of the order of 2,700 fps, and the weight of the gun some 2.5 to 3 tons.

In August 1941 a mock-up was seen and agreed. In September 1941 the War Office gave an order for 500 pieces of equipment even before the pilot models had been tested, thus expediting production. In October 1941 the pilots were tested and found to be satisfactory; production commenced and resulted in the first delivery in April 1942. The field-mounted anti-tank gun came in service generally in 1943, reaching full production in December of that year.

The problem of mounting the seventeen-pounder in a tank has been considered earlier in discussions on the development of the complete tank. A number of proposals were put forward, but the only two to reach fruition were the mounting of the seventeen-pounder in the Sherman and the design and manufacture of the Centurion (A41). The design of the Centurion was initiated in November 1943 by the Tank Board. This delay of two and a half years between initiating the design of the weapon and the design of a vehicle capable of carrying it effectively is unbelievable. Had these two designs marched more or less in parallel, many a tank man's grave in Normandy would have been left unfilled and the campaign in north-west Europe would probably have ended before Christmas 1944.

77MM TANK GUN (75MM HV)

This gun was in reality a long-barrelled 75mm, but was called the 77mm to differentiate it both from the 75mm medium-velocity gun and the seventeen-pounder. The difference between the two 75mm guns was that the medium-velocity gun was 36.5 calibres (2.75 m) and the high-velocity gun (77mm) was 50 calibres (3.75 m) in barrel length. The corresponding muzzle velocities were 2,000 and 2,750 fps, obviously giving the 77mm a much more effective performance in penetrating armour.

In early 1942 Vickers initiated the development of the high-velocity 75mm gun as described earlier. In March 1943 it was suggested that it might fit into the Cromwell turret, which made it even more attractive. Partly on the strength of that belief six prototype high-velocity 75mm guns were ordered. Progress with the prototypes was rapid, but on 23 May 1943 the AFV Liaison Committee learned that it was not possible to fit the gun into a Cromwell after all because the turret ring was too small. Once again, it is unbelievable that the designers seemed to be incapable of understanding and applying the science of measurement.

The only way of using what appeared to be – and in fact was – a very satisfactory tank gun was to design a new tank for it to go into. Action was taken immediately and the tank specification A34 was drawn up for the design and manufacture of the tank that came to be known as the Comet. Work started on the design in summer 1943, and in October 1943 modifications to the gun were initiated so that it could fire the seventeen-pounder's APCBC and HE ammunition. But the development of the tank as a complete unit was slow; a mild-steel prototype was ready in March 1944, and the first substantial month's production was 143 in January 1945. The Comets and the 77mm guns they mounted were in action with 29th Armoured Brigade only after the Rhine crossing in March 1945, and thus had less than two months operational service during the war. But the tank and its gun were well thought of and provided the tank weapon for some British armoured forces for several years after 1945.

95MM HOWITZER

This was developed as a close-support weapon in 1942. Its function was to provide immediate HE fire and an effective smoke shell. It was made from a 3.7 in gun barrel with a twenty-five-pounder breech assembly, and could fire a 25 lb projectile. Its

The Comets of 1st RTR, lined up in Berlin in June 1945 on the occasion of the presentation of decorations by FM Montgomery, show their long-barrelled 77mm guns. These were effective weapons. (Freddie Critchley)

construction, particularly the short barrel, made it exceptionally breech-heavy. This was counteracted by a massive counterbalance at the muzzle end of the barrel, an instantly recognizable characteristic in any photograph. The counterbalance was simply excess weight of 152 lb, but had to be carried to make the 95mm operational.

The 95mm was provided at an establishment of two per fighting squadron to Churchill and Cromwell units. They were allocated to the squadron leader and his second-in-command, and were used to take on targets as described earlier. Their role was questionable, in that it could have been provided by 75mm guns (although not nearly as well), or by calling on field artillery support. The mechanisms for field artillery support were readily available through the medium of Royal Artillery observation post (OP) tanks. Two of the OP tanks were on the establishment of tank regimental headquarters, and could be allocated to squadrons in contact with the enemy. They had a tank driver and wireless-operator/gunner, as well as a Royal Artillery forward observation officer (FOO) and wireless-operator.

The OP tank was able to bring down field artillery fire extremely quickly and was able to call on several field batteries, and even heavier artillery, if the occasion warranted it.

We have seen that directives in the summer of 1944 foreshadowed that the 95mm was to be phased out because of the availability of Royal Artillery support. While it was in service, however, the 95mm did carry out the function it was designed to perform.

POSTSCRIPT: USE OF ANTI-AIRCRAFT (A/A) GUNS AND FIELD GUNS (TWENTY-FIVE-POUNDER) IN AN ANTI-TANK (A/T) ROLE

The Germans used their anti-aircraft, or *Flak*, 88mm in an anti-tank role extremely successfully. The question was often asked, could the British do the same? They certainly could, as the following excerpt shows:

> The use of artillery other than anti-tank artillery in the anti-tank role was not a novel concept in 1940. The pre-war field anti-artillery (A/A) brigade, for example, normally fired an anti-tank shoot at Larkhill on its way back from summer manoeuvres. This practice was stopped in 1937 on two grounds:

> • The rapid expansion of the Army required the training syllabus to be as simple as possible.
> • It was judged unwise to complicate the design of new A/A guns with the instruments needed for the engagement of ground targets.

It must be recorded that at a meeting in January 1940 Winston Churchill suggested the use of A/A guns in an A/T role but was told it 'had been considered before but rejected'.

The needs of 1941, together with the discovery of the German use of the 88mm in an anti-tank role, combined to reintroduce the use of field A/A weapons as anti-tank guns. A problem with the 3.7 in A/A gun when firing horizontally was that in the desert the blast of the gun caused a great plume of sand, both identifying its position and making observation of the shot difficult. Two possible methods of dealing with this problem were to eliminate the effect of the blast by modification to the gun or charge, or to mount it in a self-propelled (SP) vehicle. The SP mounting was dismissed early in 1941 as being tactically disadvantageous, but the extensive use of A/T and other artillery on SP mountings by the Germans indicated before long that there were advantages conferred by mobility which far outweighed the loss of ability to traverse.

Even if the A/A guns were not used very imaginatively in an anti-tank role, the twenty-five-pounder field guns had considerable success in some desert battles. The twenty-five-pounder specification and design comprised a self-protective role for the equipment; it was provided with solid armour-piercing shot and was thus capable of effective anti-tank work.

During the 'Crusader' operations of November 1941 the twenty-five-pounder acquitted itself particularly well, as recorded in the following extracts from William Moore's *Panzerbait: 3 RTR 1940–44.*

German 88mm at Bardia, knocked out by Maj Hickey Sugden, MC, of 8th RTR on 1 January 1942. While they were a very effective anti-tank weapon, they were also quite a target. (P.N. Veale)

The sights and elevators of the 88mm knocked out by Hickey Sugden at Bardia received a direct hit from Hickey's two-pounder. This was very good shooting, but probably the only way to do it because of the two-pounder's very poor high explosive performance. (P.N. Veale)

1941

22 November:	Covered by a handful of tanks, the British field guns which had been defending the airfield over open sights much of the day extricated themselves and withdrew with what was left of the 7th Armoured Division.
23 November:	Cruwell (the German tank commander) drew up tanks of the 15th and 21st panzer divisions in line abreast to attack the 5th South African Infantry Brigade. This brigade was drawn up in laager style, and when the Germans attacked they were met with concentrated fire from forty-six twenty-five-pounders, two eighteen-pounders, and twenty-four two-pounders (the only specifically anti-tank guns). The *Afrika Korps* suffered very heavy losses, most of the enemy tanks being destroyed by the twenty-five-pounders of the South Africans and the 3rd and 4th regiments of the Royal Horse Artillery.
25 November:	The 5th Panzer Regiment lost eighteen machines to British twenty-five-pounders during an unsuccessful attack on a 4th Indian Division position, its experienced commander Oberst von Stephan dying of wounds in a British hospital.

BRITISH TANK-GUN DEVELOPMENT, 1933–45: COMMENTS

Development of British tank guns was a similar sad tale to the development of British tanks, but for very different reasons. The guns themselves, two-pounder, six-pounder, 77mm and seventeen-pounder were excellent in their anti-tank role. There are three very adverse comments to be made, however.

The time taken to put the six-pounder and the seventeen-pounder into use was excessive. It had been seen in 1937 and 1940 respectively that there would be a need for these progressive upgrades from the two-pounder. But the six-pounder was not available to field units as a ground-mounted anti-tank gun until early 1942, and as a tank-mounted gun until October 1942.

Progress with the seventeen-pounder was in some ways slightly better. The need was identified in 1940, and the gun came into service as a ground-mounted anti-tank gun in 1943. But the British tanks in which it was mounted consisted only of some 200 Challengers (A30) and the six pilot Centurions delivered a week after the war was over.

The second adverse comment is in part contained in the first, and it is that for nearly the first four years of the war there was little discernible integration between the design of tank guns and the design of a tank in which to carry them. The only possible example of integration was that the Churchill (A22) was capable of mounting the six-pounder without major modification. The two tanks finally available in very small numbers in 1945, the Comet (A34) and the Centurion (A41), were good tanks with good guns.

The third adverse comment is that the possibilities of the 3.7 in anti-aircraft guns were either ignored or blocked due to closed minds, small brains, personal vanity or complete inability to cooperate with other arms of the services. The 3.7 in gun was similar in many ways to the German 88mm. There were said to be certain difficulties in using the 3.7 in gun in a ground-mounted anti-tank role, but it was an excellent gun and ready for service in 1939. Surely the engineering skills of the British could have eliminated whatever minor operational defects it had in the anti-tank role, and thus given us immediate parity with the 88.

CHAPTER 5

Customer Complaints

The previous two chapters have shown that the development of British tanks was slow and produced, effectively, no tanks that were competitive with German tanks until after 1945; and that the British tank guns were effective as anti-tank weapons, but took a very long time to develop and supply tank units.

Did this state of affairs go unnoticed? Certainly not, and there were complaints from all levels about British equipment supplied to Britain's armoured forces. Complaints were made by Members of Parliament (MPs), cabinet ministers and senior Army officers, both in and outside the War Office; these are called in this chapter 'complaints from on high'. Then there were observations of deficiencies from what the MP Richard Stokes called 'the wrong end of the business', the tank crews themselves. These observations – which in regimental histories were not framed as complaints – are described in the section 'from the coal face'.

COMPLAINTS FROM ON HIGH

Complaints from on high are recorded from politicians and from senior Army officers, both inside and outside the War Office. Their observations and comments are in approximate chronological sequence starting in October 1936 and ending in January 1945.

OCTOBER 1936

On 17 October 1936 the Secretary of State for War prepared a memorandum on the tank situation for submission to the cabinet.

The present situation is summarised by recording the number of tanks now in service or undergoing trials in three categories:

Light tanks
A total of 209 tanks of different marks exists and these are barely sufficient for the training requirements of existing units, without taking into account the formation of new tank units. There are no war reserves of these tanks. Two-thirds of the number are of the two-man crew tank produced during the period 1931 to 1935. The two-man crew has proved to be tactically unworkable. These tanks are also inadequately armoured, being barely capable of keeping out armour-piercing rifle bullets. They are therefore obsolescent.

The remaining one-third of the 209 are three-man tanks whose production started in 1936. We believe that for their weight and size they are superior to any light tank produced by other nations. We are placing orders for 680 of these light tanks and anticipate that the majority should be delivered by April 1938.

Medium tanks

We possess a total of 166 medium tanks which again do not meet the training requirements of existing units. Of these, 164 are the Medium Mk I and Medium Mk II produced during the period 1923 to 1930. These must be now considered as obsolete and entirely unfit for war. They are indeed hardly adequate for training purposes, being worn out by long use. The remaining two are the Medium Mk III or 16-tonner. Six pilot models of this tank were produced but due to its cost and a number of other features it was decided to terminate development of the Medium Mk III.

One new medium tank is now undergoing trials and two other types are approaching completion. We have in effect no medium tanks that could be used against hostile forces.

Infantry tanks

An experimental model of an infantry tank is now undergoing trials (Note: this was the A11, or Infantry Tank Mk I). Some features of this tank constitute an advance in tank design, and may solve the problem of providing adequate armour for attacking heavily defended positions. There are however, no infantry tanks in the hands of our tank forces. The present situation is therefore that we have insufficient light tanks of modern design for the tank brigade, not to mention other units. We have no medium tanks fit for service, although new models are undergoing trials. We have a design for an infantry tank but it has not yet passed its trials.

TANK STATUS, MARCH 1938

The next comment on the tank situation comes from Gen Edmund Ironside, made on 29 March 1938. He was then the GOC Eastern Command, one of the senior commands in the British Army. He was also a soldier of immense and distinguished experience. The government had taken steps to rearm after the previous statement of October 1936, but had those eighteen months made much difference? Ironside's diary for 29 March 1938 records as follows:

The paper on our rearmament has come in. It is truly the most appalling reading. How we have come to this state is beyond believing.

Present situation (March 1938): We can put into the field two divisions only, with an incomplete quota of core troops, and deficient of many types of equipment essential for warfare under present conditions.

The main deficiencies are:

- Mechanized division: cavalry regiments are not yet equipped or trained with tanks.
- Tanks; obsolete medium tanks, no cruiser tanks; no infantry tanks, obsolete armoured cars; no light tanks (we have one unit now in Egypt).

And this is the state of our Army after two years' warning. No foreign nation would believe it if they were told.

The situation as recorded by Ironside seems to be even worse than that recorded in October 1936.

3 SEPTEMBER 1939

In July 1942 a paper was submitted to the Tank Board entitled 'Note on the Situation of our Armoured Forces'. This paper described the expansion of Britain's armoured forces over the period from 1938 to 1942. In particular it described the tank status at September 1939, October 1939 and July 1940. The situation on 3 September 1939 was as follows: The British tank forces which had responsibilities in England, Egypt and

A training exercise with Mk VI B light tanks in France, 1940. From the cap badge the unit appears to be the 13/18 Hussars. (Tank Museum 1595/C2)

other parts of the world had the following numbers of tanks available for operations or training:

834 light tanks of the Mk VI series, 77 Mks I and II and cruiser tanks, 66 Mk I infantry tanks.

By the next month the following was the situation: 1,068 light tanks were available to all units of the Army, 117 Mks I and II Cruisers tanks and 90 Mks I and II infantry tanks.

It can be seen that there had been substantial deliveries in that short period but this included only small numbers of the effective Mk II infantry tank or Matilda. The cruisers were quite adequate tanks in a limited role but the light tanks were useful only as reconnaissance vehicles. Thus the number of useful tanks available to all British tank formations in October 1939 was approximately 130.

MAY 1940

By May 1940 the tank forces of the British Army consisted of the units in Egypt, the units in France and those in England for the defence of the United Kingdom. The tanks available for fighting in France which had guns better than machine-guns were twenty-

A close-support A9 of 3rd RTR. The A9 proved a reasonably useful tank in the campaign of May/June 1940, but all of 3rd RTR's tanks were destroyed or abandoned near Calais. (Tank Museum, not numbered)

Matilda 'Good Luck' of 7th RTR appears to have run out of luck in France in May/June 1940. The Germans were able to assess what made it a formidable opponent at that time, and to plan counter-measures. (Tank Museum 9227/D2)

A9 close-support tank of 3rd RTR damaged and abandoned in Calais, June 1940. (Tank Museum 4171/F4)

three Matildas and 158 cruisers (a variety of Mks I, II and III). The twenty-three Matildas were with the 1st Tank Brigade which also had the Infantry Tank Mk I armed only with machine-guns. This brigade fought in the retreat to Dunkirk, and did splendid work in supporting units of the 50th Infantry Division at Arras. The cruisers were all with the 1st Armoured Division, which was not committed to the forces in France until several days after that campaign started. The 1st Armoured Division fought to the south of the Dunkirk perimeter and was used piecemeal in many hard-fought actions.

JULY 1940

The result of all these battles was defeat. Most of the tank crews were returned through various French ports to England, but all the tanks were left behind.

Thus in July 1940 the only tanks available for the defence of Britain were 200 light tanks and 50 infantry tanks. One of the people who took part in the campaign leading back to Dunkirk was Brig Vyvyan Pope. His role was adviser on armoured vehicles at the headquarters of Viscount Gort, commanding the British Expeditionary Force. Pope had many years of experience of armoured forces and his role as adviser was to do what he could to make sure that tanks were used effectively. He was able on one occasion to prevent tanks

Matilda 'Glanton' of 7th RTR knocked out in France, May/June 1940. The 7th and 4th RTRs made a determined counter-attack at Arras but could not hold out against the German strength. (Tank Museum 1767/E7)

making unnecessary road marches, which would have lessened their fighting capability. On other occasions he was able to advise on effective tactical use of tanks at the disposal of other commanders. His main impression, however, was one of horror at the vehicles that the tank troops had to fight with. He was finally evacuated to England but before his own evacuation he had sent a strong letter of recommendations to the War Office regarding the needs for tanks of the future. His main points were: the tanks needed thicker armour; there should be a gun for each tank (not a machine-gun); the gun should be better than the two-pounder; mechanisms that were used in every part of a tank should be simple and reliable.

In June 1940 the Tank Board was constituted to deal with the design and production of tanks. Its role and development are discussed in a later chapter, but Pope was appointed as Director Armoured Fighting Vehicles (DAFV) and soon became a member of the Tank Board. He made various recommendations to the Tank Board, and to see whether these were acted on we must look at a later comment or snapshot of the tank situation.

AUGUST 1942

In the early part of the war a body called the Select Committee on National Expenditure had been set up to monitor the spending on various weapons of war. They were required to consider not only the amount of money spent in relation to budget figures, but also whether the resources bought by the money were effective. On 26 August 1942 the committee presented a memorandum on weapons for the Army to the Prime Minister. This memorandum concentrated on the development and production of tanks and tank guns. Two quotations will be taken from this memorandum in relation to the production of tanks. The first extract from the memorandum concerns the Cromwell tank and is as follows:

It seems that when the decision was taken to produce a new six-pounder cruiser tank the only manufacturing concern to be approached was Nuffield Mechanisation and Aero. The evidence indicates that time was wasted after this initial approach. We consider that there is strong ground for saying that if there had been a clear plan in January 1941, if the present three Cromwell parent firms had been brought into conference, and if a combined programme with a clearly defined responsibility for each had been laid down, production of Cromwell tanks could have been advanced by something like six months.

The second comment in this memorandum relates to the production of the Covenanter and the Churchill.

It is a striking fact that a very large proportion of the country's manufacturing capacity, labour and materials have been used for the production of the Covenanter and the Churchill. The Covenanter is not battleworthy in the sense of being suitable for sending to the British fighting fronts. The Churchill is not yet battleworthy, although action is being taken to make it so. Our information is that over 3,000 of these two types have been produced and that the programme to which the government is committed may amount to something like six thousand.

We appreciate the circumstances in which the programme for producing the Churchill was started and also that it is too early yet to pronounce judgement on its final value. But the broad result of these two programmes raises the question whether they should not have been modified at an earlier date in the light of experience. Lessons for the future illustrated by this history are:

• the danger of attempting to proceed simultaneously with design and production, and especially of going into mass production without full preliminary tests and trials.
• the need for being continually at work on design for the future.
• the need for having a production programme planned well ahead.

This memorandum was submitted to the Prime Minister and the War Cabinet and, in due course, the Chairman of the Select Committee, Sir John Wardlaw-Milne, received a reply from Churchill dated 5 October 1942, which contained the following statements:

As you are aware, the obstacles and setbacks experienced have called for recurring attention from the government ever since the war began, and successive steps have been taken to improve our methods. In general the steps already taken accord substantially with the view expressed by your Select Committee, and since the date of your report further improvements have been effected. I append for the information of your members an account of the new arrangements at the War Office and the Ministry of Supply.

The question remains how the new system will work. Several attempted improvements have been made before which have only been partially successful. In order to make sure that this new plan fits and is made to fit the moving needs, I have accepted a suggestion made by the Minister of Production, the Secretary of State for War and the Minister of Supply that they should jointly review now and thereafter at intervals the detailed arrangements, scope and practical workings of the new organizations.

AUGUST 1943

In August 1943 Montgomery wrote to the Vice Chief of the Imperial General Staff (VCIGS) about the tank gun. He had the following comments to make:

We are badly behind the Germans in this respect, and I'm anxious as to whether we are thinking far enough ahead. History relates that in the struggle between gun and armour, the gun has always come out on top.

The penetrating power of the German tank armament is infinitely superior to the gun at present fitted to the Sherman V or the Cromwell. At 1,000 yd the Panther gun will penetrate 130 mm of armour. At this range the 75mm in the Sherman will penetrate 62 mm and the six-pounder in the Cromwell will penetrate 72 mm.

This is a very serious situation. The enemy can engage our tanks at ranges at which it is hopeless to reply with any hope of success. Being outgunned in this manner permits the enemy to reduce his armour thickness if he wishes, and to engage us at any range he desires.

To overcome this serious defect it is necessary for our tanks to make the fullest use of ground in order to bring effective fire to bear on enemy tanks. This is a definite handicap when we are the attacker. In pushing forward in a search for good fire positions, tanks often have to expose themselves and casualties follow rapidly.

I suggest that in the past we have tried to fit the gun into the tank. Instead we should select the gun and build the tank around it.

As a target figure, I consider we require a gun which will penetrate 150 mm of armour at 1,500 yd. It must be a dual purpose weapon with a good HE performance.

This will allow for a suitable margin should the enemy decide to increase his armour thickness by adding extra plates to his tanks.

The VCIGS replied to Monty and agreed with him whole-heartedly about most things. One of his comments was: 'There is a great deal in what you write regarding fitting the gun into the tank. At long last designers are alert to this fallacy. Their troubles now are to design tanks around the seventeen-pounder and a 3.7 in high-velocity gun. They are already making good progress but it would be foolish to expect immediate results.'

It is particularly interesting to see that the War Office blame the designers for this 'fallacy'. The War Office were presumably supposed to represent the requirements of the user, or possibly even to pre-empt the future requirements of the user. It surely should have been the War Office who insisted to the designers that the gun was the central item in a tank, and once having decided what gun was functionally necessary that the tank should be designed around it. The VCIGS was, however, quite correct in saying that it would be foolish to expect immediate results. It was about ten months after Monty's comments on the ineffective guns mounted in British tanks that the invasion of Europe took place over the Normandy beaches. Monty's troops were issued with some British tanks (Cromwells and Churchills) and the balance of their armour was the American Sherman. No British tank had a gun that had been suggested by Monty as being necessary. A small percentage of Shermans were up-gunned by mounting the British seventeen-pounder in their turrets. The distribution of the seventeen-pounder Sherman, or Firefly as it was called, was one tank per troop in certain armoured regiments whose basic tank was the 75mm Sherman. Thus many of the British returned to war with tanks, by Monty's definition, not appropriate to fight the Germans.

MARCH 1944

Sir John Wardlaw-Milne was a politician, and he knew that it was unwise to trust the statements and promises of other politicians. Some months after receiving Churchill's reply of 5 October 1942, he felt it was necessary once again to submit a memorandum to the Prime Minister for the consideration of the War Cabinet. He decided in September 1943 to 'resume our investigation to ascertain how far the new men and the new organization had in fact made good'.

The Select Committee on National Expenditure commenced gathering information on actions and results in relation to tank production, and on 11 March 1944 addressed the Prime Minister once again on this topic. The memorandum they submitted included a summary of the results of tank production in 1943, showing the operational value of that production (Figure 5.1) and a comparison between promises and actions (Figure 5.2).

FIGURE 5.1: OPERATIONAL VALUE OF TANKS PRODUCED, 1943

Type of tank	Percentage of total no of tanks made in 1943	Operational value as gun-tanks
Covenanter	0.5	Nil
Crusader	26	Nil
Cavalier	5	Nil
Centaur	17	Nil
Cromwell	7.5	100 per cent*
Matilda	2	Obsolescent
Valentine	24	Obsolescent
Churchill	18	100 per cent*

*will become obsolescent unless up-gunned; cannot as presently configured accept a larger gun.

Figure 5.1 shows that 48.5 per cent of the tanks produced were of no value as gun-tanks. A further 26 per cent were tanks which would be obsolete before too long. Thus just over 25 per cent of production was for tanks which were acceptable to field units, even though these were not capable of being upgraded. Figure 5.2 shows what had been promised in 1942 and what actually happened in 1943. Not much of what had been promised was achieved, and the useful dividend from actions taken was a very small return for the resources employed.

FIGURE 5.2: COMPARISON OF 'PROSPECT' 1942 WITH 'PERFORMANCE'

Main points   (a) in the 'prospect', as presented in autumn 1942
               (b) actual 'performance'

1. (a) That the Crusader had proved unreliable and was to go out of production.
   (b) Crusaders still represented 26 per cent of the total tanks produced in 1943.
2. (a) That the Infantry Tank Mk IV (Churchill), though justified for its original home-defence purpose, did not justify continuance for overseas fighting and was to go out of production at the end of the current contract (early summer 1943) and that the whole Vauxhall Group should then go over to the cruiser tanks.
   (b) The Churchill has, according to the memorandum submitted by the War Office, 'established itself as a reliable and efficient weapon having stood the test of battle experience in Tunisia and won the confidence of the troops'. (But, NB: It has been allowed to drop out of battle since Tunisia, apparently owing to the armament being judged insufficient.)
3. (a) That the Cromwell with a Meteor engine and carrying a six-pounder gun was going to be the best tank in the world, and an important factor already in 1943 fighting.
   (b) The Cromwell had up to the end of 1943 not proved in quality terms to be a vehicle of sufficiently reliable performance to be used in battle. Its production in

---

> quantity fell far short of the programme. As a result it was considered necessary to change the 'parentage' for Cromwell production in May 1943. Even if as armoured vehicles Cromwells had been adequately reliable, they would not have been sent abroad because, by the time they came into production, the General Staff had come to regard a cruiser tank equipped with a six-pounder gun as inadequate.
>
> 4.   (a) That the Centaur with Liberty engine was going to be a very close second-best to the Cromwell (in fact identical except at the highest speeds).
>
> (b) The Centaur with its Liberty engine proved so unreliable when handled by units at home that, as a gun-tank, it has been condemned. The Liberty engine is to go out of production but, in order not to break up manufacturers' organizations, production will have to continue long after condemnation as a gun-tank engine.
>
> 5.   (a) That the Centaur was to be adopted because, owing to the demands of the M.A.P. Merlin engine programme, a sufficient production of Meteor engines for the total cruiser programme could not be organized.
>
> (b) It has been found possible during 1943 to organize the production of Meteor engines on a scale which is claimed to be adequate for the whole cruiser tank programme.
>
> 6.   (a) That the whole British effort would be concentrated on the Cromwell type of cruiser tank, and that the production of an infantry tank would cease to be part of the British programme.
>
> (b) The General Staff have accepted the policy than an infantry tank of the Churchill type is an indispensable part of the British programme.

JUNE 1944

On 24 June 1944 Monty's Chief of Staff, de Guingand, wrote to him: 'If we are not careful there will be a danger of our troops developing a Tiger and Panther complex. P.J. Grigg (Sir James Grigg, Secretary of State of War) rang me up last night and said he thought there might be trouble in the Guards Armoured Division as regards the inadequacy of our tanks compared with the Germans. Naturally the reports are not being circulated.' On 25 June Monty wrote to Grigg as follows:

My Dear Secretary of State,

It has come to my notice that reports are circulating about the value of British equipment, tanks etc. compared to the Germans.

We cannot have anything of that sort at this time. We have got a good lodgement area, we have built up our strength and tomorrow we leap on the enemy. Anything that undermines confidence and morale must be stamped on ruthlessly. I have issued the enclosed letter.

Yours ever,
B.L. Montgomery

Monty also wrote to Alan Brooke, the CIGS, at this time. He said:

> I have had to stamp very heavily on reports that began to be circulated about the inadequate quality of our tanks as compared with the Germans. In cases where adverse comment is made on British equipment such reports are likely to cause a lowering of morale and a lack of confidence among the troops. It will generally be found that when the equipment at our disposal is used properly and the tactics are good, we have no difficulty in defeating the Germans.

That is all very well for Montgomery in his position as Commander-in-Chief. It is not quite so comfortable for a Cromwell or Churchill tank crew member. A brief conversation between a newly arrived tank officer and his superior officer in 1944 records: 'How does a Churchill get a Tiger?'

'It's supposed to get within 200 yd and put a shot through the periscope.'

'Has anyone ever done it?'

'No.'

AUGUST 1944

Churchill read Wardlaw-Milne's memorandum of March 1944 not long before the invasion of Normandy, and was naturally kept so involved by those responsibilities that he was not able to reply until 2 August 1944. In his response Churchill made several statements himself and provided supporting documents with statements from other people; here are some quotations:

> The situation in 1943 when Britain was able to purchase large numbers of Sherman tanks from the USA enabled a drastic reshaping of our tank production policy, and this accounts in large measure for the fact that 1943 output fell substantially short of the estimate made at the end of 1942.

> The Minister of Production and other members of the cabinet have, during 1943, kept jointly under review the working of the new organizations which were set up at the end of 1942, and are satisfied that they are functioning efficiently and smoothly.

> Reports from Normandy indicate that the Cromwell possesses speed, hardiness and cross-country ability, which make it superior in these respects to other tanks. The Cromwell is primarily a weapon of offence. The Tiger and Panther are primarily weapons of defence and are being definitely used as such in the present fighting in Normandy.

These and many other similar comments are either political double-speak or gross misrepresentations of the truth. Churchill had evidently decided to ignore inconvenient comments conveyed from the tankmen themselves through political and other intermediaries.

There were a number of MPs – only a small number – who were concerned about the short-comings of British weaponry. Sir John Wardlaw-Milne, Richard Stokes, S.S. Hammersley and Mr Ellis-Smith were MPs who raised questions from time to time.

Richard Rapier Stokes had served with distinction and gallantry in the First World War and was perhaps the most persistent of those raising questions in the House of Commons about the effectiveness of the British tanks. On 2 August 1944, Stokes raised this matter during a debate on the war situation. Hansard (Parliamentary Debates, House of Commons, Vol 402, Column 1533) records:

Stokes: My friend the general (a general in command of fighting troops in the British Army) told me that we are as far behind the Germans today in quality as we were in 1940.

Rear Admiral Beamish: The Hon. member complained just now because we are everlastingly accused in the United States of doing nothing. May I say that no matter how highly bred a dog may be, if you persist in giving him a bad name it will stick to him. The Hon. member has spent his whole time in doing everything he can to lower the prestige of the British Army.

Valentine Hector IV of 8th RTR knocked out at Sidi Rezegh, November 1941. The penetrating shot hole can be seen just to the left of the vertical identification stripes on the turret. (P.N. Veale)

Valentines of 46th RTR (23rd Armoured Brigade) knocked out in the El Alamein area, autumn 1942.

Stokes: Really and truly, if I had thought that my Hon. and gallant friend was going to make a remark like that I would not have given way. If he took the trouble to read my speeches he would be aware that all along they have been based on irrefutable facts. (Laughter)

It is all very well for Hon. members to laugh, but these men are dying. It is all very well to sit here on a soft seat. I speak as a fighting soldier. I have been at the wrong end of the business, and I am determined to protest in this House against the inadequacy of the steps which are being taken to provide our men with the proper equipment.'

The members of that House could obviously only find humour in the suffering and death of British tank crews.

Richard Stokes' facts were indeed irrefutable. Anyone who had the unpleasant task of fighting in a British tank in Normandy and north-west Europe – and many other places – will certainly agree with Mr Stokes. Those tankmen felt that no one cared sufficiently to do anything about improvement, or were too uninformed or incompetent to do so. Obviously there had to be some way in which valid information was retrieved, collated, analysed and acted upon. The recorded memories of British tank crews in the latter stages of the Second World War do not include any mention of the opportunity to discuss difficulties of British tanks with anyone who could do anything about it.

Churchills of 34th Armoured Brigade in Roosendaal, Holland, on 30 October 1944. The approach to Roosendaal was intersected with waterways and was damp, but the Churchill was very good across such country, particularly in view of its weight of 40 tons. (Henk Bredevolt)

FEBRUARY 1945

In a memo of February 1945 Monty made some very strange statements about British tanks.

> British armour has come through the campaign in western Europe with flying colours, and has proved itself superior in battle to German armour.
>
> If Rundstedt had been equipped with British armour when he attacked in the Ardennes on 16 December 1944 he would have reached the River Meuse in thirty-six hours. This would have placed the Allies in a very awkward position.
>
> If 21st Army Group had been equipped with German armour it could not have crossed the Seine on 8 August 1944 and reached Brussels on 3 September and Antwerp on 4 September, thus cutting off the whole Pas de Calais area in eight days: a very remarkable achievement which had far-reaching results.
>
> The credit for all this must go to the War Office. The British armies in June 1944 were splendidly equipped for the job that had to be done.

The problem with this memo is that it made the War Office complacent with what Monty said they had done, whether they had done it or not. Perhaps even more perniciously, this type of statement could be quoted in the House of Commons as coming from the great commanding general who was omniscient and all-seeing in these matters. Once again, one can only say that this statement was not correct.

VIEW FROM THE COAL FACE

The next group of comments on tanks relates to those made by the users themselves. Most of these have been taken from either regimental histories or from personal accounts of campaigns. In most cases these are direct recordings of the state of affairs as observed. In some cases the authors, particularly those of regimental histories, are inclined to be uncritical of the situation they saw, but the recordings of the situations themselves are revealing.

9TH LANCERS

The 9th Lancers had been converted to tanks some time before the war and in the winter of 1939 were in the 1st Armoured Division. They were then training for the part they were to play with the British Expeditionary Force when they moved over to France in the spring. The plan was that on their arrival in France they would complete their training in Normandy. During the last few weeks of their training at Wimborne in Dorset a few of their new cruiser tanks arrived. The rest of the new equipment was to be delivered when they reached France, but in fact much of that did not yet exist.

The Germans attacked on 10 May 1944, at which time the 1st Armoured Division was still in England. After many changes orders were received that vehicles and drivers were to proceed to Southampton on 17 May and the rest of the regiment were to move to the same port by rail on 20 May. Tanks, machine-guns, spare parts, equipment and stores were still arriving and because there was no time to break bulk they were loaded just as they arrived. Anything which came after the vehicles had left was carried to the port by train with the dismounted party. C Squadron's commanding officer was seen driving down the road to Southampton in his private car handing out machine-guns, belt boxes and telescopes to his tanks; it was a grim reminder of the appalling lack of readiness.

The 9th Lancers left Southampton on 20 May and arrived at Cherbourg on 21 May. They spent the next two days on maintenance and fitting guns into tanks. The general state of tank readiness can best be described by considering the state of the A Squadron tanks. They were supposed to be issued with cruiser tanks with a two-pounder gun. There were only enough tanks at the outset – and before there were any casualties – to mount two of the four troops in the squadron. The squadron's second-in-command, Capt Scott, was mounted in a fine new tank, an A9. This had a powerful 3in howitzer. Unfortunately, there was not one round of ammunition for this useful weapon. There was plenty of ammunition for the secondary armament, a Vickers machine-gun. The method of aiming this machine-gun required a telescopic sight, but there was no such sight, and if there had been it would have been of little use because there was no hole pierced into the front of the turret into which it could be fitted. This supposedly powerful tank therefore set off to meet the Germans with a rifle as its only effective weapon. Mounted in a new light tank was 2/Lt Close, but instead of armour plating its turret was made of plywood and there was no weapon other than his revolver and rifle.

It is instructive to consider the readiness of the formation in which the 9th Lancers fought, the 1st Armoured Division. On 24 May 1940 its commander, Maj Gen Evans, had as his available strength the 2nd Armoured Brigade, of which two regiments were detraining 30 miles away, the 101st Light Anti-Aircraft and Anti-Tank Regiment of the Royal Artillery, and one or two units of ancillary services.

'It was with this travesty of an armoured division,' said Maj Gen Evans, 'a formation with less than half its proper armoured strength, without any field guns or a proper complement of anti-tank and anti-aircraft guns, without bridging equipment, without infantry, without air support, without the bulk of its ancillary services, and with part of its headquarters in a three-ply wooden "armoured" command vehicle – that I was ordered to force a crossing over a defended, unfordable river, and afterwards to advance some 60 miles through four real armoured divisions to the help of the British Expeditionary Force.'

That was in 1940. The 9th Lancers returned to England, were re-equipped in so far as it was possible, and recommenced training. In 1942 they were sent to Egypt with the rest of the 2nd Armoured Brigade. In April 1942 the regiment's tank establishment was as follows: A Squadron: sixteen Crusaders; B Squadron: twenty-three Honeys and two old cruisers; C Squadron: 3 new Crusaders, 8 Honeys and 1 old cruiser.

Regimental headquarters was mounted in two 2 new Crusaders and two new Honeys.

Rumour had it that a new American medium tank (the Grant) had arrived and that shortly we would receive enough to equip the squadron. This was excellent news. At that time we were hopelessly behind the Germans in armour, firepower and reliability. The two-pounder tank gun was a miserable thing: its shell simply bounced off the standard German Mk III tank, and the German Panzer crews treated it with contempt. The German high-velocity 50mm tank gun cut easily through Crusader and Honey alike. They could sit down comfortably at 1,500 yd and with their magnificent telescopic sights pick off British tanks at leisure. Whereas we were not able to open up at anything greater than 600 yd. To be able to do this there was much concentration in training in the use of smoke.

QUEENS BAYS

The Queens Bays were also in the 2nd Armoured Brigade. Their experiences were quite similar to those of the 9th Lancers in that they were sent hurriedly to France in May 1940, were evacuated in due course and found their way to Egypt in 1942. Their story starts in February and March of 1940. They were then training with their new light

A Matilda knocked out in the desert. In the latter half of 1941 the German long-barrelled 50mm anti-tank gun and the 88mm made the Matilda vulnerable in spite of its good armour. (Tank Museum 385/C1)

tanks, the Mk VI Cs. The 7.92mm Besa machine-guns for this tank were not yet available because they were 'to follow'. A sheet of plywood covered the place where the gun mountings would fit into the turret.

It had now been decided to equip the whole division (2nd and 3rd armoured brigades) with cruiser tanks to the extent that production capacity allowed, and to abolish the light tank. Some A9 cruisers were received in April 1940; they were armed with a two-pounder gun and a Vickers .303in co-axially mounted machine-gun. The whole regiment went to the range at Linney Head for battle practices with these tanks, but there were still no guns for the Mk VI C tanks. When orders came on 3 May to be ready to go overseas within the next twelve days, no one had seen the Besa guns except for one or two NCO instructors.

Two other types of cruiser tank were now received, the A10 and the A13, which differed in certain respects from the A9 and from each other. There were still twenty-one Mk VI C tanks to make up the numbers and the final distribution within the regiment immediately before embarkation consisted of twenty-nine cruiser tanks and twenty-one light tanks.

TABLE 5.3 TANKS OF THE QUEENS BAYS, MAY 1940

	Cruisers				Light tanks	
	A9	A10	A13	Total		
Regimental HQ	–	3	–	3	–	–
A Squadron HQ	2	–	2	4	–	–
two troops, each	–	–	3	6	–	–
two troops, each	–	–	–	–	3	6
Total A Squadron	2	–	8	10	–	6
B Squadron HQ	2	–	2	4	–	–
two troops, each	–	–	3	6	–	–
two troops, each	–	–	–	–	3	6
Total B Squadron	2	–	8	10	–	6
C Squadron HQ	–	–	3	3	–	–
one troop	–	–	3	3	–	–
three troops, each	–	–	–	–	3	9
Total C Squadron	–	–	6	6	–	9
Total, Regiment	4	3	22	29	–	21

Very little was known about the driving and maintenance of the three different types of cruiser tank, as they had only just been issued. There were no spare parts or tools with them; these were to be made up on arrival overseas – as were the guns for the light tanks, which arrived just before sailing to be put on board still nailed up in their packing cases.

At the time these complications and difficulties did not seem of great importance as the announced intention was to move to a training area somewhere in France where there would be time to complete mobilization and carry out some shake-down training.

A13s of 5th RTR in France, 1940. The rhinoceros emblem of 1st Armoured Division can be seen on the front of the leading tank. None of these tanks returned to the UK. (Tank Museum 1757/D2)

Final sailing orders were received on 7 May. On 10 May the German armies attacked in Luxembourg and Holland. The 1st Armoured Division, consisting of 2nd and 3rd armoured brigades, had been ordered almost at the moment of sailing to concentrate in a new area west of Brussels. It was to this area that the advance parties of the 2nd Armoured Brigade had moved up by road some days before.

The convoy containing the Queens Bays reached Cherbourg on 20 May 1940. The unloading of vehicles was completed by the next morning.

A start was made on the quayside by taking the guns for the tanks out of their packing cases, assembling them and mounting them in the tanks. At midday the tanks and tank crews left by rail and the task of mounting the tank guns was completed on the rail flats during the journey. On 22 May tanks were unloaded at Breval, 49 miles south of Rouen.

At this point they made themselves comfortable in billets and looked forward to bringing the tanks into battleworthy condition, and giving themselves some training on the use of these new tanks. However, plans of settling down to a programme of training were soon dispelled, for within three hours of their arrival they were on the move to meet the enemy.

The regimental history comments on some of the events and conditions of their confrontation with the Germans.

The Regiment in their first action had been rushed into battle against first-class German troops of all arms without adequate time for preparation and without any artillery to support them. As a result their gallant individual efforts and those of the 4th Borders were dissipated in a number of minor actions, none of which had any chance of success or were within supporting distance of another.

An A13 of 1st Armoured Division knocked out in Rouen, May/June 1940. (Tank Museum 1762/C5)

Armaments and other equipment had had to be fitted to the cruiser and light tanks as opportunity allowed. There had been little or no time for maintenance and no chance of getting wireless sets properly netted and in good working order. Another serious handicap had been that the cruiser tanks, with the brake linings worn out, had become very difficult to steer, so that quick manoeuvre was impossible and the tanks had been easier targets for the German guns.

Many of the casualties (9 killed, 7 wounded and 12 tanks lost) might have been avoided if smoke had been available. But all the training smoke ammunition had been withdrawn before embarkation and operational smoke ammunition, which should have been put on board at Southampton, had never been received.

7TH HUSSARS

The 7th Hussars were in Egypt in 1938. They became part of what was then called Matruh Mobile Force under the command of Brig H.E. Russell. The three regiments in this brigade-size force were the 7th Hussars, 8th Hussars and 11th Hussars. Their equipment then was as follows: 7th Hussars had two squadrons of light tanks which consisted of mixed Mk IIIs, VI As and VI Bs, but had no .50in ammunition for the heavy

Valentines of 40th RTR at Thompson's Post in the northern sector of the El Alamein line, October 1942. This section of the line was the domain of the 9th Australian Division. (Tank Museum 1788/D4)

One of 40th RTR's Valentines knocked out, quite possibly in the El Alamein battles. (Tank Museum 1788/D2)

machine-guns; 8th Hussars had 15 cwt Ford trucks with Vickers light machine-guns on improvised mountings; 11th Hussars had old Rolls-Royce and Morris armoured cars, and many of the former had seen service in this area in the First World War.

During 1939 the Matruh Mobile Force was redesignated the Light Armoured Brigade; it still had the same units and formed part of the Mobile Division (Egypt).

In April 1940 this was reorganized again and the armoured segment of the division was reorganized into two homogeneous brigades. The 7th Hussars went to the Heavy Brigade and their place in the Light Brigade was taken by the 1st RTR. At the same time a reorganization of the cavalry regiments took place and both were to have two squadrons of light tanks and one of A9 cruisers. More cruisers were gradually coming out from England and A10s were expected to arrive at the rate of ten per month from July 1940 onwards. Meanwhile A9s were being issued, and, unfortunately, some of these arrived without their two-pounder guns.

By the beginning of May when the twilight war in Europe was changing to lightning war and the attitude of Italy was more menacing, the tank situation in Egypt was by no means satisfactory. It was the cruisers that would count in operations against the Italians, who were known to have a number of armoured units, and the cruiser situation in the division was bad. In the 4th Armoured Brigade (the new name for the Heavy Brigade) the headquarters had four, the 7th Hussars seven and 6th RTR twenty-three. In the 7th Armoured Brigade (formerly the Light Brigade) the headquarters and the 8th Hussars had none, while of the twenty-three in 1st RTR, eight were without their two-pounders.

That was the situation in 1940. In May 1941 the 7th Hussars expected that their final establishment of tanks would be thirty-two A9s and twenty A10s. The latter had a little more armour and were generally more solid, and it was something of a disappointment that there were to be so many A9s and that there should be no mention of the A13. However, it was a beginning and the arrival of the first seven tanks gave a lot of encouragement. They were very deficient in equipment and frequent visits to store depots only partially made up the shortages.

At many times during the campaign in North Africa a unit was required to give up its tanks to replace those of a unit that had lost many of its tanks in action. This was obviously essential from the overall strategic view, but it was immensely disheartening to those units that had become used to their vehicles and expected to have to use them in battle. The 7th Hussars had exactly this problem; no sooner had they received their new tanks than they were required to send them all up to Mersa Matruh as replacements for the 2nd RTR.

13TH/18TH ROYAL HUSSARS

The 13th/18th Royal Hussars (13/18H) returned from India and landed at Southampton in October 1938. In January 1939 they began training as the mechanized cavalry of the 1st Infantry Division, which was commanded by Maj Gen Harold Alexander. The problem confronting the commanding officer of 13/18H was a difficult one. There was very little training equipment and what there was came slowly and in small quantities. The number of instructors available for driving and maintenance, and for weapons and wireless training, was quite inadequate and large numbers of officers and NCOs had to be sent on courses. However, the great majority of soldiers who joined cavalry regiments between the wars were far more mechanically minded than horse minded, and welcomed with intense interest and keenness all forms of mechanized training. The only barrier to carrying out effective training was an appalling and disheartening lack of the necessary means of every sort with which to get down to the job of training. A limited number of light tanks arrived in due course, but most of these were well-worn training vehicles. On arrival only a small proportion were mechanically sound enough to get from the railway siding to the barracks without breaking down.

When war was declared on 3 September 1939 the 13/18H were sent as soon as possible with the 1st Infantry Division to France. They were part of the initial force that had been promised to France. The regiment was gravely deficient in equipment and certainly not fully trained. Third-line transport was only provided on the last afternoon. This consisted of bakers' vans, grocers' lorries and similar exotic vehicles, all in their peace-time glory with owners' names emblazoned on them in bright colours. Regimental pride ensured that as soon as possible these colours were hidden under a decent regimental khaki. Only three days had been spent on the ranges with the new weapon and no machine-gun had more than two ammunition belts. Out of twenty-eight tanks, only twelve had shoulder pieces and so were in a position to fight, and many drivers had hardly ever driven a tracked vehicle except on the training field.

Mk VI B light tank abandoned in France, May 1940. It does not appear to impress the young German soldier very much – nor should it have done.

The regiment fought with the 1st Infantry Division during the retreat to Dunkirk and eventually returned through the beaches of Dunkirk. Their losses were comparatively light in people but total in terms of tanks. In June 1940 the regiment became part of the 1st Armoured Reconnaissance Brigade which was guarding the coast to the west of Bournemouth. Luckily there was no enemy attack because the only weapon available was the rifle with no more than fifty rounds of ammunition per man. Towards the end of that month the regiment was equipped with standard motor cars with a little armour carrying a Bren gun. At the end of June the regiment had a strength of seventy-two of these vehicles and was moved to Essex where it was the mobile reserve for the eastern counties. Over the next year, the regiment's equipment improved in a marginal way and by August 1941 they had been re-equipped with the Covenanter tank. They found it to be a very bad tank. It was unreliable mechanically, lightly armoured and, like all British tanks at that time, had a two-pounder gun as its main armament. The 13/18H in the end were equipped with Sherman DD tanks and used them effectively on the assault on Europe in June 1944.

15TH/19TH HUSSARS

The 15th/19th Hussars (15/19H) was a regular cavalry regiment similar to the 13/18H. This regiment's turn for mechanization did not come until mid-1938. It was a

Covenanters of 9th Armoured Division training in the UK, 1941–2. The divisional emblem, the panda, can just be seen on the front of the tank in the foreground. (Tank Museum 4694/C4)

complicated, lengthy process in that the horses left but were not immediately succeeded by machines. For nine months the regiment knew only frustration and uncertainty with a few obsolete track carriers, half a dozen motorcycles and some trucks in which to train itself for the requirements of the new age. Early in 1939, however, the regiment had some modern carriers and by August of 1939 it also had a number of light tanks. But this was only a month before war broke out, and the regiment had little or no opportunity to train seriously for war. The role of the 15/19H was that of the reconnaissance regiment to the 3rd Infantry Division commanded by Maj Gen Bernard Montgomery. They fought as well as they could in the campaign of May 1940 in France, but like all other tank units they had to leave all their tanks behind.

Back in England they were reorganized as a medium machine-gun regiment and in this role their fighting vehicles were Austin cars and their main weapons Vickers machine-guns and .55in anti-tank rifles. Each squadron also had a bus in which spare men were supposed to ride to war.

Towards the end of 1940 the 15/19H was converted to an armoured regiment and brigaded into the 28th Armoured Brigade, part of the new 9th Armoured Division. From December 1940 to March 1941 the regiment was officially an armoured regiment in an armoured division. But they had no tanks. They were compelled to combine training for war in tanks with the task of remaining operationally fit to fight anywhere in England in

Austin cars. In March 1941 the regiment received its first cruiser tank, and this was followed by others in a slow but steady trickle through the succeeding months. They already had a few light tanks similar to those that they had used in France. The new cruiser tank was the Covenanter or A13 Mk III. This was a development of the cruiser with which the armoured division had been equipped in France to a very limited degree. The history of the 15/19H states that it was produced in large numbers for home defence. The regiment trained with its by now full complement of tanks during the latter part of 1941 and the first half of 1942. In May 1942 they had to send all their tanks back to the works for modification. This naturally interfered with troop training, and when they got them back again they had to send nearly half of them away for a second time for more modifications which had been forgotten. These teething troubles of the Covenanter were constantly occurring and each fault meant a modification carried out either in divisional workshops or at the manufacturers. The 9th Armoured Division was the first to be equipped with Covenanters and so bore the brunt of the disorganization caused by these mechanical faults. The 15/19H regimental history records: 'In any case the Covenanter had only been produced for home defence and its armour was little better than that of the light tank and its gun, the two-pounder, was easily outclassed by contemporary German weapons.'

Covenanters of 9th Armoured Division. These were issued to units such as the 15/19 Hussars. They had to send them all back to the manufacturers for modifications, and as soon as they had them back half of the tanks had to go back a second time in an attempt to make them work properly. Some 2,000 of these useless vehicles were produced. (Tank Museum 1833/B3)

A Mk I Churchill with turret-mounted two-pounder and hull-mounted 2in. After two years of teething troubles the Churchill eventually became mechanically reliable, but was always undergunned. (IWM H32707)

At a later stage the 15/19H was equipped with Cromwells. Their opinion of the Cromwell was not, initially, very enthusiastic. They said as follows: 'On paper the Cromwell was an enormous step forward but its behaviour to begin with, though full of promise, was very disappointing. It proved in detail unreliable; it was impossible to evacuate the driver and front machine-gunner, should they become casualties, when the turret was traversed in certain positions; the suspension, basically the same as that of the Crusader, was clearly overloaded; the steering system which had been successfully developed for the Churchill tank was erratic to the point of danger owing to the unpredictable slipping of certain brake bands when the gearbox oil got hot. It was fortunate the Cromwell as first issued was not required in 1943, and that it was possible to develop it through several marks to a high degree of reliability by the time that the Normandy invasion took place.'

While the reliability and general performance of the later marks of Cromwell were excellent, it is true to say that the Cromwells were outarmoured and outgunned by the heavier German tanks. This disparity was particularly acute in close country such as Normandy where ranges were short and the power of manoeuvre restricted. It was on their speed and manoeuvrability, in which respects they were probably the best tank on the battlefield, that the Cromwell relied for their protection and effectiveness; these qualities were of little advantage in Normandy.

A close-support (95mm) Cromwell in Normandy, 1944. The Cromwells had a good turn of speed but could not use it to any effect in the close bocage country. (Tank Museum 3579/E2)

Cromwell of the Sharpshooters (3/4 County of London Yeomanry) knocked out at Villers Bocage, June 1944. The unit was leading the 7th Armoured Division, and was effectively brought to a halt by the single Tiger tank commanded by Michael Wittman. (Tank Museum 3666/B2)

Another Cromwell tank knocked out, almost certainly in the same encounter. (Tank Museum 3579/F3)

The 15/19H was one of the few regiments in the British Army to have the Challenger (A30) issued to them. Their comments on this vehicle are not particularly complimentary; they viewed the Challenger as only a stopgap until a newly designed tank of superior qualities was available.

The 15/19H was also one of the few regiments to be re-equipped with the last British cruiser tank to see action during the war, the Comet. They found the Comet to be better armoured than the Challenger and appreciated the fact that the Comet was designed from the beginning to mount a large gun, the 77mm. Even so they found that the Comet could not stand up to attack by the high velocity German 75mm and 88mm guns except at long ranges. They also found its belly armour was insufficient to give adequate protection against anti-tank mines.

On the whole, however, they found that the Comet was a good Cruiser tank and its 77mm gun was a fine weapon fitted with a particularly efficient sighting equipment. The vision arrangements for the tank commander in the Comet were also a great improvement on those fitted to previous Cruiser tanks.

FINAL COMMENT

One person who was very vocal on the performance of British tanks during the war was Bob Crisp. Crisp was a South African, and had played cricket for South Africa before the war. He fought with great gallantry in North Africa, Greece and north-west Europe in a great variety of tanks. He comments on the tanks taken by his unit (3rd RTR) to Greece:

> Of the sixty-odd tanks 3rd RTR had taken to Greece at the beginning of 1941, not half a dozen were casualties of direct enemy action. All the others had been abandoned with broken tracks or other mechanical breakdowns. They littered the passes and defiles of Macedonia and Thessaly, stripped of their machine-guns, but otherwise intact. They were of no help to the enemy; no other army would have contemplated using them.

It is reputed that some of Crisp's strong comments on the performance of British tanks made Montgomery so angry that when Crisp was recommended for a bar to his DSO, Monty downgraded the award to an MC. Crisp eventually found a medium through whom he could make his views widely known, the MP Richard Stokes. Crisp wrote him a report in which he said:

> For four years now I have been watching shells fired from mine and other tanks bouncing off the front armour of German Panzers. I mean actually watching and actually bouncing, and that after we have wriggled and crept and rushed our tanks to within effective range for our weapons. This has meant always for at least 1,000 yd we had been within the enemy's effective range before we could fire a shot that had any hope of success.

Bob Crisp was by no means alone in thinking that British tanks needed substantial improvement. Most soldiers, however, were not outspoken risk-takers like Crisp. There was a convention in the British Army that you got on with the job without belly-aching, and it was only a bad workman who blamed his tools. This attitude quite clearly blocked the totally legitimate right to comment by those forced to use inadequate weapons. The blocking of constructive feedback was one of many other causes for inadequacy of British tanks. These will be discussed in the last chapter of this book.

CHAPTER 6

The Forges of Vulcan

MANAGEMENT OF TANK DESIGN AND PRODUCTION

OVERVIEW

Vulcan was the Roman god of fire, forging and smelting, a very appropriate deity for armoured forces. Besides many other functions, he was the maker of pieces of metalwork that were of beautiful design and great utility and much prized by those to whom he gave them. Vulcan was particularly fortunate in that he alone was responsible for deciding the purpose of what he was going to make, then designing it and finally carrying out the necessary steps of manufacture.

Any manufactured item must be taken through the three main steps of specification, design and production. As the item becomes more complex, so does the need to divide up the steps into more detailed tasks, and to assign responsibility for their achievement to appropriately qualified people. But to maintain control over these divided tasks it is vital that someone – some one person, not a department, not a committee – be made accountable for commanding and driving all those responsible for the subordinate tasks to the joint completion of the desired end result.

This chapter records and describes some of the systems set up to discharge responsibilities for tank design and production. It is assumed that the specification for a tank has been reasonably precisely defined – although we have seen that this was far from being the case. It is also assumed that details of the main tank armament are defined, and preferably that the gun is in being. Once again, this was very seldom so.

We look first at the systems and organization that were set up for the design of tanks. The next section looks at the organizations for producing tanks. Finally, the roles and usefulness of the Tank Board and the Tank Parliament are considered.

TANK DESIGN, 1918–45

In 1918 Lt Col Philip Johnson returned from France to establish the Department of Tank Design and Experiment. His immediate task was to develop the tanks for 1919, but the need for this was greatly reduced by the war ending in November 1918. Johnson's department continued with design and experimental work, however, particularly on the Medium D and some derivatives. The department worked on other designs and prototypes, including a Light Infantry Tank and a Tropical Tank.

Although Johnson was a brilliant and inventive engineer, his designs were not always practical or user-friendly. It was said of the Medium D that Johnson was the only person who could drive it properly. And the Royal Tank Corps for which his designs was intended were not impressed with a series of prototypes that were in workshops more often than they were on the road.

As a result of this ineffectual output and Treasury stringency Johnson's department was shut down in March 1923. It was not for another eight years that a design section specifically dedicated to tanks was re-established, eight years in which Britain frittered away what was and could have remained a substantial lead over any other tank designers in the world.

In 1920 a Grade II Directorate was established under the Director of Artillery with general responsibility for mechanization of the British Army (CAB 102/849). In 1927 this became the Directorate of Mechanization, and a Mechanical Warfare Board was set up whose role was to advise the Master General of Ordnance on the technical development of all types of mechanical vehicle. This covered not only tanks, but also a wide range of other vehicles.

In 1931 a design section dealing with tanks was established at Woolwich Arsenal in the Department of the Superintendent of Design whose department was accountable to both the Director of Artillery and the Director of Mechanization. This shared accountability was reinforced by the fact that all the design sections (guns, ammunition, small arms, tanks and wheeled vehicles) were gathered together in one building. Maj G. Macleod Ross, appointed to the tank section in 1933, recorded that:

> This proximity was a stroke of genius, enhanced by the fact that personnel came from all three services and the Royal Marines. This melding of all those responsible for a variety of weapons proved of inestimable value whenever an unusual requirement arose. A discussion with officers of other sections often provided a solution. For example, when the standard of tank armour rose to 80 mm, the turret of the tank became too heavy to rotate manually, much less to lay on target. Reference to Capt Kerrison's work at the Naval Ordnance Laboratory on anti-aircraft directors for following aerial targets resulted in his experience providing us with hydraulic traversing gear manufactured by Power Mountings Ltd.

The process of design and prototyping as described by Macleod Ross in the mid-1930s went as follows. Once a broad specification had been drawn up the Tank Design Section asked the Mechanization Board to provide information and dimensions on items such as the engine, engine cooling and transmission. This information was obtained by the Mechanization Board from the appropriate experts. The Tank Design Section produced a line drawing to instruct the pattern makers, who then produced a plywood and timber mock-up. This reproduced the tank in such a way that its ergonomics and suitability for fighting could be evaluated at full scale and in three dimensions, rather than through the medium of a set of drawings. The mock-up was shown to the Tank Gunnery School, Tank School instructors, and any other interested War Office branches. While this was happening the tank's engine was being modified to fit the hull design. When the mock-up was approved, a request was made to the Treasury for funds to proceed to the next step.

The next step, once the funds had been approved, was for the Tank Design Section to prepare detailed drawings of the hull assembly. These were used by the Woolwich Arsenal Royal Carriage Factory to make two identical mild-steel pilots.

The pilot hulls were assembled to all the automotive components, and the turret with its main gun. The pilots were driven to Farnborough for automotive tests and to Lulworth for gunnery tests. Faults were corrected and then application made to the Treasury for funds to manufacture production models. Manufacture would normally be put in the hands of a sub-contracted industrial firm.

Up to 1937 there were only two establishments with the competence to build complete tanks to the required standards of quality. These were the Woolwich Arsenal Royal Carriage Factory and Vickers, operating in particular at its Carden-Loyd subsidiary at Chertsey. The Tank Design Section were responsible for monitoring the processes of manufacture, as well as for supplying the designs.

The facilities and resources controlled by the Superintendent of Design were shared by the Director of Artillery and the Director of Mechanization, the latter through the intermediary of the Mechanization Board (a renaming of the Mechanical Warfare Board on 31 May 1934) and its chairman. The chairman, evidently in order to expand his empire, set in train steps to separate the tank design functions from the other design functions administered by the Superintendent of Design.

As a result of various complaints and manoeuvrings during the second half of 1934 a Committee was appointed to examine the administration and work of the Design Department at Woolwich as a whole (WO 32/3660). The members of the Committee were Col A.E. Davidson, President of the Institution of Mechanical Engineers, Mr W.A. Stanier, Chief Mechanical Engineer of the London, Midland & Scottish Railway, and Mr F.W. Hawkesworth of the Great Western Railway.

The purpose of the committee's investigation was not divulged at the time (January and February 1935) but became apparent in March 1935 when the Tank Design Section was allowed to read the terms of reference of the investigating Committee. One paragraph stated: 'The ideal organization which the Director of Mechanization would like to see would be one in which he had under his direct control – probably under the Mechanization Board – a Development Branch coordinating applied research, design and development. This would enable him to keep in the closest contact with it, and not via other directorates and branches. The Superintendent of Design controls the allocation of all draftsmen, and there is no guarantee that the sections in which the Director of Mechanization is concerned are always employed on designs for which the Director is waiting.'

The report of the committee called for a second Deputy Superintendent of Design to take charge of the design of tanks and wheeled vehicles, and to report directly to the Chairman of the Mechanization Board. This was the first step in cutting adrift the design of guns from tanks, a divorce of gun from tank that was to disarm the British tank for the next ten years. It laid the ground for continued undergunning of tanks, long after the Director of Artillery had developed first the six-pounder tank and anti-tank gun and later the seventeen-pounder.

This separation was most unhelpful, especially in the long run. In the short run something just as serious was the shortage of draftsmen. During the period from 7 September 1936 to 10 September 1937 the progress of design of the A12E1 (Matilda II) was slower than had been anticipated due to the difficulty of obtaining draftsmen and designers. This design was being done at the Vulcan Foundry; from November 1936 to May 1937 Vulcan employed only two draftsmen on the Matilda II.

It was at this time that the British rearmament programme was beginning to take its first feeble steps towards providing effective weapons for their armoured forces. The number of draftsmen allocated to Matilda II was one indication of how apathetically the programme was being undertaken. Another most unfortunate circumstance in the progressing of tank design was the loss of some of the best tank designers employed by civilian firms, namely F.R. Smith, who died in 1930; Sir George Buchan, who died in 1928; and Sir John Carden, who was killed in 1935.

The loss of John Carden was the most serious of the three. His obituary, published in *The Times* on 12 December 1935, two days after his death in a plane crash, records:

> The death of Sir John Carden is a heavy blow to mechanization in the British Army, and it comes at a particularly unfortunate time. For a number of years past the progress of tank design in this country has largely depended on the mechanical genius of Sir John. Apart from his efforts, results have been disappointing. Thus one may measure the loss that his death entails at a time when the modernization of the Army and its re-equipment is about to be undertaken on a proper scale.

There was some talk of sabotage, because his plane was returning from Belgium where he had been investigating a German fifth-column supposedly undermining the reliability of Belgian Army equipment. And a previous attempt on his life had been made by loosening the brakes of his car.

As well as the loss of civilian designers, the Tank Design Section at Woolwich working for the Director of Mechanization also lost two of its senior designers in 1937. Campbell Clarke, the Deputy Superintendent of Design was appointed as Director of Artillery. He subsequently fulfilled this role brilliantly, but many thought that as Director of Mechanization he could have made an even greater contribution to Britain's preparedness for war. Also, in 1937 Macleod Ross, who had been Assistant and then Deputy Superintendent of Design, left after failing to gain the confidence of two directors of mechanization.

The loss of senior designers was very significant and unfortunate, but the lack of design staff and draftsmen to implement their designs was equally significant. Some of the reasons for this shortfall are described:

> The design and development facilities at the disposal of the Mechanization Board were totally inadequate. Neither lack of financial inducements nor the system of military rotation were responsible for the lack of staff. Many first class engineers had worked at Woolwich as civilian draftsmen, designers and research engineers.

Throughout the prewar period the technical training there was as good if not better than anywhere else in the country. It was the desire for useful work, as much as the need for bigger salaries and more consistent supervisors, which made so many members of the Woolwich staff leave it for work with private industry.

A measure of what could be achieved by a government designer is the regenerative steering system developed by Dr H.E.(Ted) Merritt, an outstanding design contribution of British tank technology in the prewar period. Work almost as important was carried out at Woolwich on armour. Had there been a persistent and coherent picture of what a tank had to be like, designers could have been motivated to remain and persevere with a challenging and valuable task.

Dr H.E. Merritt joined the Tank Design Section in 1937 from the engineering firm David Brown & Co. of Huddersfield, and immediately started on the regenerative steering system mentioned above. After a short while he became concerned with the organizational failings of the Mechanization Board and its subordinate departments, as well as with the activities of its senior officers. In early 1939 he wrote: 'My military boss sits on the windowsill all day and only appears in the forefront when there is a War Office demonstration in the offing. Then he claims the credit for anything creditable.'

Ted Merritt's disillusionment resulted in his handing in his resignation in May 1939. This caused great consternation, and the Director General of Munitions Production, Rear Adm Harold Brown, asked to see him. After an interview Brown asked Merritt for a written report, part of which read:

> The latest example of tank design: the Deputy Superintendent of Design designed a tank one Saturday afternoon, took it to the Director of Mechanization on Monday and on Tuesday the latter decided to go straight to production. The Director said it would revolutionize tank design and immediately ordered 500 Meadows 300hp engines, after refusing for three years to embark on a new engine.

Merritt did not resign immediately, but by November 1940 he was back with David Brown, his transmission patented and 600 being built for the A22 (Churchill).

Macleod Ross commented on the continuing departure of people experienced in tank design from the place they were really needed:

> The jettisoning of these experienced officers resulted in more than waste of their accumulated experience. It ensured a loss of continuity of thought and purpose, so that their successors, in their ignorance, repeated mistakes and embarked on ideas many of which had been explored, reconciled or discarded years before. Rediscovery became the order of the day, with its attendant waste of time and energy; doubts dispelled some years before were resurrected – as for example the fire hazard of petrol versus diesel – all at a time when production was crying out for a set of finalized drawings on which to manufacture a tank.

DESIGN UNDER THE MINISTRY OF SUPPLY, 1939

The Ministry of Supply was set up in the summer of 1939 with Dr Leslie Burgin as its head. The principal reason for doing this was to relieve the War Office and the Secretary of State for War, Leslie Hore-Belisha, of the very large responsibility for provisioning the Army and to a lesser degree the other services. It was anticipated that the appointment of experienced businessmen to senior positions in the new ministry would result in a supply system exhibiting greater drive, efficiency and promptitude.

The design and production of tanks became the responsibility of the Director General of Tanks and Transport (DGTT), Sir Peter Bennett. The Mechanization Board continued for the time being, and had responsibility for the new Department of Tank Design (DTD). There was thus a gap between the users (War Office General Staff) and the designers and producers, the gap being formalized by the Ministry of Supply and the War Office reporting along separate chains to the cabinet.

At this stage there were separations of varying degrees of organizational severity between user and designer, gun designer and tank designer, and designer and manufacturer.

These organizational separations could have been remedied to some degree by effective communication and understanding – beside reasonable personal rapport – between the parties. The evidence shows that in general these remedies were not applied.

Early in 1940 tank design capability in Britain consisted of the Department of Tank Design and the design department at Vickers. Vickers had a strong and independent tank design department, and long experience of heavy engineering in the field of armaments generally. The vehicles it designed were to meet a War Office requirement or specification, but the War Office had no control over the execution of that specification. Most importantly, the firm's designs were intended for production in its own factories and therefore the designs were influenced by the need for efficient and economic manufacture – a normal business practice in any engineering organization.

Over the period 1936–40 other engineering firms acquired skills in the design and construction of tanks, albeit slowly. Vulcan Foundry worked on Matilda II; Nuffield Mechanisation and Aero, specially set up for designing and producing tanks, developed Cruiser Tanks Mk III, Mk IV and Mk VI; Vauxhall developed the A22 (Churchill), using work done by Harland and Wolff and the Department of Tank Design. Other work was done by the London Midland & Scottish Railway Company, Leyland Motors and the Birmingham Railway Carriage and Wagon Company.

Not everyone was happy with the situation immediately prior to Dunkirk, however. There was a small group of Members of the House of Commons who were determined to do their best to ensure that British forces had appropriate weapons with which to fight. They felt that they were having to fight against not only bureaucratic mismanagement at the War Office and in the Ministry of Supply, but against opposition within parliament and in the committees and boards that proliferated at the beginning of the war with a speed similar to that of bacterial growth. Two MPs who fought strongly and continuously for better fighting equipment were Mr Richard Stokes and Mr S.S. Hammersley. Hammersley wrote to the Minister of Supply, Herbert Morrison, on 14 May 1940:

> The War Office have now no say in the Mechanization Board (after its transfer to the Ministry of Supply). The Ministry of Supply have to appeal for all their information on tank design and construction to a body that is inadequately equipped in experience and personnel to design a tank suitable for warfare in France. The Mechanization Board therefore is in a position to stonewall everybody. That is what it has done. That is why we have no suitable tanks.

ACTION AFTER THE FALL OF FRANCE, MAY–JUNE 1940

When France fell the British Army left France through Dunkirk, Cherbourg and any other port it could use. The British Army escaped but effectively all its equipment was left behind. This meant that a massive programme of re-equipment had to be put in train. To deal with the current shortage of tanks and the need to develop progressively more powerful tanks, the government set up the Tank Board in May 1940. The functions, activities and vicissitudes of this body will be discussed in more detail in a later section, but its basic function was to canalize knowledge and experience in the provision of tanks to ensure that the armoured forces had weapons to meet current and future perceived threats.

Changes immediately after Dunkirk were intended to increase tank production; collaboration in design between the Mechanization Board and the firms designing tanks was not envisaged in the new arrangement.

The Ministry of Supply was responsible for transmitting specifications to the industrial firms mentioned above, who would then prepare designs for subsequent manufacture. The Department of Tank Design (DTD) was a department for modification of design rather than for design itself. New projects were given to the various firms, and DTD rectified the faults in current production vehicles. This arrangement was formally laid down in January 1941 and subsequent alterations in organizational titles and responsibility did not alter it. Design was in effect split into two groups, one supervising commercial design groups and the other correcting faults in the tanks produced by those commercial designers.

This was a gross misuse of tank design resources. In the urgent days of autumn 1940, however, production was the only thing that mattered to the government. They had to take a decision on this matter, and they did. And it was found possible to use DTD's resources to good developmental purposes; in the early stages of the design of the Churchill tank, a number of engineers were seconded from Woolwich to Vauxhall Motors, the Churchill's 'parent'. They were able to provide the specialist knowledge on tank design which is obviously different to that needed for the manufacture of a family car.

The policy of the Ministry of Supply remained the same in respect of tank design for at least the period from late 1940 to late 1942. That is, design of new tanks should be done by those who were going to produce, and the DTD would merely correct faults in the products. The industrial firms producing tanks, however, felt quite rightly they could design more efficiently and economically if they could take part in the discussions on the specification for a new tank. In September 1942 they approached the Ministry of Supply with a request for industrial representatives to attend the meetings of the Tank Board. The Minister denied this request.

The request seems reasonable and the denial obstructive. It is difficult to see that security could be involved, because the firm subsequently designing and manufacturing to meet a specification will have far more detailed knowledge about the configuration and capability of the tank than anyone else. It is also certain that much subsequent interactive questioning would be eliminated, and many good ideas would be put forward by the industrial firms which could enhance the end product and provide savings in both time and cost.

In his letter conveying his denial to the industrial firms the Minister of Supply also made clear his policy, as at September 1942, in respect of tank design:

> It is the definite policy of this Ministry to use to the maximum extent possible the design facilities available in the various industrial establishments engaged on tank work. The Department of Tank Design's role will be confined as far as possible to that of consultant, and as a source from which manufacturers can obtain advice and general information based on broad experience.

The Department of Tank Design was growing steadily in 1942, and was acquiring by experience an ever more commanding role in tank development. The armament of the tank was becoming the chief factor in design – as indeed it should have been. All tank guns were designed under the authority of the Director of Artillery (except some of those produced by Vickers), and this led to a greater control by the Ministry of the design of the tank turret and superstructure.

Turretry, armour, stowage and many other factors of design became a matter of expertise transcending that available to an industrial firm. This expertise, in the period from late 1942 to the end of the war, resided very largely in the Department of Tank Design. Part of the DTD's strength stemmed from its having incorporated many senior officers from industrial firms on to its staff. Just as in earlier days the Mechanization Board had lent staff to design firms, so the reverse process strengthened the DTD.

The strength was magnificently demonstrated in the design and production of the Centurion tank. In July and August 1943 the DTD was authorized to start the development of a heavy cruiser tank under the designation of A41. Design was carried out and the first mock-up was viewed in May 1944. After approval twenty pilot models were ordered, and manufacture of these pilots was split between the Royal Ordnance Factory Woolwich and the Royal Ordnance Factory Nottingham.

The first six pilots produced were sent to Germany in May 1945, a week after the war ended. Between 1945 and 1962 more than 4,400 Centurions were built for the home and export market, and it served with distinction and the great approval of those who fought in it. Even in 1990 large numbers remained in service with Denmark, Israel, Jordan, South Africa, Sweden and Switzerland. One-third of the Centurions produced came from Vickers' Elswick works and the remainder from the Royal Ordnance factories. In the end then, it was from Government resources of design and production that Britain's only good tank of the Second World War came. The tragedy for the tank crews was that those resources were marshalled too late.

The history of the design of British tanks from 1919 to 1945 is indeed a sad tale. It shows that the skills and resources were there, but they were harnessed and managed extremely ineptly.

RESPONSIBILITY FOR TANK PRODUCTION, 1933–45

The overall responsibility for tank production included the responsibility for tank design described in the previous section, and there is therefore some overlap between this section and that.

To make it clearer what departments were involved in supplying tanks to the armoured units, the organization chart for the Army Council (as it was in 1933) is shown in Figure 6.1. The two members of the Army Council principally concerned with tank production were the Chief of the Imperial General Staff (CIGS) and the Master General of Ordnance (MGO). Their main responsibilities in respect of the provision of tanks (which were only a small part of their overall tasks) are described below.

CIGS

The Department of the Chief of the Imperial General Staff was responsible for stating the users' requirements. Figure 6.1 shows that the CIGS had three main directorates responsible for carrying out the duties of the General Staff. These were: The Director of Operations and Intelligence (DOI), the Director of Staff Duties (DSD) and the Director of Military Training (DMT). In respect of provisioning the Army with its requirements these three directorates had the following tasks.

Operations and Intelligence forecast the type of warfare for which provision should be made, and provided evidence of the anticipated opposition; Staff Duties prepared functional specifications for the weapons themselves and stated the quantities needed to satisfy the proposed establishment of the particular section of the Army; Military Training was responsible for training the troops in the technicalities of the weapons and in the tactical doctrine of their employment.

MGO

The first of the departments accountable to the MGO was headed by the Director of Artillery who was responsible for the design and provision of artillery weapons to the Army. There were some overlaps or shady areas in respect of the extent of his responsibilities, and the design and provision of infantry weapons was transferred to him only in 1934. There was a continuing problem in respect of tank and anti-tank guns. The Director of Artillery provided the guns, but for the tanks someone else provided the mounting. The demarcation between the task of providing the gun and the task of mounting it caused many problems during the course of the Second World War.

FIGURE 6.1 THE ARMY COUNCIL 1933

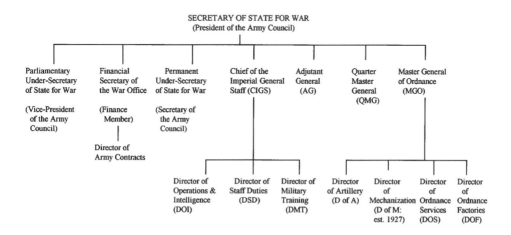

The second Directorate under the MGO was that of Mechanization, a position which had been created in 1927. Up to that time a second Director of Artillery had carried responsibility for tanks and transport, and organizationally the Director of Mechanization was the junior partner. After 1927 the Director of Mechanization was responsible to the MGO for tanks and transport, and in 1934 he took over the additional responsibility for engineer and signal equipment.

The Director of Ordnance Services was responsible for the supply of 'general' stores. He was concerned with storage, distribution and repair. He operated through the Royal Army Ordnance Corps (RAOC) and employed a large number of civilian workers as well as soldiers. He was responsible for the ordnance workshops and depots in which all the operations of repair, inspection and storage were carried out. His departments thus had a significant effect on the continued ability of weapons to discharge their required functions.

The Director of Ordnance Factories was the person responsible for production of specified classes of weaponry. The Royal Ordnance factories can trace their existence back to the seventeenth century; in the mid-1930s they employed some 8,000 people, and continued to fulfil the role of providing artillery and equipment to the services which they had done for so many years.

Up to about 1935 the requirements for the Army were not large. Financial stringency meant not only small forces, but also small quantities of weapons being issued to them. When rearmament started in the mid-1930s it became clear that the Department of the Master General of Ordnance was ill staffed to undertake a substantial production programme. The production required would have to be undertaken by civilian industrial firms, and those firms would have to be monitored effectively by someone acting for the user. Of the four directorates reporting to the MGO the Directors of Artillery & Mechanization were serving soldiers, the Director of Ordnance Services was not greatly concerned with production matters and the Director of Ordnance Factories had his hands full with his own production.

The person who appeared to have the right title to deal with production by firms external to the Army was the Director of Army Contracts. His position is shown in Figure 6.1 as reporting to the Financial Secretary of the War Office. Thus he was in a different organizational chain to that of either the CIGS or the MGO.

The Director of Army Contracts was placed under the finance member, not only because it was felt that contracts should be under immediate ministerial control, but so that the Director of Army Contracts might be beyond any suspicion of being in collusion with the supply branches. War Office doctrine in this respect was re-endorsed in February 1936. It was felt that a department that required production urgently would not be concerned about the prices that they would pay. Thus the Director of Army Contracts maintained his complete independence from both the user and the supplier of weaponry. While it was true that the Director of Army Contracts was a person adept in contractual negotiations and conditions, he had little knowledge of the technicalities of the weapons that were required. It would thus be difficult for him or his staff to make informed decisions about the technical suitability of manufacturers with whom they were going to place contracts.

Various proposals were put forward to solve the problem of obtaining production of military hardware in a way which was both effective and free from possibilities of collusion. A solution was proposed by Lord Weir, who had been asked by the government to investigate and prepare a report on the whole field of armament production. This included naval and air armament production as well as military, but it was upon the problems of the War Office that he concentrated. He pointed out that the Army's problems were particularly severe. The Admiralty had already convened their own body of professional contractors. The Air Ministry had already made (in 1936) a successful beginning in adapting their organization to the new conditions. Lord Weir considered that the Army was facing a task the magnitude of which it had not had to deal with in the last eighteen years. His main recommendation in a report submitted in January 1936 was as follows:

That there must come into existence at the War Office a munitions supply department covering every phase of supply. This department can not only buy something which someone makes and desires to sell under normal commercial procedures, but has sufficient technical production, inspectional, commercial and financial experience to enter into the contracts that are necessary. There may be as many as 100 firms which will be required to create new facilities and adapt existing facilities to enable them to supply highly technical products of which they may have had no previous experience. In addition, this munitions supply department must make the fullest use of the professional sources of supply and be responsible for the Royal Ordnance factories and their expansion. Somehow the War Office will have to rearrange its internal structure so that it will have a munitions supply department with a head responsible to the Secretary of State for War for carrying out this programme of munitions supply.

Lord Weir's report was considered by the Committee of Imperial Defence and in June of 1936 the position of Director General of Munitions (DGM) was created. The first head of this department was engineer Vice Adm Sir Harold Brown who had been engineer in chief of the Royal Navy. Two new directorates were formed to work under him. The first was called the Directorate of Industrial Planning, which combined the planning duties previously performed by the directorates of Army Contracts and Ordnance Factories. The second was a Directorate of Progress which relieved the Director of Army Contracts of the responsibility of watching the progress of munitions contracts, and also reviewed designs from the production point of view.

An attempt was made to define the responsibilities of the various departments concerned with munitions production. The CIGS remained the representative of the user, describing in functional terms the weaponry required to meet the user's role. This functional requirement was translated into a detailed specification for manufacture by the Master General of Ordnance. The development of the specification could include research, design, and production and evaluation of prototypes. The end result of the MGO's work was to place a clearly specified demand on the Director General of Munitions (DGM).

The DGM was then responsible for satisfying the demand. This could be done either by the Royal Ordnance factories or by industrial firms under contract. The two directorates of Industrial Planning and Progress provided the detailed management functions of planning and monitoring. The MGO's next responsibility was to inspect the finished product which had been manufactured under the authority of the DGM.

The DGM also had the power to expedite production once a specified demand had been made. However, he had no authority – or responsibility – to deal with delays before the demand was made. Thus the provision of weaponry could be delayed by the user not being able to make up his mind what he wanted, the designer having difficulty in drawing up a design suitable for the user's needs and the facilities for production, or manufacturing delays, including sourcing factory capacity, shortage of labour, shortage of machine tools and other specialist equipment, and shortage of material.

During the period from mid-1936 to the end of 1937 there developed a move for the transfer of responsibility for industrial production more and more from the purely military arm (the MGO) to the Director General of Munitions – retitled during this period as the Director General of Munitions Production, or DGMP.

A suitable moment for this to happen was on the retirement of the current MGO, Gen Sir Hugh Elles, in 1938. Sir Hugh was the last MGO, and on his retirement his department was transferred to the DGMP's directorate. The functions of the department remained unchanged, and its head was now called the Deputy Master General of Ordnance (DMGO) reporting to the DGMP.

During 1938, however, the centre of interest was shifting. The question was not what the War Office should do to put its supply organization on a full rearmament basis, but whether the War Office should handle the responsibility for supply at all. There was an increasing demand for the institution of a Ministry of Supply. Some of the arguments for and against a Ministry of Supply were put forward by Lord Weir. He said: 'Given powers of interference and control, the most valuable facilities – skilled labour and executive personnel – would become available to play an effective part in both production and organization. On the other hand interference in peace time would produce entirely novel difficulties and dangers gravely affecting the financial and economic stability of the country.'

This was the problem for the government: they wanted in some way to increase the output of military hardware, but at the same time without using up capacity that could be used for producing the goods that kept Britain prosperous. There was the problem of opposition from business people, who could see that they would be asked to make small runs of unusual things probably without much profit, and also from the unions who were likely to be opposed to the direction of their members into places of work that were not necessarily their own choice.

This debate about creating a Ministry of Supply continued until 1939, during which time there were many who thought that the creation of such a ministry was essential to ensure that rearmament proceeded at a reasonable pace. But the government decided that the best way to proceed was to obtain the cooperation of industry and labour. They felt that any form of compulsion, which was implied in the creation of a Ministry of Labour, would have negative rather than positive effects. After the Munich Crisis of September 1938 it was apparent that there were still enormous military deficiencies in terms of equipment; the question was again raised as to whether a Ministry of Supply with powers of compulsion should be created. The government's position on the subject was expressed by the Minister for the Coordination of Defence, Sir Thomas Inskip. He contended that neither the international nor the supply situation was serious enough to warrant the dislocations that imposing controls would entail. He pointed out that the real bottlenecks in production were the result of technical problems that compulsion could not affect and he noted that industry had cooperated fully up to that time. It was his opinion that compulsion would only be necessary when cooperation failed.

It is questionable whether in fact the cooperation had succeeded. The state of preparedness revealed at the Munich Crisis was such that no one could really believe that cooperation was achieving positive results.

In January 1939 Inskip started to reverse his position. He suggested that the deterioration of the international situation made war imminent, and that the government should begin to set up the organization which would allow munitions production to be placed on a war footing. It was clear that appeasement was a failure, and that it was only a matter of time before Germany went to war. It was also clear that Britain's plans for the mobilization of her resources on the outbreak of war were inadequate. He was told by Arthur Robinson, his adviser on supply questions, that if the nation had to go to war under the plans as they were then constituted, chaos would result.

In the light of this Inskip prepared a paper for the Committee of Imperial Defence recommending that a Ministry of Supply be set up. Inskip presented this paper to the cabinet and explained that he was doing so because he and the Committee of Imperial Defence had the feeling that the situation had changed so far for the worse since Munich that the decision then made no longer held good. He presented his paper and within a few days Prime Minister Chamberlain asked him to resign.

The fall of Prague on 15 March 1939 forced the government to confront the reality it had been trying so hard to deny. They first suggested that the elimination of Czechoslovakia had changed nothing, but the weight of public opinion made the government realize that such a position was no longer tenable. Reluctantly the government turned to serious preparation for war.

On 19 April 1939 a proposal was again put before the cabinet for the creation of a Ministry of Supply in peace-time. The ministry that was suggested would take over all Army supply and the procurement of the stores used in common by the three services. The Royal Navy and the Royal Air Force (RAF) would continue to be responsible for the purchase of their specialized equipment such as aircraft and ships stores.

The Ministry of Supply bill that the Cabinet finally authorized in May 1939 was the weakest version that was politically acceptable. The Ministry of Supply would take over all Army supply and the procurement of stores used in common by the three services. The Royal Navy and the RAF would continue to be responsible for the purchase of their specialized naval and air force equipment. Under the legislation the government would be able, in the event of war, to turn the ministry into a body encompassing all demands of all three services. The legislation also provided powers to compel contractors to submit to investigation on costings and binding arbitration on prices. However, it did not give any extra powers for dealing with the aircraft industry's observable profiteering.

There was strong feeling in the House of Commons that favoured the taking of much more sweeping powers to control both industry and labour, but the government resisted increased powers in order not to alienate either group. Despite the obvious failure of cooperation the government clung to it as the basis of the rearmament programme.

The organization of the Ministry of Supply included those departments which its creation was designed to incorporate, as for example the Directorate of Munitions Production and those departments in the Board of Trade responsible for raw materials.

With the outbreak of war on 3 September 1939 it became clear, as we have seen earlier, that the tank supply position was extremely grave. This required immediate attention, and by October 1939 the organization of the Ministry of Supply was increased by the creation of the Director General of Tanks and Transport.

The Controller of Mechanization Development was given the design hierarchy which had previously existed under the Director of Mechanization. There was no significant change to that hierarchy in its new organizational location.

As a result of the initial recommendations made in June 1940 by the Tank Board – whose creation and recommendations are discussed in the sections on the Tank Board and the Tank Parliament – further changes were made regarding the provision of tanks. The most important changes were the creation of a director whose sole responsibility was for tank production and another whose only responsibility was for tank design. As described in the previous section of this chapter, the Departmeny of Tank Design (DTD) was responsible only for assisting industrial firms in the design of tanks and for design modifications found to be necessary to achieve desired performance. It was not until 1943 that the DTD was given the opportunity to do the complete design of a tank, and it then produced the extremely successful A41 or Centurion.

From June 1940 to September 1942 various alterations were made to the organizational structure. By the end of that period, three years after the start of the war, many of the responsibilities for tank design and production had been brought together under one person accountable to the Minister of Supply (Figure 6.2). The holder of the position of Chairman, AFV Division, was Cdr E.R. Micklem, a retired naval officer who had held a senior position with Vickers until his appointment as CAFV. He was appointed Chairman of the Tank Board at the same time. The organization of the AFV Division changed little from this time until the end of the war. It appeared a satisfactory structure, but its output of competitively battleworthy tanks issued to tank units before May 1945 was very small. These were the Comets issued to the 29th Armoured Brigade in March 1945 and used by them until the end of the war in Europe.

The major criticism to be made of the organizational structure is that there was still a gap between the design of tank guns and the design of tanks in which to mount them. This gap could – and should – have been closed by the secondment of a team from the Directorate of Artillery to the AFV Division. Unfortunately, no such instruction was issued in time for it to do anything useful for tank units fighting in the battlefields.

THE TANK BOARD

When confronted with a problem the knee-jerk response of most government bodies is to form a committee. This may be given the alternative title of a 'board', and under rare circumstances that of a 'parliament'. The British government may well lay claim to being the founders of this method, and its purveyors to the rest of the world.

In the spring of 1940 a number of criticisms were directed at the Ministry of Supply, one of the main ones being the quality and quantity of tanks being delivered to Britain's armoured forces. The most persistent of the critics were Lord Lloyd, Sir Albert Stern, and two MPs: Mr S.S. Hammersley and Col Gretton. We have seen that the deficiencies in quantity and quality stemmed from actions preceding by many years the formation of the Ministry of Supply in August 1939; none the less, the Ministry of Supply was now responsible and action had to be taken now. In October 1939 the Director General of Tanks and Transport (DGTT) was responsible for the development and production of tanks, and had departments to deal with these two functions. Development of tank guns was the

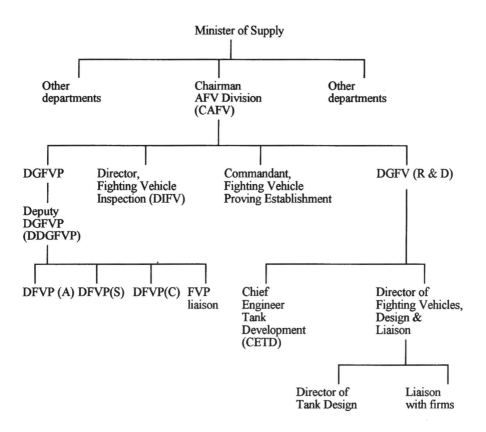

(Departments related to provision of tanks)

FIGURE 6.2: MINISTRY OF SUPPLY ORGANIZATIONAL STRUCTURE, SEPTEMBER 1942

responsibility of the Director of Artillery, now under the Director General of Munitions Production (DGMP), a separate division of the Ministry of Supply to that of the DGTT; but liaison between tank gun and tank development staff was obviously quite possible.

The two main types of action that can be taken to deal with such a problem as the deficiencies in quantity and quality of tanks are: either to make a single person accountable for the delivery of tanks of the required quantity and quality, to discuss with that person the resources needed to achieve the accountability, and to make those resources available; or to appoint a committee with responsibility for investigation and advice.

Naturally, it was the second type of action that was taken. On 29 May 1940 a Tank Board was appointed. The terms of reference agreed by the Minister of Supply and the Secretary of State for War make it plain that the board was regarded as a temporary, or at any rate an advisory body, somewhat like a Royal Commission. It was called upon 'to consider the whole situation regarding the production and design of tanks and to advise the Minister of Supply as to future action'. The members appointed on 29 May 1940 were the Chairman, Sir Alexander Roger of BSA, who had done the same job in the Ministry of Munitions in the First World War; Mr A.A.M. Durrant, a chief engineer of the London Passenger Transport Board; Mr J.H. Moyses, Managing Director of Birmingham Railway Carriage and Wagon Company, and Mr G.W. Thompson, Member of the General Council of the Trades Union Congress.

They conducted their initial enquiry with admirable speed, and reported on 7 June 1940:

- Army requirements should be confined to the minimum number of types in order to achieve standardization of design.
- The Army must state its demands unequivocally and through one focal point. The fundamentals of these demands should be expressed in terms of armament, production, performance and numbers.
- Control of the organization in the Ministry of Supply should be in the hands of civilians engaged in rapid commercial methods.
- Assuming that a civilian Director General remained in charge of both tanks and wheeled vehicles (the DGTT, then Mr Peter Bennett), a General Manager should be appointed to devote his entire time to the tank department, with subordinate civilians charged respectively with design and production responsibility.
- Tank construction should be simplified, and responsibility for complete assembly should be vested in the Ministry to avoid vehicles being issued without vital equipment.

Most of these changes were made to the organization and procedures of the Ministry of Supply. One change that might or might not have been intended was the replacement of Peter Bennett with Mr Geoffrey Burton. Maj Gen Campbell Clarke, the Director of Artillery, made the following comments on Peter Bennett when he was DGTT: 'My impression is that he is able, energetic and devoid of frills; but like many business executives of his type he feels he has to be careful in avoiding the toes of the military, who are hardly human. Possibly he has his reasons for maintaining this theory.'

When Peter Bennett had been replaced by Geoffrey Burton, Campbell Clarke wrote further on 9 August 1940: 'You saw no doubt the unexpected departure of Peter Bennett who, with less than no help from his Director of Mechanization (Maj Gen A.E. Davidson), had pulled round the production side extraordinarily well. His leaving was the result of a political intrigue arranged by a back-bencher MP and some business friends. The only gain was the retirement of the Director of Mechanization. Not only did Davidson go, but the appointment of Director of Mechanization was liquidated also.'

By July 1940 the structure under the DGTT was substantially changed. There remained a Director of Mechanization for wheeled vehicles, but responsibilities for tanks were divided between the Director of Tank Production and the Director of Tank Design.

To achieve the 'one focal point' for Army demands two senior Army officers with substantial experience in tank operations were appointed to the Tank Board. They were Maj Gen Vyvyan Pope, who had served in the retreat to Dunkirk and made pungent observations on the performance of tanks in that campaign, and Brig Douglas Pratt, who had commanded the 1st Army Tank Brigade (4th RTR and 7th RTR) during the same campaign.

With the addition of Geoffrey Burton and the two Army officers the Tank Board began to work in accordance with its terms of reference. Its performance was judged to be particularly ineffective until early October 1940, and this by one of its own members, Vyvyan Pope.

On 7 October Pope wrote to the Assistant Chief of the Imperial General Staff. He started by expressing his anxiety about the progress of the Tank Board. He then recorded the initial action taken by the Chairman and the three independent members, resulting in the report of 7 June. He went on:

> At its first full meeting on 24 June 1940 the Board was directed by the Minister of Supply.
>
> (a)   To examine the specification of the new A22 tank.
> (b)   To consider the views of Sir Albert Stern's committee.
> (c)   To consider any matters which might later be referred to it.
>
> Up to the present date the board has met eight times, namely:
>   Thrice in the last week of June (A22 specification)
>   Twice in July (Sir Albert Stern's Committee)
>   Twice in the first week of August (Sir Alexander Roger's departure)
>   Once in September (Tank gun deficiencies).
> The Chairman has gone on a mission to India and one of the non-departmental members has been employed under the Ministry of Supply and no longer attends meetings. The Board, therefore, has no Chairman or Deputy Chairman and consists of only two non-departmental members in addition to the departmental representatives.
> Since 19 July when the Board last met Sir Albert Stern's committee, the only matters referred to the Board have been:
>
> (a)   The question of whether Sir Alexander Roger could be spared to undertake a mission to India (by the Ministry of Supply).
> (b)   Shortages in tank gun and other connected equipment (by the War Office representatives).
>   I may add that the question of purchases in the USA was not referred to the Board and that no general information on tank production is circulated.
>   It appears that the Board is in grave danger of lapsing into impotence through inertia; it also appears that there are widely divergent views as to its proper functions.

On the one hand there is the view that it is required as a purely advisory body only which has no power of initiation and should consider only matters specifically laid before it.

On the other hand, there is the view expressed in your paper to the Secretary of State for War of 3 April 1940 which envisages an active coordinating body in a supervising capacity possessed of powers of initiation.

I strongly support the latter view and I feel that the present decline into relative ineptitude of the Board is deplorable and not in the interests of the country. Unless, however, vigorous and immediate measures are taken to strengthen and revitalize the Board, it would be preferable for it to be formally disbanded. At present it is in the invidious position of having been formed with a good deal of publicity and thereby securing for itself apparent responsibility for tank production, which it is practically powerless to influence in any direction.

Signed V.V. Pope, Director, Armoured Fighting Vehicles.

On 29 December 1940 the Minister of Supply, Sir Andrew Duncan, sent a cable to Sir Alexander Roger in India telling him that he had been superseded by Sir James Lithgow. On 14 December 1940 the War Office nominated Maj Gen G.N. Macready, the ACIGS, and Maj Gen Stewart, Inspector of the Royal Armoured Corps, as alternate members in place of Brig Pratt who had gone to the United States as part of a team to buy American tanks for the British Army. On 8 January 1941 the Tank Board had the following terms of reference and composition: To consider the design, development and production of Armoured Fighting Vehicles, including their armament and equipment, and to take decisions thereon in order to meet as expeditiously as possibly the requirements of the War Office; and to advise the Minister on such questions as he may refer to them.

In July 1941 Lord Beaverbrook was appointed Minister of Supply. As Minister of Aircraft Production his dominant energy had driven the aircraft industry to make aircraft of high quality in sufficient numbers to defend Britain and to strike back. It was hoped he could do the same for Army equipment. In respect of tank production one of his earlier actions was to appoint, on 26 July 1941, a new Tank Board, and on 6 August 1941 the Tank Board's terms of reference were revised, thus: To consider General Staff specifications, types and programmes of armoured fighting vehicles including their armament and to take decisions thereon. To receive design and production progress reports.

In February 1942 Lord Beaverbrook moved on to the Ministry of Production and Sir Andrew Duncan again became Minister of Supply. On 2 May 1942 the Tank Board was reconstituted under Lord Weir and its terms of reference were once again slightly modified, thus: The Tank Board will be responsible to the Minister of Supply for settlement of all major questions of policy in regard to development and production of tanks and armoured fighting vehicles and will give particular attention to the qualitative aspects of the tank programme, e.g. reliability, mobility, armour and armament.

On 29 June 1942 Mr W.A. Robotham of Rolls-Royce joined the Board, as well as Maj Gen E.V. Rowcroft, Director of Mechanical Engineering. The changing structures of the Ministry of Supply and the changing members and terms of reference of the Tank Board did not go unnoticed. The Select Committee on National Expenditure (SCNE) forwarded a report to the Prime Minister on 26 August 1942 (from which extracts have previously been quoted) in which they commented on the organization for the provision of tanks to the armoured forces (Cmd 6865 page 14).

> On the Ministry of Supply side, the past history of the organization affecting tanks – especially the nebulous and constantly changing Tank Board – reveals obvious weakness. In spite of recent changes, we feel that more should be done to reduce the multiplicity of committees and to advance in the direction of placing responsibility on individuals rather than on committees. The organization hitherto has not been on a self-contained functional basis, with the result that a large number of cross-connections has had to be kept up. The paramount need is to have some individual of independent mind and driving force filling the position of Chief Executive Officer for the production of tanks.

In a period of just over two years there had been four different chairmen, twenty-seven different members and at least four major changes in the terms of reference. This ensured that there would be no clarity of purpose, no continuity of thought, and no drive to achieve useable results.

In early September 1942, however, Cdr Micklem was appointed Chairman of the AFV Division of the Ministry of Supply (as we have seen in an earlier section), and was at the same time appointed fifth Chairman of the Tank Board. He was also given executive control over research and development, design, testing and supply of tanks. It was all three years too late, and as we have seen the output of all of this resource and time was some 200 Comets delivered in February 1945 as the only really battleworthy tanks provided in just under six years of war.

THE TANK PARLIAMENT

As a dedicated parliamentarian Winston Churchill was a champion of the process and powers of debate. When it was apparent in spring 1941 that Britain's armoured forces were still not as strong as they should be he decided to convene a 'Tank Parliament' to discuss the matter with those most competent to contribute to such a debate. This was in spite of the fact that existing bodies such as the cabinet, the Tank Board, the War Office and the Ministry of Supply were all equally competent to discuss the matter.

The 'Tank Parliament' held its initial meeting on 5 May 1941 at 10 Downing Street with Winston himself in the chair. Others present were: Lord Beaverbrook, Sir Andrew Duncan, Minister of Supply; Sir William Brown, Sir Harold Brown, Sir James Lithgow, then Chairman of the Tank Board but soon to be superseded by Mr Geoffrey Burton; Maj Gen Crawford of the Ministry of Supply; and David Margesson, Secretary of State for War. Those representing the War Office and the armoured forces were: Lt Gen Sir Robert Haining, VCIGS; Maj Gen Macready, ACIGS, Gen Sir Alan Brooke, then C-in-C Home

Forces; Lt Gen Giffard Martel, Commander Royal Armoured Corps; Maj Gen V.V. Pope, Director Armoured Fighting Vehicles; and Maj Gens Norrie, Crocker, Macready, Burrows and Hobart, commanding the 1st, 6th, 8th, 9th, and 11th Armoured Divisions respectively. The remaining participant was Churchill's Principal Scientific Adviser, Prof Frederick Lindemann. This formidable body was put in the picture by Churchill.

The Prime Minister said that he had wished to make a general examination of the present position and prospects of armoured formations, and for this reason had decided to set up a 'Tank Parliament', at which there could be free discussion and exchange of views.

It was necessary for them to consider not only 1941 and 1942, but also 1943. Reviewing the progress of events since the last war, and the experiences of the present day, when they had seen large armies paralysed by comparatively small forces of armoured fighting vehicles, it was evident that Britain's tank programme was a matter of the greatest importance. Last summer, when Britain had so little, it had been necessary, they were told, to concentrate on existing types; but at the same time the A22 (Churchill) had been designed, and this would be the staple article for late 1941, and possibly for 1942. They would have to do better than that for 1943. Looking at the broad strategy of the war, Churchill believed Britain might have to reckon with a break eastwards by the Germans, with the object of nullifying the blockade. This would cause a steady drain on their resources, and they should do their best to pulverize them by our air bombardment. This might not, however, be decisive, and they must therefore come back to consideration of what could be done on land. They had to look ahead to the utilization of the large resources of Britain and the United States of America, and fashion the means to win.

In a recent directive Churchill had set as the aim for 1942 the equivalent of fifteen armoured divisions. For 1943, they had to aim perhaps at twenty-five. People had spoken of creating a balanced Army, but if Britain could land really powerful forces of tanks at various places in the enemy's enormous coastline, it could reckon on the uprising populations to assist it. The ultimate programme had therefore to be examined, and with it had to go a programme for all the vessels which would be required for overseas operations. With this end in view, he wanted to discuss, at successive meetings, all aspects of armoured warfare with a view to framing decisions for the future.

The first topic discussed was the present tank programme. It was stated that the three principal factors affecting the production of reliable tanks were: insistence on speed, armour and obstacle-crossing performance. There was no mention of tank guns. The second topic was planning for the future, in relation to which the Commander RAC, Lt Gen Martel, stated that planning should take into account four things:

- We could not build too many tanks.
- We should now get our training establishments organized on a very large scale.
- We should make certain of having a repair and maintenance organization which could cope with large forces.
- We should get the cooperation between armoured forces and the RAF on a sound footing.

The final topic discussed in any detail was the organization of the armoured division, discussion of which resulted in no clear decision. Three more meetings of the Tank Parliament were held, two of which were in May and the last in June 1941. The topics of tank production, repairs and maintenance, and cooperation in various ways with the RAF were further pursued, and the topics of tank and anti-tank gun development and Anglo-American cooperation were introduced.

By this time Churchill seems to have realized that the idea of the Tank Parliament was a complete waste of time, and that the results from it would be platitudes and posturing.

At the end of the fourth meeting on 19 June 1941 Churchill said that he was content to leave matters as they were, and to review them again in the light of the reports on the recent operations in the Western Desert. He proposed to call another meeting to consider these reports when they were ready. There is no record of the Tank Parliament ever meeting again.

CHAPTER 7

Teaching Your Grandmother

Scene: 18 June 1944 Ste-Honorine-de-Ducy, Normandy
The half-track was covered with the fine white dust of the Normandy lanes, and the
replacement crews in the back were the same colour. It drove down the battered main
street of the village, turned into an orchard with the B Squadron sign on a tree by the
gateway, and stopped.

'Right, you lucky lads, this is your new home,' said the Corporal in the front. 'Jump
out and bring all your kit with you, and we'll see where the Sergeant-Major wants you
to go.'

The six replacements formed up in front of the sergeant-major.

'What have we got here, Corporal?'

'Two driver mechs, two gunner-ops, and two driver-ops, Sir. Here's the list.'

'Thanks, Corporal. Most urgent one is a gunner-op for 5 Able. Watters, where are
you?'

'Here, Sir.'

'Right, get your gear and the Corporal will take you to Mr Benskin. Their tanks are
over there, lined along the hedge.'

Charlie Watters and Cpl Wrightson walked over towards the 5 Troop Tanks.

'Whose Mr Benskin, Corp?'

'He's the Troop Leader. The squadron had a bit of a pasting four or five days ago, and
they've had to make changes all round, promote people and that sort of thing. You'll be
all right with Benskin, he's a decent sort of chap. That's him over there.'

The Corporal and Charlie walked up to Lt. Tim Benskin, halted and saluted.

'This is your replacement gunner, Sir, name of Watters. Just brought him up from the
Forward Delivery Squadron.'

'Thanks, Corporal, leave him with me and we'll get him settled in.'

'Sir.'

Tim Benskin turned to Charlie.

'You'll be Sgt Jackman's gunner, Watters. We'll go and meet him in just a moment,
but first I'd like to know what training and experience you've had. Where did you join?'

'56th Training Regiment, Sir, and trained as a gunner-op.'

'Get much gunnery practice – actually firing, I mean?'

'Gunnery camp at Warcop, Sir. Fired four rounds and two belts of Besa.'

'Stripped a 75mm?'

'No Sir, only a six-pounder.'

'Willing to learn?'

'Definitely, Sir.'

'That's good, because it sounds as though you've quite a bit to catch up on, and this troop is on standby for a counter-attack from first light tomorrow. But Sgt Jackman's had a lot of experience, and you'll be the first replacement in his crew. They'll look after you. Get your kit and we'll go over to meet him.'

It took Charlie Watters several weeks before he was a really effective member of his Cromwell. He had to learn how to fire and maintain its 75mm main armament, the operating drills used by the crew to maximize their fighting efficiency, and all the replenishment and housekeeping systems to keep the tank and its crew ready to fight at any time. He realized that in all of his previous training – nearly twelve months at 56th Training Regiment RAC and 43rd RTR – he had not learnt as much about being an operational tank soldier as he did in his first week with 5th RTR of 7th Armoured Division which he had joined at Ste Honorine.

Later on he asked other younger members of the troop what previous training they had had to prepare them for battle, and found that it had been much the same as his. It troubled Charlie to think that they were all so ill prepared. Another thing that troubled Charlie was the story told about the division's bloody nose at Villers Bocage on 13 June 1944, which caused the casualties and thus the need for him as one of the replacements. It seemed, although no one senior was willing to admit it, that the leadership at the higher levels had not been very good. And the divisional commander and the armoured brigade commander had both been sacked in the early days of August as a result of the Villers Bocage and other cock-ups.

Charlie Watters is an imaginary soldier – and if there is a real Charlie Watters out there, this wasn't him. But his situation is real enough, and 5th RTR was at Ste-Honorine-de-Ducy a few days after 7th Armoured Division received that substantial rebuff at Villers Bocage. During the next few weeks after that date Brig 'Loony' Hinde, commanding 22nd Armoured Brigade, Maj Gen George Erskine, commanding 7th Armoured Division, and Lt Gen G.C. Bucknall, commanding 30th Corps, were all relieved of their commands. It was not that their courage was in doubt, or that their ability to command at a certain level was in question; it was simply that they had been promoted to a level above their current competence, and to which they showed no aptitude to grow.

The story of Charlie Watters presents explicitly or implicitly the training that was needed to provide an effective, ferocious and fearsome fighting tank force. The training was needed in the categories of individual trade skills, collective skills, leadership and motivation to kill.

Trade skills included all those technical tasks needed to fight, supply and maintain tanks, their crews and their support echelons. Collective skills are needed so that people work together effectively. These skills are required at all levels of the military establishment, i.e. a tank crew, a troop, a squadron, a regiment and so on up. The skills are learned by formal training, by exercises and by battle experience; they are reinforced by leadership, laid-down procedures, feedback and discipline. Such systems and skills have been part of the success of good armies throughout history. Gen 'Black Bob' Craufurd's Light Division had such a system, instituted in 1809 in the Peninsular War. One of the division's chroniclers, Johnny Kincaid, recorded that:

'Seven minutes sufficed to get the whole division under arms in the middle of the night and fifteen to bring it in order of battle to its alarm posts, with the baggage loaded and assembled under escort in the rear. And this not upon a concerted signal or a trial, but at all times and certain.'

Leadership skills are needed at all levels of a military organization, and they have a substantial bearing on the learning and implementation of collective skills. It is at the higher levels of command, however, that skills of military leadership become so important. Irrespective of the competence of the sub-units of a military force, its effectiveness is almost completely determined by the skills of its commander.

The last main category is training in motivation to kill, with the complementary skill – if it can be called a skill – a preparedness to die. It is a paradox that the military force that is most prepared to die is least likely to do so. How to train people to adopt these attitudes is a most difficult problem.

Before considering what training was given, we need to note some factors that apply specifically to the training of armoured forces.

The time needed to acquire competencies can vary from a few weeks to many months. Some of the skills are quite simple to learn, and the period to acquire competence can be reduced greatly providing there is the opportunity for continuous practice. Other skills, particularly those for senior command, may take years to learn.

Military skills are normally learnt by full-time training, although it can be done part-time very effectively, as for example in a Territorial unit; but in time of war almost all the initial training is done by continuous attendance of trainees at establishments dedicated to training. These establishments must therefore be constructed in appropriate quantities, and then equipped with instructors, equipment and all logistical support.

Effective training demands extensive familiarization with, and use of, weapons the trainee will use in action. There must therefore be suitable areas in which this can be done, and there are three requirements of particular importance. Tank drivers and commanders must learn what are the outer limits of capability of their vehicles, and how best to take them over different types of ground. Gunners must have suitable ranges where the full potential of their weapons can be practised. There must also be areas where units of all sizes can manoeuvre as formations. Such areas should, as far as possible, simulate the terrain to be expected in battle; they should also be large enough to allow considerable variety in the exercises or manoeuvres undertaken.

TRAINING GIVEN TO TANK SOLDIERS

Training of armoured forces before 1939 was on a very small scale for two reasons: the number of tank soldiers was small, and the amount of reasonable equipment on which to train was minuscule. Some very useful training was carried out, however, particularly by commanders such as Percy Hobart in Egypt. The units that became part of the Western Desert Force and subsequently the 7th Armoured Division, had every reason to thank Hobart for the rigorous drills he had imposed on them.

In general terms, however, most armoured troops were very poorly trained when war broke out in 1939. The problems in implementing the required training programmes were exacerbated in the early stages of the war by: shortages of equipment and instructors, and the large number of people that had to be trained.

The equipment available for all users was small in quantity and largely obsolete when the war started in September 1939. What could be used for field units should obviously have been allocated to them, but that left obsolete vehicles or nothing for training. In many cases training was done with placards which announced 'I am a tank'; the movements over ground of the depressed individual holding such a placard were a poor way of simulating tactical movements, and definitely taught him nothing about driving.

The shortage of instructors had some similarities to the shortage of equipment. The tank training establishments, particularly at Bovington and Lulworth, were professional establishments staffed by professionals. But they were far too few to cope with the expansions planned just before the war and during its first few months; and in any event the process of mechanization of cavalry units was not complete, and territorial yeomanry units were substantially behind them. Finally, the numbers of people requiring training increased at an exponential rate.

A review of all training given to armoured forces would be a immense task, and it is not intended to do that here. We will instead pick out various points in time and look at the training that was being done and some of the factors affecting that training. One of the most useful sources for information on the training of armoured forces consists of the reports of the Directorate of the Royal Armoured Corps (DRAC), later the Directorate of Armoured Fighting Vehicles (DAFV). This report was prepared every six months and generally, but not always in the early years, included a report on training. The first DRAC report (PRO WO/165/89) covered the period September 1939–June 1940, and contained no mention of training; in view of the catastrophic events occurring at the end of the period this is not really surprising. The second report, DAFV No. 2 (PRO WO/165/89) covered the period from 1 May 1940 to 31 December 1940 and the major activity in relation to training was one of expansion. The training regiments were increased from seven to fourteen, and the Officer Cadet Training Units (OCTUs) for tank officers were increased from two to four. The training for tank soldiers was divided into three stages: general military training (foot and rifle drill, and basic infantry skills); operational training (tank crew skills of driving, gunnery and wireless); and operational crew training before joining a service unit.

Report No. 3 makes no mention of training, but in the fourth report (PRO WO 165/42), covering the period from 1 July 1941 to 31 December 1941, the effect of expansion was particularly apparent. Three actions were taken to increase the numbers of tank soldiers: seventeen infantry battalions were converted to tank regiments, becoming RAC regiments 141 to 157 inclusive; the 42nd Infantry Division was converted to the 42nd Armoured Division (from 15 September 1941 to 31 March 1942) and the Guards Armoured Division was formed from infantry battalions of the Brigade of Guards (from 28 July to 30 October 1941).

Training appropriate to their disciplines and rank was given to the following members of the seventeen converting battalions: senior officers, instructors, other regimental officers, technical adjutants, quartermasters, warrant officers, fitters, motor mechanics, electricians, quartermaster sergeants, technical quartermaster sergeants and tank crews.

The training was given at various establishments, which included the Royal Armoured Corps OCTU at Sandhurst, RAC Training Regiments, the AFV schools at Bovington and Lulworth, the RAC Tactical School, civil training centres (for technical tradesmen), and the RAOC Depot at Chilwell, and by attachment to field units. The duration of the courses or attachments varied between six and fourteen weeks.

This conversion programme was in itself a massive exercise, and was superimposed on the normal intakes to meet the demands of the remainder of the Royal Armoured Corps; it must be remembered that during this period there were substantial losses in tank crews in North Africa which had to be made good as soon as possible.

Various other methods of training were used over the complete duration of the war, in some cases building up from practically nothing, reaching a peak, and winding down towards the end of the war. These included the development of pamphlets, the production of films and courses given by civilian manufacturers such as CAV, Lucas, Ford Motors, Vauxhall Motors, Solex, Pye Radio, etc.

A further complication for training generally occurred in 1942, as recorded in reports nos 5 and 6. This was the need to implement the scheme 'Bolero', the clearing of Southern Command area for the arrival of American forces. The effect of this on recent

April 1942: a group of recruits outside their tented living quarters at the 56th Training Regiment, Catterick, Yorkshire: Back row: Bill Alp, Fred Benham and Chris Brixey; front row: Dennis Cook, Peter Beale and Bertie Cross.

One of the most important tasks for a tank crew was to make the most of the rations provided. A member of an 8th RTR tank troop cooks bully and eggs on a sand and petrol cooker, Western Desert, early 1942. (P.N. Veale)

Sometimes the acquisition of rations requires bargaining with local providers; members of 8th RTR bargain with the Bedouin, exchanging cigarettes for eggs in 1942. (P.N. Veale)

intakes at the 52nd Training Regiment at Bovington is described by one of the newly joined tank soldiers: 'For reasons known only to the military it was decided that large numbers of the 52nd TR should be moved in mid-March 1942 to the 56th TR at Catterick in Yorkshire. At least the train journey, including entraining and detraining, gave two days respite from the rigours of square bashing. By this time anyway the recruits had gained some toughness, just what was needed for military manoeuvres on the roads and moors of Yorkshire in winter.' This disruption was amplified by the training load caused by the introduction of Sherman and Cromwell tanks, but was ameliorated by more tanks and equipment generally being made available for training.

DRAC Report No. 7 (1 January 1943–30 June 1943) indicates that training programmes were operating smoothly, with only minor ripples. There was a shortage of 75mm guns for training, and a training programme for instructors in tank waterproofing was instituted. The waterproofing programme was well timed, in that tank units landing over the Normandy beaches waterproofed their tanks in April and May 1944. One person who had direct experience of the waterproofing programme was Sgt Bob Anderson of 9th RTR. He joined 12 Troop in early 1943 after his previous unit, 156th RAC, had been disbanded: 'Later in 1943 I was sent on a tank sealing course to Bovington. On completion of the course I did not rejoin the 9th but was detailed to supervise sealing tanks and other vehicles at Crawley where I stayed for the remainder of the year. I finally got back to the 9th in January 1944.' He was certainly of immense help in his squadron's waterproofing programme later in 1944.

In the period covered by Report No. 7 two new gunnery ranges were completed. These were at Kircudbright in South-West Scotland and at Warcop in Cumbria. The existing ranges were at Castlemartin and Minehead, as well as classification ranges at Lulworth and Hornsea. There were also thirteen less elaborate ranges under five area commands in Britain (north, east, south-east, south and Scotland).

DRAC Report No. 8 (1 July 1943–31 December 1943) records that the need to practice firing HE shell from the 75mm revealed that the ranges at Lulworth, Kircudbright and Warcop were too short for safe firing of 75mm HE. At Warcop it was possible to select firing points further back. At Kirkcudbright this was impossible, and a long-range annex was selected at Creetown some miles further west. At Lulworth, the report says: 'Fortunately, it was possible to obtain a larger area in the immediate vicinity; if this had not been possible the Gunnery School would have been forced to move, and that would have had major repercussions.' The acquisition of the larger area was not quite so fortunate for some, however. Patrick Wright, in his book *The Village that Died for England*, said that, 'Towards the end of 1943 it was decided to evacuate the Tyneham valley and also the sparsely settled heath that now forms the main long distance gunnery range. In all 225 people in 102 properties are reported to have been affected.'

Those people were reassured by Maj Gen Miller of Southern Command: 'The government appreciate that this is no small sacrifice which you are asked to make, but they are sure that you will give this further help towards winning the war with a good heart.'

A similar sort of problem was recorded in the same report in relation to collective training. 'Field formations were generally handicapped during this period by the need to concentrate a large proportion of effort on individual training, by the need to conserve

*Replenishment of ammunition was a vital part of tank routine in action. Sgt Harry Simmons of 10 Troop
9th RTR practises loading ammunition through the pannier door of his Churchill in 1943.* (IWM H32698)

operational tanks, and by the shortage of really suitable training areas. The last named
factor, always inevitable in this small and intensively farmed country, was further
aggravated by the needs of the US forces for training areas.'

By the middle of 1942, as we have seen, training systems were generally operating
very effectively, and problems were dealt with as they arose. The DRAC reports on
training become more and more routine, and in Report No. 10, for the period from
1 July 1944 to 31 December 1944 the topic of training for postwar RAC field units was
dealt with in detail. Report No. 10 did, however, draw attention to one weakness relating
to crew training. Crew training had to be completed for a tankman to be considered
capable of undertaking troop training or any higher training. During the war crew

An essential part of a tank crewman's training was learning to become part of his crew, his troop, and his squadron. The sense of comradeship is evident in this group from an RTR squadron in the Ardennes, January 1945. (Henk Bredevolt)

training was done either in a special brigade or in a special crew training regiment within the training organization. Report No. 10 considered that both of these had failed, and that it was essential for there to be continuity between the individual and crew training.

TRAINING FOR TANK OFFICERS

PRE-1939

In spite of becoming 'Royal' in 1923 the Tank Corps was the first choice of very few of those who had chosen the career of Army officer in the 1920s. One person who did want to join the tanks was Nigel Duncan, subsequently Maj Gen N.W. Duncan CB, CBE, DSO, a distinguished tank officer. He recorded his memories during an interview in 1978; he was asked about training at Sandhurst, and replied: 'Once you were turned out from Sandhurst you were nominally a platoon commander. What you actually came out as was a chap who knew his footdrill absolutely inside out, a rifle shot varying in standard – I was a marksman with the rifle and the Lewis gun. You had a smattering of military law, accounting and military history, which in actual fact was a complete waste of time.' The interviewer asked a question about tanks: 'Had what you've already referred to as the one-month wonder, the tank, attracted sufficient attention for the instructors at Sandhurst to make any mention of it?' 'Oh no, it wasn't even mentioned. And when I suggested joining a tank unit I was told not to be stupid. It was an extremely odd arm which had had a limited effect in France, and was unlikely to continue for long. I was to give up all idea of serving in anything so stupid, and in any case tank officers were not very nice people.'

Nigel Duncan progressed in the Army and in 1935 went to the Staff College. His 1978 interviewer asked him about the Staff College instructors' attitude to armour: 'Armour teaching was disgraceful at Staff College. The handling of armour was virtually ignored.' The students of 1935 were those who would have to command or employ armoured formations between 1939 and 1945. No wonder there were so few who could do it competently.

Two other groups of officers who would command tanks at various levels in the Second World War were those in the cavalry and those in the yeomanry. The experience and background of both groups taught them dash and unflinching courage, but not always the ability to deal intelligently with military problems on the battlefield. There was also a lack of enthusiasm for supplanting horses by tanks. Their state of training can perhaps be exemplified by the Yeomanry Colonel whose unit was being inspected by his divisional commander just prior to leaving England for the Middle East in the very early years of the Second World War: The General asked the Colonel whether everything was in order. 'Oh I think so, George,' replied the Colonel. The General pressed a little more firmly: ammunition? vehicles? other ranks' training? communications? The Colonel scratched his head and said: 'Dash it, George, I don't know about any of that – but we've got forty dozen of champagne, well crated, and the pack of foxhounds is in fine fettle.'

WARTIME TRAINING FOR TANK OFFICERS

The general method for training tank officers for most of the war consisted of these steps:

- Training as a tank soldier to acquire the basic tank crew skills.
- Evaluation for potential to be an officer; the evaluation was normally in two stages, first at the training regiment and then at a War Office Selection Board (WOSB).
- If recommended by the WOSB, 2–3 months training as a pre-cadet at a Pre-OCTU; if satisfactory at this stage, six months' training at an RAC OCTU, one of which was at the Royal Military Academy at Sandhurst.

A record of something of the flavour of Sandhurst in 1942–3 is given by an ex-cadet: 'Sandhurst in 1942 was a strange mixture of peace-time traditions and war-time necessities. The place where cadets could buy morning and afternoon tea, for example, was the Fancy Goods Store or FGS. Morning tea for many consisted of six grilled sausages and a pint of milk, soon burnt up by unremitting exercise. There was some classroom training, but most of the time was spent outside on such activities as square drill, cross-country map reading, route marches, obstacle courses, and physical training.'

It is interesting to note that no mention is made of commanding tanks or learning tank troop tactics in the field at Sandhurst. There was a small element of training in tanks, however, because an accident is well remembered. The tanks used for training were the notoriously unreliable Covenanters, with their equally unreliable turret hatch clip. Christopher Hibbert, subsequently the distinguished military historian, was travelling fast across country when the clip came unlatched, the hatch came forward, and Christopher suffered some rearrangement to his teeth.

When a tank officer reached his field unit he could reasonably expect some training in being a troop commander. Whether this happened depended to some degree on where the unit was – if there were any facilities or space for troop training – but much more importantly on whether there was a policy of training within the unit. This policy was generally a reflection of the training policy of higher formations in which the unit served.

Every biography of Montgomery stresses the major importance he attached to training at all levels. In his training exercises he would say before the exercise what was going to be learnt, carry out the exercise, and then ram home the lessons learnt and still to be learnt in a detailed post-exercise review. This approach to training was mildly ridiculed by some senior commanders, admired by others, but not followed by many. In the two years before D-Day many troop commanders would manoeuvre their tanks in the field for no more than days, certainly not weeks.

TRAINING TO KILL

It is a regrettable thing that being at war means killing other humans; but it is equally regrettable to bring troops into the front line who have not got, in Montgomery's phrase, 'the light of battle' in their eyes. It has been said that 'If you are not prepared to kill, but more importantly, if you are not prepared to die, you will not survive.' This is a very hard lesson to learn, and an even harder one to teach. But it has been proved over and over again in the course of history that a resolute group of soldiers, prepared if necessary to die, will almost always suffer much lower casualties than those who are less willing to defend themselves.

There is the story of the well-trained and magnificently disciplined group of 300 soldiers who were led by their commander against a group of several thousand enemy. The enemy commander was incredulous and contemptuous until, at the orders of their commander, one of the 300 threw himself over a cliff and another killed himself by falling on his sword. Astounded and amazed at such discipline the enemy commander at once yielded. The willing sacrifice of two undoubtedly saved the lives of many. It is, however, an extreme change from the customs of civilian life to the requirements of military urgency, and to guide recruits along that path of change is a major challenge to the military trainer. And yet it is a necessary change.

In the war against the French fought in Spain and Portugal by Wellington's forces between 1808 and 1814 many recruits came to the British units with no experience of war. They were immediately made aware of the realities of war.

'Do you see those men on the plain?' barked old Maj O'Hara of the Rifles to the latest batch of 'Johnny Newcomes' as they looked down from the rocky heights. 'Es, Zur.' 'Well, those are the French and our enemies. You must kill those fellows and not allow them to kill you. You must learn to do as those old birds do and get cover where you can. Recollect, recruits, you come here to kill and not be killed. Bear this in mind; if you don't kill the French, they'll kill you!'

Was any thought given to this aspect of military training in the Second World War? Certainly it was to those troops such as commandos and paratroops, and to a limited degree to the infantry forming part of standard infantry divisions. For armoured troops it is rather more difficult to generate combative attitudes. John Powell was a wireless operator in a Churchill tank unit that fought in Normandy. Before leaving England for France, and having been with his unit for just over a year, John had the following comments on the training he had had: 'Generally a very amiable and variable fourteen months of simulated battle training which honed our skills and general competence and made our troops, squadrons and the battalion as a whole into reasonably effective units. We didn't learn much about being "under fire", but we became passably good at managing our vehicles, navigating and communicating. And most of the gunners felt confident about hitting a half-way decently presented target.' John was wounded in the Normandy fighting, and he was a typically efficient and courageous soldier of that unit. His comments, however, use some interesting phrases such as 'amiable and variable simulated battle training', 'didn't learn much about being "under fire"', and 'passably good at managing our vehicles'. It sounds as though instilling aggression into its soldiers was not part of the training programme of that particular tank brigade. It is reasonable to assume that it was the same in many other tank units, as well as many other fighting formations.

This problem has been documented by Brig James Hargest of the New Zealand Army (PRO CAB106/1060). Hargest had a brilliant record in the First World War, and in the Second World War he commanded the 5th New Zealand Infantry Brigade in Greece, Crete and Libya. He was appointed as an observer to the British XXX Corps and served as such from 6 June to 10 July 1944 in Normandy. He was attached for much of that time to the 50th (Tees and Tyneside) Infantry Division, and was tragically killed on his farewell visit to it. His observations are thus those of a person with immense ability and experience in 'sharp end' soldiering. Hargest comments on many aspects of the Normandy fighting, and selections from his report illustrate the attitudes and morale of infantry and tank soldiers. The first quotation related to the 50th Infantry Division:

The men are tired after eighteen days of unrelieved strain (25 June). They are supposed to infiltrate the enemy's position – first by patrolling, then by moving on from one firm base to another. They achieve nothing – only sustain grave casualties. Their advances have no impetus. The moment the enemy spandaus or mortars open up the troops go to earth and stay there, lose men and morale. It's all wrong. Had we young officers of spirit and training to push these patrols we might achieve something. The soldier from Britain will accept losses without losing morale providing he sees some results – but this niggling is hard on him.

179

Speaking with other officers I come to these conclusions. The morale of the infantry officer and soldier is not high. This applies to new troops as well as to veterans. Officers are not keen on patrol work as an example. Even senior officers grumble about being too long in the line and have the opinion that they are being 'used'. Last week I saw the 15th Scottish (Infantry Division) in action (26 June). They began their battle on Monday and by the next Saturday they were relieved – used up. The troops have not that spirit essential to victory. It appears to me that the Higher Command will do well to rely on air, artillery and tanks. Our level of morale frightens me.

Any tank soldier who watched the infantry in action had the greatest sympathy for their wretchedly exposed task and the unflinching courage with which most of them carried it out. But Hargest was an infantry soldier, and he was observing what happened while it was happening. He also observed tank units in the early weeks of the Normandy invasion, and was not particularly impressed with them either. 'Our tanks are badly led and fought. Only our superior numbers and our magnificent artillery support keeps them in the field at all. They violate most of the elementary principles of war. They bunch up – they are the reverse of aggressive – they are not possessed of the will to attack the enemy. At the moment we suffer because of incompatibility and the lack of the will to fight in the armoured corps.' He gives two examples of this lack.

On 12 June I came across a whole squadron of tanks in a field supported by SP guns. They told me there was a Tiger tank in Verrière about 1,000 yd to the left front, and in reply to my query why they did not attack they said it was very powerful. On 17 June a tank of the 8th Armoured Brigade sat passively at a British roadblock while several German scout cars and an SP gun moved down a straight road. The tank did not fire although the target was a perfect one. Neither did it call on the tanks in its troop nearby for support. The infantry Brigade Commander sent down a message asking that the gun and cars be taken on. The reply was, 'If I do he will reply to my fire.' After a delay of twenty minutes and only after an infantry anti-tank gun had come into action beside it did the tank fire. Its third round got what looked like a direct hit on one vehicle – after a few shots it relapsed into silence and was only persuaded to fire again later.

This lack of aggression was observed by Hargest and others in many infantry and tank units. There were of course many brave soldiers or 'warriors' at all levels of units, but the overwhelming impression was that the German soldier had been trained to act with much greater aggression and hostility, and was much more prepared to die. Why were British soldiers not trained in the same way? It is extremely difficult to provide a definitive and researched answer to this question, but two points can be made. Except for those forces – commando and paratroops – who could expect fierce hand-to-hand combat as part of their role, it was not seen as particularly necessary to give lethal close-combat training to other units. This was particularly so for tank soldiers, because who could see the likelihood of being involved in an incident such as happened to Capt Cornaby of A Section, 3rd Carabiniers on 2 March 1945 just south west of Mandalay?

He had halted his tank to engage a party of Japanese, his guns were in action and the attention of the entire crew was focused on the action. Suddenly a Japanese officer broke out of the scrub and climbed on to the back of the tank. The Japanese officer used his sword to kill Cornaby, kicked his body down into the tank, and followed him down and killed the gunner. The loader, Tpr Jenkins, had just time to draw his pistol and fire all six chambers, the Japanese stabbing and slashing at the same time. Jenkins finally managed to use Cornaby's pistol to end the Japanese officer's life. The ability to defend oneself with ferocity at all times was taught in very few units, partly because it seemed an unlikely occurrence, and partly because of an unwillingness by the British government to encourage such training.

The second point to be made in relation to the lack of aggression demonstrated by many British troops is concerned with community attitudes. Realistic training to fight requires that soldiers be taught not only the necessary skills, e.g. with rifle, machine-gun, tank-gun, mortar, etc., but also the necessary attitudes of hostility, ferocity and desire to inflict injury or death – and that of willingness to die. The trainers who could instil such attitudes were unlikely to exhibit much gentleness or Christian restraint in their training programmes. It was also probable that there would be – and should be – danger in some of the training exercises. If the methods of such exercises could be observed by the public or communicated by the trainees, the reactions of a civilian and democratic population would very obviously be largely negative. Church leaders, journalists, MPs and indeed many average citizens might be horrified by teaching that was clearly unmoral, and which could lead to all kinds of subsequent psychological problems in those so taught.

To be realistic, as we have said, there must be some danger in training. The use of all weapons, even under the carefully controlled conditions of a firing range, is inherently risky. Anyone who has ever been in charge of a range practice with live grenades will acknowledge the extreme relief when a practice is over, providing there have been no accidents and no unexploded grenades to deal with. There are potential dangers in tank gunnery ranges also, as this extract from a tank unit history shows.

On a tank gunnery range there were mock targets of enemy soldiers (men), tanks (hornets) and anti-tank guns (ants). These were exposed at pre-arranged times during a gunnery practice, and the tanks engaged them as accurately as they could. From time to time firing was stopped, the targets checked for hits by the tank guns and repaired as necessary. The unfortunate people who had to manipulate the targets were called the butt-parties. It was a job that was lengthy, boring, and occasionally highly dangerous. There was a system of signalling which indicated when a tank could fire and when it absolutely could not. When the signals indicated 'no firing' then the butt-parties could emerge from their bunkers and go to the targets, check hits, and make repairs. Sometimes, however, signals were difficult to see, crews were careless or over-enthusiastic, commanders were flustered or distracted. As mentioned earlier, some of the simulated targets were cut-outs of men. One tank commander ordered his gunner: 'Men, 800 yd, fire.' But the gunner had

Chapel range, Castlemartin, West Wales; a Comet prepares to fire. The area is bleak and featureless, and looks out to sea.

Chapel range: the Comet 77mm fires at artificial targets down range. The commander observes the shot through the dust and smoke created by firing so that he can take corrective action.

Chapel range: a half squadron shoot, where two tank troops and a headquarters tank have moved progressively through a tactical action, moving to planned bounds and engaging targets as they are observed.

glimpsed something out of the corner of his eye, quickly traversed the turret and started to fire at the target. 'No, no, no,' screamed the commander, 'those aren't men.' 'Yes they are,' replied the gunner sturdily, 'they're running.'

The thesis of this section is that unless soldiers are trained to be aggressive, to take the battle to the enemy, and to be willing to die, they will suffer unnecessary casualties. It is a paradox for a soldier that the more you are prepared to put yourself at risk, the less likely you are to reap the consequences of that risk; the more you are prepared to die the less likely you are to die. Presumably German soldiers were trained to be aggressive and to take risks; whether given this training or not, many formations behaved as if they had been. A particular group of such German troops were the Waffen SS, and among these one division which fought with continuous resolution, tenacity, ferocity and courage was the 12th SS Panzer Division, *Hitler Jügend*. This division fought more or less continuously for ninety days in Normandy, and during that time was reduced from 10,000 to a few hundred men. But its reputation for fighting and fearlessness acted to protect it from much more rapid extinction, discouraging Allied forces from pressing home attacks against such a determined force.

Some British commanders did take steps to instil aggression into their troops by such methods as example, exhortation, training and various combinations of these. The commanders quoted below are all in charge of infantry or senior (infantry and armour) formations.

The first is Maj Gen Orde Wingate of the Chindits in Burma, speaking to all ranks of the 1st Cameronians (Scottish Rifles) in December 1943 not long before Operation Thursday, the second operation of the Chindits behind Japanese lines. He fixed one of the Cameronian soldiers with his eye and said in his peculiar rasping and intimidating voice, 'You're going to die.' He moved his gaze to another soldier. 'Many of you are going to die, or to suffer wounds, or near-starvation. All of you will meet hardship worse than anything you have ever imagined.'

The second is Maj Gen Bill Slim, recently promoted to the command of the 10th Indian Division in Iraq in spring 1941. He gathered all his officers together in a hangar at Habbaniyah and gave them his thoughts about war: 'We have already trained our men to the highest possible level of skill with their weapons and in the use of minor tactics. But in the end every important battle develops to a point where there is no real control by senior commanders. Each soldier feels himself to be alone. Discipline may have got him to the place where he is, and discipline may hold him there for a time. Cooperation with other men in the same situation can help him to move forward. Self-preservation will make him defend himself to the death, if there is no other way. But what makes him go on, alone, determined to break the will of the enemy opposite him, is morale. The dominant feeling of the battlefield is loneliness, and morale, only morale, individual morale as a foundation under training and discipline, will bring victory.'

The third commander fought in North Africa and Burma. Maj Gen Pete Rees led the 19th Indian Division in Burma very much by example, his preferred command position being with the forward infantry sections of his most forward battalion. John Masters was appointed divisional G-1 (the senior staff officer of the division) early in 1945, and at his first meeting with Maj Gen Rees recorded: 'His divisional pennant, a scarlet flag bearing the gold device of a hand thrusting a dagger, fluttered from the top of the radio mast of his jeep. The whole set-up would have been instantly recognizable at a mile on a foggy day. The enemy were about 200 yd away.'

The last example is Montgomery, and relates to his willingness to authorize very realistic training. In the instructions for Operation Lightfoot (the Battle of El Alamein, beginning on 23 October 1942), paragraph 32 says: 'There will be a great weight of artillery fire available for the break-in battle. During the training period prior to the battle infantry and other arms must be accustomed to advancing under the close protection of artillery fire and mortar fire.

We must have realism in our training and use live ammunition in our exercises with troops, even if this results in a few casualties. I will accept full responsibility for any casualties that may occur in this way.'

The four generals whose methods have been briefly described above were four of Britain's most successful. Perhaps their success was in substantial part due to their inculcation of fighting and aggressive spirit into the troops in their formations. It is equally certain that many formations that were not so successful could attribute their failures partly to a lack of fighting spirit. Tank troops in particular were given very little training or indoctrination in aggression. Many behaved with courage and a few were

Valentines training with Polish troops in the UK in 1943; the scene appears very cluttered, which it almost certainly was, because one of the major problems for formation training in the UK was lack of space. (Tank Museum 4752/D6)

naturally aggressive, but this lack of training made them unprepared for the realities of war, and caused many unnecessary casualties. The system of training must take the blame for these casualties.

TRAINING FOR HIGHER COMMAND

The effectiveness of a military formation is dependent to a very large degree on the way that it is handled. It is obviously possible for dedicated troops to achieve results in spite of inept leadership; British troops in various wars, of which the Boer War was a particularly good example, have been described as 'lions led by donkeys'. The lions sometimes gained the required military objectives in spite of the donkeys, but at terrible cost. How much better for an army and its soldiers if its leaders were able to command so that they gained their objectives but at the same time conserved their resources? In the Peninsular War an emotional sentry in an exposed position once greeted his C-in-C Wellington with the words, 'God bless your crooked nose; I would sooner see it than 10,000 men'; not conventional, but heartfelt. The development of a person to carry out a nominated task depends on selecting a person with appropriate potential, and then

15 Troop, Royal Armoured Corps Officer Cadet Training Unit, Sandhurst, October 1942. The six-month OCTU course taught cadets something about physical fitness and square drill, but not much about commanding a troop of tanks. Front row (sitting cross-legged on the ground): Christopher Hibbert, Peter Beale, Russell Brown and Dennis Cook.

providing training to convert that potential to competence. At lower levels of military command processes for selecting NCOs and junior officers can be – and were – implemented, evaluated and modified as necessary. The War Office Selection Board (WOSB) procedure became an effective selection process for officers during the Second World War, and its principles have been widely and effectively applied since.

The problem of selecting the right people for higher command is much more difficult for several reasons: the required qualities are harder to define, quantify and measure; the opportunities for validation are very much fewer; personal opinions and political pressures are likely to distort decision-making processes; and very often the promotion to higher command may have the effect of revealing unsuspected frailties or hidden talents. One of the principal ways by which senior commanders were appointed during the Second World War was by the nomination of the CIGS, Gen Sir Alan Brooke. He was responsible, taking into account the advice of his colleagues, for the selection of the commanders of Britain's field forces. His experience of command and his sound judgement of people ensured that most of his choices were good, but the task was not easy. The difficulties arose in part because so many potential leaders of higher formations had been killed in the First World War and there were not enough left of appropriate quality to fill all the positions. Once he had picked someone and that person had proved himself, Brooke left him free to operate in his own way. This meant that up to a certain point Brooke would not interfere, but when a situation appeared to require action he did not hesitate to take it. When Montgomery arrived in England on leave in June 1943 Brooke noted that: 'He requires a lot of educating to make him see the war as a whole outside the Eighth Army orbit. He wants guiding and watching continually and I do not think that Alexander [then Montgomery's immediate superior] is sufficiently strong with him.'

Appointments at the very senior level, i.e. those appointed by Brooke, were also subject to political factors, both national and international. Eisenhower's nomination as the commander of Operation Torch (the invasion of Tunisia) was due partly to compromise between the American and the British Chiefs of Staff, partly due to Eisenhower's undoubted ability to weld together an international team, but in no way due to his previous experience of higher command in battle – which was nil.

At a level below that of theatre and Army commander, selections and appointments were made in consultation between the Prime Minister and cabinet, the War Office represented by the CIGS, and the theatre or Army commanders themselves. As described above, Brooke was generally reluctant to countermand the selections made by the man on the spot. This could result in bad choices or good choices. Auchinleck made a number of bad choices such as Ritchie, Corbett, and Dorman-Smith; Montgomery made some good choices such as Leese and Horrocks.

Gen Sir Alan Cunningham, recently dismissed as commanding general of the Eighth Army in Egypt, takes the salute at a passing-out parade at the RAC OCTU Sandhurst, February 1943. Behind the General stands the spruce figure of Brig Errol Pryor-Palmer, commandant of the OCTU.

When a senior commander has been appointed he is likely to need training to help fill in the gaps in his experience and knowledge. It is likely that he will have had experience in command at levels below that to which he has just been promoted, and will also have had Staff College training in the handling and logistics of higher formations. But the training in direct command of his present formation and, in particular, the command of formations containing different types of division – how could that be done, and how was it done?

Obviously the most direct way of learning how to command higher formations is to command them in battle. Two problems with this are that mistakes result in unnecessary casualties, and it is not often that a commander gets feedback on his mistakes and how to correct them. After an unsuccessful battle a commander is likely to be very defensive and attribute perceived failures to circumstances outside his control. And after a successful battle the normal response is congratulation without comment – sometimes the congratulations are omitted as well. As one of the rare examples of congratulations and comment, Lt Gen Brian Horrocks commanded XIII Corps in the Battle of Alam Halfa from 30 August to 7 September 1942. Horrocks carried out Montgomery's instructions for the battle, which was a success for the Eight Army, and after it Horrocks felt that congratulations were in order. He was therefore slightly chagrined to receive a letter from Monty on 8 September containing: congratulations; a reminder that Horrocks was now a corps commander and not a divisional commander; and a listing of four or five things that he had done wrong mainly because he had interfered too much with the tasks of his subordinate commanders.

Montgomery commented on some of his other subordinate commanders during and after the Battle of El Alamein (23 October–4 November 1942).

Lt Gen Herbert Lumsden commanded X Corps in this battle, and on 26 October Monty noted in his diary: 'I have just discovered Lumsden has been fighting this battle without having his Corps Commander Royal Artillery (CCRA, responsible for all the artillery in the corps) with him. I have ordered the CCRA up at once. There is no doubt that these Royal Armoured Corps generals (Lumsden was a cavalryman) do not understand the cooperation of all arms in battle. I have had many examples of this since the battle started. Lumsden is not really a high-class soldier.' It seems unlikely that Montgomery was as constructive in his criticism to Lumsden as he was to Horrocks, because Lumsden was sent back to England in December 1942 and Horrocks took over X Corps.

Monty also had comments about other senior commanders during the battle of Alamein as his diary records for 27 October.

It is a sticky fight and artillery plays a great part of it. But the armoured divisionals' commanders do not know anything about artillery; they are used to having it decentralized by batteries; there is no Commander Royal Artillery (CRA) who understands how to handle a division's artillery; they have never been trained by their divisional commanders or the CCRAs. The commanders of armoured divisions are quite unfit to train anything in their divisions except the armour; they are therefore not really fit to command armoured divisions.

Officer training within a field unit; map-reading is a vital skill for all tank commanders, and some of that training can be done by indoor exercises, such as those shown here. (IWM H32705)

Another method of training senior commanders is by 'exercises' at the end of which the competence of the participants in their various roles is critiqued. An 'exercise' in this context is a simulation of a battle, including approach marches, in which the equivalent of between one and four divisions take part. Exercises were used by various commanders at different times, but the most effective exponent of the exercise as a training method was undoubtedly Montgomery. As commander of V Corps in 1940–41 he progressively developed the length and scope of the exercise to include the basic infantry divisions plus armour plus the RAF in a close-support role. The exercises were preceded by sand-table programmes to describe the lessons to be learnt, and were followed by a detailed critique by Monty in which he commended good performance and exposed weaknesses that needed to be corrected.

On 27 April 1941 Monty was transferred to the command of XII Corps which was stationed in the south-east corner of England, the main danger area for an invasion by the German Army. In June he carried out Exercise Binge to study the use of XII Corps in defeating invasion. In his post-mortem on the exercise – which was delivered to 2,000 XII Corps officers – he said: 'A great deal went wrong on this exercise. The Army is not a mutual congratulation society; great issues are at stake; if we lose the battle in Kent we may lose the war. The problem in this exercise was not that the troops lacked enthusiasm or fitness, but simply that commanders had no notion how to put a modern Army into Battle.' He then proceeded to tell them how, and for many of them in front of a large number of their subordinate officers. His exposition also made it clear that an underlying problem for the British Army was the decline of military knowledge and expertise as the Army was expanded to meet its wartime commitments. Monty was certainly going to do all he could to reverse that decline at all levels of command, but particularly at the top.

How did the commanders of higher formations perform in response to the training and development they had received by battle experience, exercises, and any other methods that were employed? This should be considered in three categories, all related to the use of armoured forces:

- Commanders of Army tank brigades (subsequently renamed armoured brigades); the main function of an Army tank brigade was the direct support of an infantry formation, generally a division.
- Commanders of armoured divisions; the role of an armoured division was not quite so easy to define, but certainly included the exploitation of breakthroughs, pursuit, and in many battles a significant part in the set-piece attack to provide a breakthrough.
- Commanders of corps, generally including infantry and armoured formations and supporting arms.

Commanders of Army tank brigades generally performed effectively. Their role was relatively simple, in that they were normally under the command of an infantry formation and had no other arms to worry about. Many of these brigades were armed with Churchills, and a number of them ultimately formed part of the 79th Armoured Division with its range of specialized armour. The 21st Tank Brigade performed so well in support of the 1st Canadian Infantry Division in Italy that the brigade was authorized to wear a maple leaf on its black diabolo formation sign.

Commanders of armoured divisions can only be described as a mixed bag, and there were not many who managed armoured divisions as well as Rommel or the American John Wood. Pip Roberts of 11th Armoured Division was certainly well up with that class, closely followed by Allan Adair of the Guards Armoured Division. The 7th Armoured Division had a fine reputation until Normandy, but it did have a high turnover of commanders both in North Africa and in north-west Europe.

In the use of armour by corps commanders we again have a mixed bag. Richard O'Connor was brilliant when he commanded the Western Desert Force in 1940–41, but he was captured shortly after his victory at Beda Fomm. The habit in the desert for most of 1941 and 1942 was for formations to be broken down into brigade-size groups, and cooperation between infantry and tanks was far from good. Adding to this the previously mentioned lack of understanding about how to use artillery, it is immediately evident that corps commanders were not well trained themselves, were not trained by their Army commanders (Wavell, followed by Auchinleck), and were not capable of training their subordinate commanders. Some of these corps commanders were killed or replaced (Gott, Lumsden, Ramsden), and certainly Leese and Horrocks from mid-1942 onwards made more effective use of their resources. In this they were greatly helped by the reversion to divisional formations and tighter control promulgated and enforced by their Army C-in-C, Montgomery.

Horrocks, as recorded earlier, was given feedback on his performance immediately after the Battle of Alam Halfa. He does not mention many other instances of feedback, but it is to be assumed that they happened. He does, however, record in his autobiography an interesting observation on what he considers to be useful training for a senior commander, although quite inadvertently obtained. On 21 October 1914 Horrocks was wounded and taken prisoner near Ypres, and in spite of escaping several times he was always recaptured and was not free until 11 November 1918. He then applied to go to help the White Russians, and once again became a prisoner of war, this time to the Bolsheviks. When finally released and back in England he had spent more than five years of his Army career in prison, and had seen little fighting. He commented on this philosophically: 'I wonder whether the varied experiences of those years were not an excellent preparation for the stresses and strains of command in war. I had learned to live rough and depend on nobody but myself, and, having experienced the seamy side of life to the full, I was unlikely to be taken by surprise, however unexpected the crisis might be. Orthodox military life in those days (1920) was not calculated to develop the qualities or robust initiative so necessary in a commander on the battlefield.'

Horrocks as a corps commander used armour effectively in North Africa, and in Normandy after he was appointed to replace Bucknall as the commander of XXX Corps. After the capture of Antwerp, however, he made what turned out to be a major error in not pushing on to Woensdrecht and cutting off the retreat of the German Fifteenth Army. He also had further difficulties in making good use of armour in the advance to Arnhem. All this he acknowledged with great honesty, and the verdict must be that he was one corps commander who was competent to handle armour; the same could be said of Oliver Leese in North Africa.

After North Africa the opportunities for using armour were somewhat reduced until the commencement of the Normandy campaign. The 7th Armoured Division was not well handled in the initial stages of this campaign, either by its divisional commander, Erskine, or by his corps commander, Bucknall, and in August 1944 both commanders were sacked. The 11th Armoured and Guards Armoured divisions had good commanders in the persons of Roberts and Adair, and worked effectively under various corps commanders.

The two major actions for British armour in the first four months of the campaign in north-west Europe were Operation Goodwood and the advance to Antwerp. Goodwood started on 18 July 1944, and its objective was to open up the country to the east as far as Caen and if possible break through to the open going to the south and south-east of that city. The main thrust was to be provided by VIII Corps consisting of the 7th, 11th and Guards Armoured divisions, with very significant support being provided by I Corps, XII Corps and II Canadian Corps. The commander of VIII Corps was Richard O'Connor. He had achieved a brilliant armoured success in North Africa in 1940, but had then had the misfortune to be taken prisoner. He escaped and eventually returned to England and was appointed to the command of VIII Corps. Goodwood was an unfortunate battle in many ways. There was not nearly enough room for three armoured divisions in the British bridgehead to the east of the River Orne, there were insufficient tracks through the minefields, RAF bombs and Royal Navy shells produced enormous craters that hampered movement and the German defence was brilliantly sited in great depth and was very courageously fought.

Possibly O'Connor could have widened the minefield corridors, left the infantry brigade of the 11th Armoured with its armoured brigade, and applied more ginger to the 7th and Guards Armoured Divisions. But possibly also the operation had strategic rather than tactical objectives, essentially to force German armour to remain on the British front of the Normandy bridgehead rather than transfer to the American front. It certainly seems unfair to criticize O'Connor too strongly when it appears that the mistakes in the operation were made by Dempsey or Montgomery. But it is also true that in the time that O'Connor was in this theatre of operations (he was sacked by Montgomery in November 1944 for refusing to put in a negative report on an American divisional commander temporarily serving under VIII Corps) he did not make a particularly strong impression as an effective corps commander.

To summarize what has been recorded about British commanders' handling of armoured forces, it is clear that in the great majority of cases they were neither well selected nor well trained – if indeed they were trained at all. The results of this were many battles in which the tank crews fought with great gallantry only to lose their lives unnecessarily because of the incompetence of their formation (division and corps) commanders. Examples of such battles are those of 1941 and 1942 in North Africa, and the disastrous Operation Goodwood in Normandy.

The causes of the widespread incompetence have in part been described earlier, and are here summarized and amplified:

- Many of those who could have become the required commanders had been lost in the terrible blood-letting of the First World War.
- Selection procedures for higher command were understood by few, and implemented by fewer.
- There was little systematic feedback to document and analyse battles so that successful methods could be reinforced and unsuccessful methods eliminated or modified.

Training with tanks by manoeuvring over the ground was very important for all tank commanders; equally important was feedback on how the exercise went; from their expressions this group appear to have done not too well.

Of particular concern is the last point, the lack of feedback. This appears to be an endemic British problem. The Report by Kirke on the lessons to be learnt from the First World War was eventually published in 1933, fifteen years after the war was over. In relation to the campaign in Normandy, Liddell Hart wrote in 1952: 'Seven years have passed since the war ended, yet the significance of the comparative odds in Normandy in relation to the results has never been brought out in any official report, history or training manual; there has been too much glorification of the campaign and too little objective investigation.' Lack of feedback is a fundamental management failing, and incompetent management caused most of the deficiencies in the preparedness of the British Army.

EVALUATION OF TRAINING

The discussions on training in the previous sections of this chapter have covered four segments of training required for the effective employment of armoured troops, namely: the technical and basic skills to be a tank soldier, basic training for tank officers, training to kill, and training to be a senior commander employing armoured troops. How effective was the training given in these categories during the Second World War? Taking each in turn we can say the following:

Sometimes it was necessary to give training for a very specific purpose; the tanks here are about to leave the hangar where they are, go to the 'hards' on the sea shore, and embark on a Tank Landing Craft; this exercise was in preparation for the Normandy landings. (IWM H32689)

- Technical training, both individual and collective, was good: up to mid-1941 it was greatly hampered by lack of equipment and instructors, but in early 1942 training systems for the basic skills of tank soldiering were working well. Collective training was always constrained by lack of space and pressure on what space there was. Gunnery training was even more constrained by lack of space and availability of ranges. Crew training was criticized by some field units, but the system generally responded to such criticisms and took reasonable corrective action.

- Training for tank officers was generally less effective. This was because much of the formal training, e.g. at Sandhurst, was training to be an officer rather than to be someone specifically capable of handling a small group of tanks. It was assumed that the tank-oriented training would be given to an officer when he reached his field unit; but the quality of that training depended on the enthusiasm of his unit for training, the ability of the unit's senior officers to make training challenging and beneficial, and the space in which to carry out the training. Many tank officers will remember endless days maintaining tanks in a tank park; useful in getting to know your crews and tanks, but not helpful in learning how to manoeuvre a troop of tanks in action.

- Training to kill: soldiers at the sharp end of an Army must always be willing to show aggression towards the enemy, and to put that aggression into effect whenever possible. There are a number of people who are naturally aggressive, always ready to do anything they can to discomfort the enemy 'with maximum prejudice'. The great majority of war-time soldiers are not of this temperament, however, and paradoxically must be trained to risk more to have a better chance of survival. Training can be reinforced by example, and in tank units the sight of a squadron leader advancing with determination against the enemy will make all his tank commanders willing to do the same. But sometimes the example was not there, and often the provision of the example resulted in the death or wounding of the squadron leader. Then, unless the tank commanders and crews had 'fire in their bellies', aggression would very likely die and the attack falter. A majority of tank crews were not trained to have that 'fire in the belly', and this resulted, for example, in the sluggishness observed in the British tank crews in Normandy, as observed by Brig James Hargest.

- Training for command of higher formations containing armour. An objective assessment of the performance of senior commanders employing armour suggests that they were mainly incompetent. If asked to nominate effective commanders of British armour most soldiers who fought in the Second World War would name Richard O'Connor and Pip Roberts, and these at divisional level only. There was clearly a great deficiency in the way that commanders at this level were trained and developed, and although there were only a few of them their incompetence – or the incompetence of the system – caused the unnecessary deaths of very large numbers of soldiers.

CHAPTER 8

The Bone Points Where?

War is a dangerous business, and people who fight run a high risk of dying. There are, however, certain ways in which that risk can be reduced, the two main ways being: proper preparation of soldiers before they join battle; and provision of equipment which will allow them to be competitive with the enemy they face.

This book has dealt with soldiers of one arm only, tanks. It is undoubtedly true that British service people of all services fought under similar disadvantages of insufficient training and inadequate equipment. We who fought with tanks acknowledge the tribulations of all the other service people, and this account expresses on their behalf as well as ours the indignation and anger we felt – and still feel – at being commanded by uncaring, incompetent and disinterested politicians, to fight under the conditions we did.

This chapter recapitulates the facts presented in previous chapters, and suggests the causes behind those facts. There is no intention to look for specific 'guilty men', but all of the causes described resulted from human action or inaction. It is suggested finally that there must have been an overarching responsibility for all of those causes.

THE ARMY AS 'CINDERELLA'

The causes of the Second World War were to a large extent contained in the terms by which the First World War was formally concluded, the Treaty of Versailles. The terms of the treaty have been seen subsequently to have been unnecessarily harsh – and indeed the treatment meted out to Germany at the end of the Second World War was much more constructive. The result of Versailles in Germany was to build up a strong desire to recover her position and pride, and contained in this was a willingness to use aggression if necessary.

The view of the British people, on the other hand, was that they had made immense sacrifices but above all they had won; it would never be necessary to do it again. Given that this was true, it was obvious that all that Britain needed armed forces for was to protect her overseas possessions and the communications with them. This attitude was formalized in the Ten Year Rule which stated the proposition that Britain would not need to face aggression for at least ten years. This rule was renewed year by year, thus procrastinating the need to provide effective armed forces.

At the beginning of the 1930s it became apparent that there were aggressive forces in the world, and that their hostility might become focused directly or indirectly on Britain. Mussolini had become dictator of Italy; Japan had invaded Manchuria; and Hitler had come to power in Germany. In 1935 Mussolini invaded Abyssinia, and in 1936 Hitler reoccupied the Rhineland. Britain had become progressively more concerned about rearmament, and had to consider the three main roles of the armed forces: defence of Britain, defence of the empire and communications with it, and the provision of a Continental Force to support continental allies.

Of the three services the Royal Navy was perceived as being vital at all times, particularly for the defence of Britain and the communication links with the empire. The government became convinced of the need for a strong RAF, and allocated substantial sums to the provision of planes and their crews. The Army, on the other hand, suffered because the Continental Force was seen as being unnecessary until early 1939. That force would be mainly composed of Army units, and thus the Army became 'Cinderella' in third place.

Having been in this position for some years the Army was very ill prepared in 1939, and the Army's tank forces had suffered from inadequate preparation and funding more than all its other arms. The reasons for this have been described in previous paragraphs, but fundamental to the lack of preparation was shortage of money. A country's revenue is limited by its economic circumstances and by perceptions as to what is politically safe to demand as tax contributions from its citizens. The Depression of 1930–31 had hit Britain's finances hard, and the pace of recovery was slow. Money spent on armaments was money diverted from economic recovery. This understandable concern of the Treasury was reinforced by the attitude of the then Chancellor of the Exchequer, Neville Chamberlain. His view was that aggression could be contained by diplomacy and appeasement, and that armaments should be used as a last resort. He maintained this view when he became Prime Minister.

The 'Cinderella' position of the Army from 1936 to 1939 was therefore caused by: the legacy of the Depression, Treasury stringency, and downgrading of the Army's role by making the Continental Force a low priority. The risk of having an ill-prepared Army was judged to be less than the risk of economic downturn. There were undoubtedly more votes in spending money to generate jobs then in spending money on rearmament.

HOW SHOULD TANKS BE USED?

The tank was a weapon developed in the First World War with the two main purposes of crushing defensive wire entanglements and bringing supporting fire as a direct accompaniment to advancing infantry. In spite of mechanical unreliability and an appalling internal environment for their crews, tanks were very effective in achieving their two main purposes. Champions of the tank, particularly members of the Royal Tank Corps (RTC), put forward very strongly the view that it was the weapon that won the war. The view must be put in context. The total number of RTC battalions formed or being formed by the end of 1918 was thirty-six; of those only numbers 1 to 17 saw significant action. The total number of all ranks of the RTC killed between 1916 and 1918 was 1,319; this should be compared with the 19,240 (mainly infantry) killed on 1 July 1916, the first day of the Somme, and the 908,000 killed from all ranks, arms and services of the British Empire during the whole of the First World War.

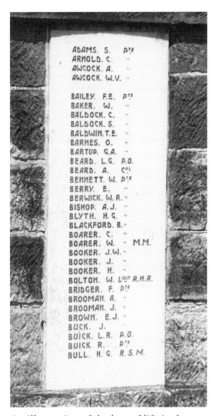

An illustration of the loss of life in the First World War, demonstrating why many people in Britain in the 1920s and 1930s thought that fighting was not worthwhile. A single panel of the War Memorial at All Saints, Crowborough, Sussex, leads to the conclusion that of the young men (aged twenty to forty) able to join the services in that village one-third were killed and the remainder wounded. Among those killed were the author's uncle, John William Booker, and kinsfolk Joseph Booker and Hercules Booker.

Had that war continued into the next year the tanks' contribution would have been much greater. Plan 1919 envisaged the use of many thousands of tanks of improved performance and varying capabilities, particularly the Whippet tanks with their much greater speed and potential for pursuit, raiding and disruption of the enemy's rear.

The tank was viewed after 1918 as a sufficiently useful weapon that it should be kept as a military resource. But those in charge of the Army at that time did not have the ability, experience, motivation or time to plan how to develop the potential of the new weapon. The efforts of tank enthusiasts such as Fuller, Lindsay, Broad and Hobart were hampered by their positions in the military hierarchy, the disagreements between them on the way that tanks should be used, the lack of funding, and the perception that they were out to enhance the status and role of the RTC at the expense of other arms.

Lack of funding, besides restricting the number and types of tanks available, also meant that experimental manoeuvres could be carried out very infrequently. Manoeuvres that were executed were valuable, progressive, and thought-provoking. But most of the experimental work was in the head or on paper, not in the field. It was generally those with the most forceful personality who won any argument, unsupported by physical activities.

The account of changing tactical doctrine and organization of armoured formations show that it was not until 1944 that Maj Gen Roberts, then commanding the 11th Armoured Division, could say: 'Throughout the war the tactics used within an armoured division and its organization were continually changing. It was not until our third battle in Normandy that we got it right, and that was an organization of complete flexibility.'

The causes of the uncertainty regarding tactics and organization were clearly the following: a lack of funding to develop tanks of appropriate quantity, and to carry out experimental manoeuvres in their use; the lack of time or motivation immediately after the First World War to evaluate what tanks had done and what they could do; the perception by other people in the Army that the RTC was over-selling its case, and were out to aggrandize the RTC at the expense of other arms. In spite of what Fuller and

Liddell Hart have written, the most senior officers in the Army were constructive rather than obstructive regarding the development and use of tanks. They were a valuable weapon, but had to be integrated with all those others that still had useful functions to perform.

TANK AND TANK GUN DEVELOPMENT

The designers and manufacturers of tanks gradually became aware that a tank should be built to accept a particular gun, rather than the other way round. In all the years up to 1945 there were only two tanks that were built to mount guns that were required by the armoured forces. These were the Comet (A34), mounting the 77mm, and the Centurion (A41), mounting the seventeen-pounder. Up to the end of the war only 200 Comets had been issued to field units, and no Centurions.

For much of the time there was uncertainty regarding the function of the tank gun. It could either be an anti-tank gun, in which case it needed to fire an armour-piercing projectile at high velocity; or it could be a gun whose main purpose was to destroy 'soft' targets using high-explosive shells. For effective use of HE shells it was in some ways better that their flight velocity should be slower so that there would be less chance of them ricocheting past the target. The third possibility was to have a multi-purpose gun, such as the short-barrelled medium-velocity 75mm, which had a projectile heavy enough to deliver an effective weight of explosive, but at the same time had sufficient muzzle velocity to deliver a projectile to knock out some enemy tanks.

War Office thinking, if that is not a contradiction in terms, changed regularly on the function that the tank gun should fulfil. The guns actually produced for use in tanks – two-pounder, six-pounder, 77mm and seventeen-pounder – were all excellent anti-tank guns in their prime, particularly with the use of APCBC and APDS ammunition. The HE capabilities of the two-pounder and six-pounder were completely ineffective, but those of the 77mm and seventeen-pounder were good, with the proviso mentioned above that their muzzle velocities were high.

The real problem for tank crews was that the six-pounder and the seventeen-pounder were very slow in development, i.e. from initial concept to the time of delivery to tank units. The reasons for this, as have been discussed in earlier chapters, were: lack of motivation or resources to commence development after need was recognized; competition for manufacturing facilities; and no suitable turret into which to mount the manufactured gun.

It has to be observed that there was in being from 1939 an excellent potential anti-tank gun in the 3.7in A/A gun. And A/A guns normally fired an anti-tank shoot at Larkhill on their way back from summer manoeuvres until the practice was stopped in 1937. It can only be that the amour-propre of senior officers in the Royal Artillery decided that they would allow no one else to do anything with their guns. And as for learning from the almost identical situation in which the Germans used their 88mm A/A gun very successfully – how could senior British officers debase themselves by learning from the enemy?

The development of British tanks was not integrated with that of tank guns, as we have seen, and that was no help at all in developing the complete tank. Several different roles were defined for tanks: light tanks for reconnaissance, mediums as the core of a powerful mobile force, cruisers to add speed to that mobile force, infantry tanks to provide direct close-at-hand support to infantry formations and assault tanks to crack heavily defended localities.

The results of trying to meet so many different needs were that none of them was satisfied. This was compounded by the lack or withdrawal of design skills, and by the extremely low level of funding. The amount of money spent on tracked vehicles in the years from 1931 to 1937 was:

Year	£,000 (approx.)	Percentage of Army Expenditure
1931–2	350	0.9
1932–3	300	0.8
1933–4	350	0.9
1934–5	500	1.25
1935–6	650	1.45
1936–7	850	1.55

The amounts and percentages increased substantially as the war progressed, but what value was achieved for the additional expenditure? The lineage of British tanks shown in Figure 3.3 reveals that in the period 1930–35 work was done on fifty-seven different designs of tank. Of these fifty-seven, twenty-eight were never produced in a suitable form for issue to field units. All the remaining designs were issued to field units in varying quantities, although some were judged unfit ever to be used in action. Of those delivered to field units to be used in action, 75 per cent were useless at the time they were delivered.

The failure of the process of tank design and production meant two things: there was an enormous waste of resource for very little useful output; and tank crews were required for most of the war to fight with inadequate equipment, causing many unnecessary deaths to themselves and to the people they were supporting.

The causes of this failure were: an inability or unwillingness to define what was required; lack of integration between gun and tank design; inadequate resources, including money, manpower and facilities for design and manufacture; inability to identify and focus on chains of equipment development so that models could be upgraded to meet increasing enemy strength; and a lack of feedback – or, as the next set of comments will show, a complete lack of interest in any feedback that was made.

CUSTOMER COMPLAINTS

The list of customers who complained about the tanks delivered to the Army is a long one, and includes representatives from all levels within the Army as well as a number of senior politicians. Some of those mentioned in earlier chapters were: the Secretary of State for War in 1936; Gen Sir Edmund Ironside as GOC Eastern Command in 1938; Brig Vyvyan Pope; Gen Bernard Montgomery; the Select Committee on National Expenditure, headed by Sir John Wardlaw-Milne; Richard Stokes, MP, and several other MPs. These were just a few of the complainants from on high.

There were plenty of additional complaints from the people at the coal face, the tank crews, but these complaints appeared to be treated as if they were made by an ignorant peasantry, and in any event the barriers to communication from the lowest echelon were almost impenetrable. A tank crew member who complained about his equipment as being inferior to that of the opposition would be told very smartly: 'Get on with your job, man. It's not your business to think about that sort of thing.' And if the complaint was made and lodged at a higher level, say by a tank troop leader to his commanding officer, the response would be couched in such terms as: 'Stop belly-aching. It's our job to do the best we can with what we're given. Perhaps you're a bit windy, eh?'

Such responses, and they are very definitely typical, inhibited any objective or reasonable comments about matters that were obviously in need of correction. The culture of any authoritarian organization, civilian or milliary, stifles attempts to convey useful information that could be interpreted as a criticism of those higher in the hierarchy. The culture imputes omniscience to those higher in the scale, and as people move up the scale so they become more defensive and less willing to hear.

One of the few people at the 'coal face' to make adverse comments, as we have already seen, was Maj Bob Crisp, DSO, MC, of the Royal Tank Regiment. His temperament was such that he did not much care what he said or who he said it to if he thought it was worth saying. But the only reward he got was to have his award of a second DSO downgraded to an MC – and this by one of the more senior complainers, the hypocritical Montgomery.

To identify problems and to take action to correct those problems it is essential that there be feedback. This will allow the provider of the item, in this case a tank, to compare its actual performance with what was intended or expected. The content of feedback must be objective, accurate and impartial, and it should not be blocked, distorted or attenuated until it reaches the point of comparison. Action resulting from feedback on tank performance was effectively nil, as can be seen from the previously related sad tale of tank development.

The record of the British Army in seeking and using feedback is poor. This is illustrated very vividly in the way they learned lessons from the First World War. A committee was eventually set up to examine the military operations of that war, and analyse what failures there were to be corrected and what successes to reinforce. That war ended in 1918, and fifteen years later, in 1933, the Kirke Committee submitted its report on lessons to be learned. The Kirke report was critical of the High Command of the Army, especially that in France. The recently appointed CIGS, Sir Archibald Montgomery-Massingberd, who had served in a senior position in France, immediately took steps to block the dissemination of the report, thus denying the opportunity to make any improvements suggested in it.

This general lack of feedback occurred after the Second World War also. In 1952 Basil Liddell Hart wrote: 'Seven years have passed since the war ended, yet the significance of the comparative odds in Normandy in relation to the results has never been brought out in any official report, history, or training manual. There has been too much glorification of the campaign and too little objective investigation.'

This unwillingness for self-evaluation or criticism is in direct and marked contrast to attitudes in the Russian Army. Their tank forces were routed in 1941, and in spite of the T-34 received several bloody noses in 1942. But under the aegis of *Stavka* they examined what had gone wrong, developed solutions and implemented them. This process of continuous feedback resulted in the magnificent tanks they deployed in 1944 and 1945, characterized not only by excellent equipment but also by very professional handling at the operational and tactical levels.

Blocks to the feedback process at the lowest level have already been described, as well as one at the very highest. There were also blocks or distortions when the topic of tanks was discussed in parliament. As mentioned earlier, John Wardlaw-Milne and Richard

Graves at the War Cemetery of Fontenay-le-Pesnel, Tessel, Normandy. Left foreground is the grave of Frederick Richard Smart, and right foreground that of Arthur James Bennell. These two graves and tens of thousands of others are filled with the bodies of good men because of the incompetence, disinterest and malice of the politicians who formed the British governments in the 1920s, 1930s and 1940s.

Stokes, as well as a few other MPs, suggested on a number of occasions that the design and production of tanks should be improved. The record shows that they were either ridiculed or fobbed off with political double-speak, and that no action was taken on any of the weaknesses they described.

Even more pernicious were the occasional comments on the excellent qualities of British tanks from senior Army commanders such as Leese, Montgomery and others. Monty said in February 1945 that Germans using British tanks would have done much better in the recent Ardennes that if they had been using their own tanks, and that the British would have had difficulty in making the dash from Normandy to Holland had they been using German tanks instead of British. This statement is not only farcical in the eyes of the tank crews in the north-west Europe campaign, but criminal. It is instructive to go to the Tank Museum at Bovington and make an even superficial comparison between the British Cromwell and Churchill on the one hand and their opponents the German Mk IV, Panther and Tiger on the other.

Statements such as Monty's, however, were nectar to most British MPs and all members of the cabinet. Why should they be concerned to listen to the expendable tank crews when the great and good generals were satisfied?

THE FORGES OF VULCAN

Responsibility for design and production of tanks was spread over a wide range of organizations during the period 1919–45. The organizations changed, the organizational structures changed, and the people staffing those structures changed constantly.

During the 1920s tank design was reduced to a very small section in the War Department hierarchy, and tank production was minuscule. Tank design was hindered by uncertainty as to what the users wanted. Tank design was done either independently or contractually by Vickers' and Vickers' Sir John Carden was probably the best British tank designer between the wars. Unfortunately he was killed in 1935, and other significant tank designers died too. The functions of the Department of Tank Design (DTD) became more and more advisory rather than executive, and the DTD was able to help companies enter into tank design and production to speed up the process of rearmament. Companies taking part were Nuffield Mechanisations and Aero, Vulcan Foundry, Harland and Wolff, Leyland, and Vauxhall Motors. Until 1943 the DTD provided advice and comments on the designs put forward by private companies such as these, and did not carry out the function implied in their title, namely the design of a complete tank. By 1943, however, the DTD had acquired substantial know-how and very knowledgeable designers. In 1943 they commenced design of the A41 or Centurion, a very successful tank which has had a working life of more than fifty years.

Up to the mid-1930s, tanks were manufactured either by the Royal Ordnance factories or by Vickers. Between 1936 and 1945 other firms became engaged in tank manufacture, including all of those who carried out tank design. There were many problems associated with tank manufacture: most of the organizations were not set up for the assembly of large units of production; the quality standards required were unexpectedly stringent, and the 'craft' approach of many engineering companies meant endless trouble in making parts fit together; there were shortages of raw materials and components, which in the case of the Churchill caused frequent breakdowns when sub-optimal substitutes were used; and some tanks, such as the Matildas, required complicated and very time-consuming methods of assembly.

The overall responsibility for the production of munitions, including tanks, was until 1936 that of the Master General of Ordnance (MGO). In 1936 it was transferred to the Director General of Munitions (DGM), whose title was changed in 1938 to the Director General of Munitions Production (DGMP). In March 1939 the DGMP's department was transferred to the Minister of Supply. The Minister of Supply and the Secretary of State for War represented two separate channels reporting to the cabinet, thus causing an organizational separation between the users and the producers of tanks. There was already a separation between the producers and the designers of tanks as complete units, and between the designers of tank guns and the designers of the tanks into which they were to be mounted.

In October 1939, in response to the realization that the tank supply position was extremely grave, the organization of the Ministry of Supply was improved by the creation of the post of Director General of Tanks and Transport. Between then and September 1942 various other changes were made to the organizational structure of the Ministry of Supply. At that point, however, many of the responsibilities for tank design and production were brought together under the single position of Chairman, Armoured Fighting Vehicle Division (CAFVD), accountable to the Minister of Supply. This structure is shown in Figure 6.2 of Chapter 6, and shows that all significant functions of tank design, development, proving, production and inspection were in the same division. The only functions not included were those of tank gun design and production. There were few further changes in the structure of the AFV Division, but its performance did not win much praise from the Select Committee on National Expenditure, and the only satisfactory tanks produced in nearly six years were a few hundred Comets and twenty prototype Centurions.

The débâcle of Dunkirk in May/June 1940 made it clear that very few if any tanks would be returning from France. It turned out that the number of tanks available to defend the United Kingdom was 200 light tanks and fifty infantry tanks. Obviously some very drastic action was necessary. What could be more drastic than forming a committee and calling it the Tank Board? This strange excrescence on the bodies of the Ministry of Supply and the War Office jointly lasted until the end of the war, had five chairmen, five terms of reference and twenty members during the first two years of its existence. In September 1942 Cdr Micklem was appointed CAFVD and Chairman of the Tank Board at the same time.

It can be seen that the one thing lacking in the processes for design and manufacture of tanks was clear-cut assignment of responsibility to one person. This was approached with the appointment of Micklem as CAFVD, but much effort was dissipated in the first three years of the war by uncertain requirements, division of control and responsibility, and no effective feedback to someone who had the authority to take corrective action.

The Select Committee on National Expenditure submitted a follow-up report on the tank situation to the Prime Minister on 11 March 1944. In it they made an interesting suggestion that would have sheeted home accountability for the quality and effectiveness of tanks. That was to identify by name the organization delivering the tank to operational units, and making the organization responsible for ensuring that the tank met all operational and quality specifications. As it turned out, of course, too close an identification with this responsibility might have been a source of embarrassment rather than pride.

TRAINING

In the earlier chapter we reviewed the training that was needed and the training that was given to meet armoured forces' needs, namely: technical training, collective training and junior leadership, motivation to kill, and the command of divisions, corps or armies either composed of or including armoured forces.

The evidence is that the technical training and the collective training were done well, although in the first eighteen to twenty-four months of the war there was a painful shortage of equipment. There was one problem, however, which existed at the beginning of the war and became worse as it went along, and that was the shortage of space for exercising tanks and their weapons. Gunnery ranges required progressively more area as tank guns became more powerful; and the few available ranges were under such demand that a field unit was lucky if it was able to fire its guns more than twice a year, each time for perhaps three or four days. And the individual gunner would be lucky if he went round the range more than twice during each visit.

Practising driving a tank allowed for more opportunity, because training regiments were close to moors and heaths with variable terrain. But on reaching a field unit it was quite seldom that the tanks were close to training areas, and these were normally accessible only when a unit went on a formal exercise. Here again the limited area made it difficult to carry out realistic manoeuvres for a squadron or a regiment, and even then the manoeuvres were often repetitive because of the limited space.

The whole problem of space became more acute when substantial and ever-increasing American forces started to land in Britain in 1942. A serious result of the cramped opportunities was some unwillingness to use a battlefield without constraint – and it was during their first encounters with a hostile foe on unknown ground that many casualties occurred, partly because of an inability to use the ground.

Training people to be motivated to kill is a major problem for a national conscript Army. There are so many taboos against taking life that it is difficult to train soldiers to accept that killing their enemies is their prime function, and should be done whenever the opportunity affords. This motivation is different from courage. Many tank units and soldiers demonstrated marvellous courage in many actions, the charges of the yeomanry and cavalry regiments of the 9th Armoured Brigade in the Battle of El Alamein being an example.

But motivation to kill means a ferocious and ruthless pursuit of any weakness in an enemy, and at the same time a recognition that one's own death may be the price – at a substantial cost to the enemy. Aggressiveness was certainly taught to special troops such as commandos, rangers and paratroopers, but it was much more difficult to teach to tank troops, partly because theirs is a much more arm's length battle.

The causes of the lack of this type of training were several. It would appear first that it was not recognized as being necessary. The perception was that 'a soldier is a soldier is a soldier' – and besides being brutal and licentious he is automatically aggressive and brave and motivated to kill. This is quite untrue, obviously; all soldiers are civilians who have donned a uniform for the honour or defence of their country.

The second cause is that concerned and assorted do-gooders were worried that aggressive training would create a large population of psychopaths who would wreak havoc when they were finally demobilized. Some such people were sufficiently vocal for notice to be taken of them with resulting modifications to training programmes.

The third cause is that realistic training is likely to cause casualties in the training process. To see whether a person will advance under fire he must do just that; and the margin for error in a simulation was sufficiently close that there were casualties. Such casualties were particularly grievous to their loved ones, and strong representations were made to mitigate the severity of such training. In a democracy a government must take action on these representations, even though lack of this training will mean that many more soldiers die in the real battles.

During the whole of the Second World War Britain's armoured forces were seldom well commanded and seldom well used by the generals commanding more senior formations in

which they were included. Commanders of armoured divisions in France in 1940 had no chance; those in the desert from 1940 to 1943 changed frequently, and tanks were often used in small packets rather than in divisions. The only name that would immediately spring to mind as an effective armoured leader was Richard O'Connor, and he had the misfortune to be taken prisoner very soon after his initial triumph against the Italians. The most successful tank commander in north-west Europe 1944–5 was Pip Roberts, but his fellow commanders of armoured divisions were either suspended or could best be described as workmanlike.

It must be said that commanders of senior formations were often selected for the wrong reasons, and were not trained in what they were required to do. There appeared to be no detailed doctrine or instruction as to how an armoured commander should lead, and little or no feedback and analysis of successful and unsuccessful actions undertaken by British tanks – and even less analysis of the way in which German, Russian and American tank forces performed. Causes of this relatively poor performance of armoured commanders were: uncertainty regarding the role of armour; lack of doctrine for carrying out a role, even if uncertain; lack of training for senior commanders, and lack of feedback on their performance; and frequent changes of commanders before they had the opportunity to develop their skills and experience to meet the requirements of their position.

RESPONSIBILITY OF THE BRITISH GOVERNMENT

This book as a whole and the recapitulation in the earlier sections of this chapter have shown how ill prepared British armoured troops were for war in 1939, and how slowly their preparedness improved during the war itself. In this chapter we have looked at some of the causes for the lack of preparation.

The underlying cause was the uncertainty regarding what tanks were supposed to do. From this stemmed uncertainty as to what sort of tank gun was needed, followed by uncertainty as to what tank was needed to mount the gun. These uncertainties led to many chains of doubt, change, multiple designs and wasted resources, as well as to the difficulty of defining tactical and operational doctrine. This created difficulties in setting up training programmes and delivering training.

Another major cause of the poor preparation was the unfocused organization for tank design and manufacture. Lack of a firm specification, as described in the previous paragraph, was obviously a weak platform from which to start. This was compounded grossly by the divisions of responsibility and accountability, and the lack for several years of one person in charge of all aspects of design and production.

The other main cause was the lack of an objective, quick-acting, transparent method of feeding back problems and complaints so that suitable corrective action could be taken. Several people made great efforts to bring faults to the attention of those who could influence or take action, but there is little evidence that their efforts were successful; and there is significant evidence that parliament, the cabinet and senior members of the War Office took steps to block or divert critical comments.

The House of Commons was a particularly good blocker of feedback, as we have seen in relation to the criticisms voiced by Wardlaw-Milne and Stokes. It is to be presumed that the Cabinet and the parliament have, in the British system, the ultimate responsibility for running the country. One of the major responsibilities at all times, but particularly in time of war, is that for national security. It is the government that is responsible for assessing security risks, judging how those risks should be contained, and providing and arming the forces needed for that containment.

The record of the British government from the early 1930s to 1945 demonstrates either gross incompetence in providing for national security or a lack of concern at the death of people in the armed services, as if it were a matter of no consequence. To care so little about the equipment they were asked to use, the leaders they were given and the preparatory training they received, can best be described as criminal. The government from 1935 to 1945 is that which must be condemned, and at whose door must be laid the blame for thousands of unnecessary deaths.

Even if the government was responsible, however, it was elected. It may be that the British people got the government they deserved, and can blame only themselves for their own deaths or those of their children in the war.

The mood of the British people when the war ended in 1918 was, naturally, that they never wanted to fight a war again. The numbers of people killed – 60,000, for example in the Battle of the Somme in only a few days – resulted in the horrendously long lists of names carved in war memorials throughout Britain. These memorials were a constant reminder of the tragedy and loss caused by war. The British could also say that they won; why should they have to be prepared to fight again? As we have seen in the terms of the Treaty of Versailles, France and, to a lesser degree, Britain were determined that Germany would never be able to fight again. If this were the case then there would be no need to fight. There was a strong and totally understandable reaction in favour of pacifism or the abrogation of armed force in the settlement of disputes between nations. This applied in Britain and in France, and probably in many other countries, but one place where it certainly did not apply was Germany. They felt, with some reason, that they had been gravely disadvantaged by the terms of the peace treaty; the only way they could resume their position in the world was by recovery, and possibly by aggression.

In Britain in the 1930s many people were inclined towards pacifism, illustrated by the fact that George Lansbury, who was for a time the leader of the Labour opposition, was a dedicated pacifist. He had a substantial following which did not necessarily have anything to do with his or their affiliation. Two instances show something of the mood of the people of Britain during this time.

In 1933 the Oxford Union debated the topic, 'This house is not prepared to fight for king and country'. The final vote was in favour of the motion, although many of the people who voted that way almost certainly did fight and die for their country. But the perception in other countries was quite clearly that if people at one of Britain's senior universities felt that way about fighting, Britain's predominant attitude was that of pacifism. The second instance reinforced that perception.

In 1935 the League of Nations fostered what was called a 'Peace Ballot'. In Britain 11 million people proclaimed their unshakeable faith in the league as an instrument of peace. On all questions of defence this completely shackled the government. This was brought out by Prime Minister Stanley Baldwin who said, on 12 November 1936 in the House of Commons, 'Supposing I had gone to the country and said that we must rearm. Does anyone think that this pacifist democracy would have rallied to that cry at that moment? I cannot think of anything that would have made the loss of the election from my point of view more certain.'

The election had then just been won by Stanley Baldwin's government. Prior to the election Baldwin's main supporter, Neville Chamberlain, had said privately, in relation to rearmament: 'We must hurry on our own rearmament and in the course of the next 4–5 years we shall probably have to spend an extra £120 million in doing so. We are not yet sufficiently advanced to reveal our ideas to the public but, of course, we cannot deny the general charge of rearmament, and, no doubt, if we try to keep our ideas secret until after the election, we should either fail or, if we succeed, lay ourselves open to the far more damaging accusation that we had deliberately deceived the people. In view of these considerations I suggest that we should take the bold course of actually appealing to the country on a defence programme.' Baldwin did not follow the bolder course.

Using Britain's tank forces as an example, we have seen how ill prepared Britain was in 1939 to fight a hostile foe. The improvement in preparedness over six years of war was certainly unspectacular. There were many causes for this, as we have described, but the responsibility for these causes can be traced back to the actions or inactions of governments, particularly those in power from 1935 to 1945. But if a country gets the government it deserves, then the voters of 1935 are ultimately responsible for the unnecessary deaths of thousands and thousands of service people.

If there is any risk of future conflict – which of course there is – we should think very carefully about our national security and the people (ourselves, our children and our grandchildren) who may have to provide that security. Let us be as sure as we can that if they have to fight they are better prepared and equipped than we were in the war of 1939–45.

Bibliography

PRIMARY SOURCES

The two principal sources of primary documents are the Tank Museum Library at Bovington and the Public Record Office at Kew. Having defined the required topics and sub-topics the identification and procurement of documents at the Tank Museum was efficiently and expeditiously carried out by the Librarian, David Fletcher, and his staff. The search for primary documents at the PRO was greatly helped by a 'Guide to Sources in the PRO Relating to Armoured Warfare and the Mechanisation of the British Army' prepared by Mr A.J. (Tony) Williams of the PRO staff, and was available as an unpublished document at the Reference Desk. Many documents were accessed and consulted, principally from the letter-codes AVIA, CAB, PREM and WO.

SECONDARY SOURCES

ADDISON, P. and CALDER, A. T*ime to Kill*, London, Pimlico, 1997
BARCLAY, Brig. C.N. *History of the 16th/5th Lancers 1925–61*, Aldershot, Gale and Polden, 1963
BARNETT, C. *The Audit of War,* London, Macmillan, 1986
BEALE, P. *Tank Tracks*, Stroud, Sutton Publishing, 1995
BEDDINGTON, Maj Gen W.R. *History of the Queens Bays 1929–45*, Winchester, Warren & Son, 1954
BRIGHT, J. *The 9th Royal Lancers 1936–45*, Aldershot, Gale & Polden, 1951
BRYANT, A. *Triumph in the West*, London, Collins, 1959
CALVOCORESSI, P., *et al.*, *Total War* (2nd edn), London, Penguin, 1995
CARVER, Lord, *The Seven Ages of the British Army*, London, Grafton Books, 1986
COLVILLE, J.R., *Man of Valour*, London, Collins, 1972
COURAGE, Maj G. *The History of the 15th/19th Hussars 1939–45*, Aldershot, Gale and Polden, 1949
CRISP, R. *Brazen Chariots,* Aylesbury, Frederick Muller, 1959
DARNELL, D.S. *4th Hussar*, Aldershot, Gale & Polden, 1959
DAVY, Brig G.M.O. *The Seventh and Three Enemies*, Cambridge, W. Heffer, 1952
D'ESTE, C. *Decision in Normandy*, New York, E.P. Dutton, 1983
DIXON, N. *On the Psychology of Military Incompetence*, London, Pimlico, 1976
ELLIS, C. *Tanks of World War 2*, London, Octopus Books, 1981
ESSAME, H. *The 43rd Wessex Division at war 1944–1945*, London, William Clowes, 1952
EVANS, Maj Gen R. *The 5th Royal Inniskilling Dragoon Guards*, Aldershot, Gale & Polden, 1951
FEILING, K. *Life of Neville Chamberlain*, London, Macmillan, 1946
FLETCHER, D. *Mechanised Force*, London, HMSO, 1991
——. *The Great Tank Scandal*, London, HMSO, 1991
——. *The Universal Tank*, London, HMSO, 1993
FORTY, G. *A Pictorial History of the Royal Tank Regiment*, Tunbridge Wells, Spellmount, 1988
FOSS, C. and MACKENZIE, P. *The Vickers Tanks*, Wellingborough, Patrick Stephens, 1988
FULLER, J.F.C. *The Conduct of War 1789–1961*, London, Eyre Methuen, 1972
HARRIS, J.P. *Men, Ideas and Tanks*, Manchester, Manchester University Press, 1995
HARRIS, J.P. and TOASE, F.N. *Armoured Warfare*, London, Batsford, 1990
GILBERT, M. *Second World War*, London, Weidenfeld and Nicolson, 1989
GREENWOOD, R.T. (ed. Barry Greenwood), *One Day At a Time: A Diary of the Second World War*, (published privately 1988)
HALSTED, M. *Shots in the Sand*, Portsmouth, Gooday Publishers, 1990

HAMILTON, N. *Monty: The Making of a General*, London, Coronet, 1981
HAMILTON, S. *Armoured Odyssey*, London, Tom Donovan, 1995
HORNE, A. *The Lonely Leader*, London, Macmillan, 1994
HORROCKS, B. *A Full Life*, London, Collins, 1960
——. *Corps Commander,* London, Magnum Books, 1977
JEFFREY, K. (Ed.), *Correspondence of Sir Henry Wilson*, London, Bodley Head, 1985
KENNEDY, Sir J. *The Business of War*, London, Hutchinson, 1957
LEWIN, R. *Man of Armour*, London, Leo Cooper, 1976
LIDDELL HART, B.H. *History of the Second World War*, London, Pan Books, 1970
LIDDELL HART, B.H. *The Tanks: History of the Royal Tank Regiment 1914–1945*, London, Cassell, 1959
McKEE, A. *Caen: Anvil of Victory*, London, Papermac, 1964
MACKSEY, K. *Tank Facts and Feats*, London, Guinness Superlatives, 1976
MACKSEY, K. *Tank Versus Tank*, London, Guild Publishing, 1988
MACKSEY, K. *Tank Warfare*, London, Rupert Hart-Davis, 1971
MACLEOD, Col R. (ed.) *The Ironside Diaries 1937–1940*, London, Constable, 1962
MASTERS, J. *The Road past Mandalay*, London, Michael Joseph, 1961
MILLER, Maj Gen C. *History of the 13th/18th Hussars 1922–47*, London, Chisman Bradshaw, 1949
MONTGOMERY, The Viscount, *Normandy to the Baltic*, Boston, Houghton Mifflin, 1948
——. *Memoirs*, London, Collins, 1958
MOORE, W. *Panzerbait: 3rd RTR 1940–44*, London, Leo Cooper, 1991
NICHOLSON, H. *Diaries and Letters 1930–39*, London, Collins, 1966
NOCKOLDS, H. *The Magic of a Name*, London, G.T. Foulis, 1949
OGORKIEWICZ, R. *Armoured Forces*, London, Arms & Armour Press, 1970
ORGILL, D. *The Tank*, London, Heinemann, 1970
PERRETT, B. *The Churchill*, London, Ian Allan, 1974
——. *The Churchill Tank*, London, Osprey, 1980
——. *Tank Tracks to Rangoon*, London, Robert Hale, 1987
PETT, Lt Col P.W. *History of the Royal Wiltshire Yeomanry 1920–1945*, London, Matheson & Co., 1946
POSTAN, M.M. *British War Production*, London, HMSO, 1952
POSTAN, M.M., HAY, D., and SCOTT, J.D. *Design & Development of Weapons*, London, HMSO, 1964
REDDISH, A. *Normandy 1944 From the Hull of a Sherman*, Poole, Kew Ewing, 1995
ROSS, G.M. *The Business of Tanks 1933–1945*, Ilfracombe, Arthur Stockwell, 1976
SCHULMAN, M. *Defeat in the West*, London, Secker and Warburg, 1951
SCOTT, J.D. & HUGHES, R. *The Administration of War Production*, London, HMSO, 1955
SMITHERS, A.J. *A New Excalibur*, London, Leo Cooper, 1986
——. *Rude Mechanicals*, London, Leo Cooper, 1987
SUETER, Sir M. *The Evolution of the Tank*, London, Hutchinson, 1937
THE TANK CORPS, *Honour and Awards 1916–1919*, Birmingham, Midland Medals, 1982
THE TANK MUSEUM. *Churchill Tank*, London, HMSO, 1983
TRYTHALL, A. *Boney Fuller*, London, Cassell, 1977
34th ARMOURED BRIGADE (1945), *The Story of 34 Armoured Brigade*, published privately, Germany, 1945
VAUXHALL MOTORS. *Driver's Handbook for the Churchill Tank*, details of imprint not given, 1944
WHITAKER, W.D. and WHITAKER, S. *The Battle of the Scheldt*, London, Souvenir Press, 1945
WHITAKER, W.D. and S. *Rhineland: The Battle to End the War*, London, Leo Cooper, 1989
WHITE, B.T. *Tanks of World War II*, London, Peerage Books, 1972
——. *British Tank Markings and Names*, London, Arms & Armour Press, 1978
WHITEHEAD, W. *Dieppe 1942*, Glasgow, Richard Drew Publishing, 1982
WILLIAMS-ELLIS, C. and WILLIAMS-ELLIS, A. *The Tank Corps*, 1919
WILMOT, C. *The Struggle for Europe*, London, Collins, 1952
WILSON, A. *Flame Thrower*, London, William Kimber & Co. Ltd, 1956
YOUNG, D. *Rommel, the Desert Fox*, London, Fontana, 1950

Index

Guide to the Index

1. The index is in three main sections: (a) Armies and formations (by country) (b) Armoured Fighting Vehicles (c) All other entries.
2. Where a serving officer's rank is shown it by no means implies that it was the most senior rank he attained.
3. References in italics relate to illustrations.